Who Lost America?

CAN AMERICA'S DEMOCRATIC IDENTITY
AND GOVERNMENT SURVIVE OUR ETHICAL,
POLITICAL AND ECONOMIC FAILURES?

Bromwell Ault

authorHOUSE®

AuthorHouse™
1663 Liberty Drive
Bloomington, IN 47403
www.authorhouse.com
Phone: 1-800-839-8640

First published by AuthorHouse 10/24/2011

ISBN: 978-1-4634-7446-1 (sc)
ISBN: 978-1-4634-7445-4 (hc)
ISBN: 978-1-4634-7444-7 (e)

Library of Congress Control Number: 2011915365

Printed in the United States of America

FOR
Norman Holmes Pearson, Emory S. Basford,
Arthur B. Darling, Ben Long and Douglas
Knight --- exceptional teachers from long ago
whose presence and guidance linger on.

Acknowledgements

In the course of a book's publication its author requires the services of people of different and essential talents without which publication would not be possible. I am indebted to Sandra Beck who consistently converts the chaos of my manuscript first drafts into a readable typescript. Prepublication production involving typesetting and proofing has been provided by Banyan Printing in Lake Worth, FL. All of Banyan's highly skilled staff are unfailingly helpful, and I am particularly appreciative of those with whom I have the most frequent contact ---Tina, Bonnie, Ed, Chris, Amy, Larry and CEO Roger.

With thanks to all,
BA

Table of Contents

Who Lost America?

Introduction

Things as vast as governments, especially ours, can reveal themselves in small ways and events. A couple of these that date to the Constitution have recently shown how much our process and tradition have been hijacked by party politics.

Every year in late January the President appears before both houses of Congress and an extensive list of guests to deliver his State of the Union speech. While previously this took the form of a relatively brief and factual presentation of past, present and anticipated problems facing the nation, today it has devolved into a menu of political options and responses carefully selected to benefit the President, his administration and his party.

As the President enters and makes his way towards the podium, he is besieged by efforts of those on or near each side of the aisle to either make some physical or verbal contact. Upon assuming the podium he is met with a prolonged round of applause that defies his feigned attempts to end it and begin his speech. At some point in his speech the President ususally declares that "The State of the Union is strong". This has become a tradition and touches upon several emotional and historical bases. It is familiar to all; it provides a note of positive pride and strength; and it creates a sense of unity that binds us to each other and to our past. The problem is that it is a lie centered on its two key words – "union" and "strong".

The proof of this is to be found in the audience's response to the rest of the speech which, having put on display the requisite image of unity, then generally reverts to the reality of our polarization in which the members of the party in power engage in uncontrollable applause, even for the most minor of statements, while the out party maintains an awkward but determined silence.

It is not often that an event so clearly titled is just as clearly contradicted by reality. Why should we care about this brief moment that is regularly described by reporters and observers as political theatre? The answer has come to be that we should care not for what it offers, but for what it disguises. Complacency is not in order. Throughout our world unseen opportunity or circumstance determine history. The small is entry to the large, as the keyhole, window and door are to the room beyond.

The evening is an exercise in bonding and self-importance. It is slight of hand. It is the Midway. And, for the public hoping for substance, it is merely a menu, not a meal.

In recent years we have embarked upon another congressional charade which belittles its origin and purpose. We refer to the Senate confirmation hearings for Supreme Court nominees. These were once relatively non-partisan inquiries into the candidate's career and general legal thought process, and included any comments he/she might want to make as to service on the court, if confirmed. Not so today, when both parties press for assurance by the nominee that his/her decisions will coincide with the inquiring senator's political/judicial preferences.

The result of this far more aggressive interpretation of the confirmation process has led to the spectacle of Court nominees deflecting very specific questions with answers so general that the value of the process is now questionable. Elena Kagan's two days of testimony in July 2010 is the most recent example and stands as a lesson in artful dodging and how to craft answers that do not yield the information requested. But Kagan's evasion came as no surprise, as Justices Roberts' and Alioto's hearings and others before them had established "legal precedent".

In my first volume, <u>Eminent Disdain</u> (Author House, 2009), I explored the multiple failures of many of our institutions to provide the intended protections for which they had been created. This is no minor symptom for, as government has grown, its institutions have come in contact with most of our private or public social and economic elements.

In the past century, through a combination of circumstances, our country has assumed an identity contrary to our early character and beliefs. The difference in the two is considerable and yet they are both parts of the same whole. <u>Eminent Disdain</u> identified the most notable contradictions and failures of our democracy's recent progress. In this collection we take the next step of relating our failures to our politics and policies.

None of this will be easy. As a matter of acknowledged fact, the chance of success at best is slim, but possible. It rests entirely on the will of America's citizens to become involved, to stay involved and to demand more from the two major parties and their candidates who run for office.

The effort that will be necessary will require us to reexamine many relations between government and the people. Among these are various forms of our national security; the role and responsibility of a Congress that has enjoyed an incumbent reelection rate of over 90%; systemic corruption of elected representatives by special interests at local, state and federal levels; a new tax policy; defining the interaction between the private sector, the public and government as a benefit to each; establishing fiscal restraints and responsibilities to end the runaway spending programs and their enormous debt increases of the Bush II and Obama administrations;

and reestablishing meaningful ethics and budgetary mechanisms to replace our present failures.

We will have to address the control of our political process by the Ideological Imperative recognizing that its embrace by both parties has sounded the death knell for American centrist government. One of the great follies of the last fifty years has been the way we have moved money and power in vast amounts to the edges of our political scale.

Right or left, it makes no difference. Democracy is a tender plant. Without a rational and principled center it will always be at risk to be crushed by the forces that have formed on its flanks. While we think we may be extending democracy to our fringes, it is possible that something entirely different will come back to us. Without a center everything is up for grabs – including our history, our tradition <u>and our democracy, itself</u>.

Something as basic as religious freedom must be viewed from the perspective of facing a global Muslim fundamentalism willing to employ extreme violence and terrorism to resist the West's territorial, cultural and military presence in Muslim lands.

In all of these areas the policies put forth by our government can be much improved if we attempt to remake our government. The word "remake" may sound to some as a call for radicalism. It is not intended in that way, but rather to convey the sense that we must make repairs to our government so that it looks and feels better to us, sounds better to others — and works better for everyone.

We cannot be vague about this. We must be clear about our purpose and our methods, for only by being open and encouraging will we be effective in convincing others to join with us.

There is always a delicate balance involved in applying the popular will to the conduct of government. In our electoral system, which lacks a mechanism for change by vote between elections, today's error does not linger long in our conscience. Memory is short and habit strong, and we are easily distracted from our failures by oncoming events. But as these failures multiply, they become increasingly difficult to pass along from one election, or one generation, to the next. They become an accumulation, then a burden and finally, perhaps, a critical mass with the power to destroy itself and those who created it. We are at such a moment and its outcome, one way or the other, will be determined by the American people.

They can do nothing and trust to politics as usual, or they can rise to the occasion and commence the way back to an open and informed democracy. To accomplish the latter they will need the kind of help and leadership that America has had before, but has allowed to slip away.

There will be pain at every level of our society as roles, habits, customs, protections and benefits are re-evaluated in the new view of national interest. The most pain will be felt, as it should, by those special interests who have persuaded past governments that the national interest is a mirror image of their own. Whether by economic, social or political pressures, and regardless of their acquired special status, they will have to be realigned with our historical democracy, not the pay-to-play version that now plies its trade on Capitol Hill.

This widespread pain will not be permanent, for, as it works its way through the system, it will provide catharsis that will cleanse our government and renew our strength.

There is always the question that hangs over entrenched politics of "What is reality?" Is it what we are or what we claim to be? If allowed, it can fuel itself, but we are not there yet, as we see in our State of the Union speech and confirmation hearings. Our politics and government are wrapped in multiple layers of cant and hypocrisy that can only be removed by public determination. We must undertake the challenge of breaking old habits and building new responses. We must remind ourselves that the first step away from the old is also the first step towards the new, and that we have the courage to take it.

I think this is possible and that in doing so Americans will reveal new strengths and older truths. And, who knows? Along the way we might return to a real State of the Union speech?

Technology and "progress" have a way of overwhelming cultures that are not spiritually, geographically, economically or politically resistant. And it is the ever shifting mix of these elements which determines whether different cultures will succumb or survive.

The objectivity required to evaluate any society is often obscured or deflected by the momentum of its growth. America is a prime example of this as we can see by looking at a few past and present attitudes.

Think back to our pre-national, colonial period and its views on sex, money, religion and politics and then compare them to those we hold today. We might well think "you can't get here from there".

America was particularly susceptible to cultural drift because of its newness and because it was an experiment for which it could write its own rules. It not only lacked the centuries of tradition of its European forebears, but it strongly desired to keep itself separate and free from their errors. Young America's course on the sea of change was that of a bobbing, moving float, whereas our Spanish, French, English and Dutch predecessors were more like buoys attached by tradition to the anchor of their prior histories.

The transforming changes that have taken place in our culture have created an identity crisis for our country marked by confusion of our ideals and institutions. The process required to repair them is what I refer to as American Renewal.

Our times do not favor the success of any broad idealistic reawakening in America. Quite simply, we are too divided and too unconcerned. And our institutions are not strong enough to play their part, as it is they who will be called upon to provide the necessary legislative, managerial and oversight functions.

Institutions, however, can be reformed or strengthened one by one through our electoral process, thereby making the American people the ultimate determinant of success or failure. To provide them with the requisite means and opportunity, they will need to be armed with more information and motivation than our two parties have offered in the past.

We are at a stage of political consciousness when opposition within the two parties produces anger and isolation and where actions beyond their control suggest panic. Both responses are excessive, unnecessary and damaging to our nation.

Americans can do better, much better. And they must! But at this point they need some help in getting started on their way to reclaiming their country. There is nothing inherently radical in what we propose. It is neither liberal nor conservative, Democratic nor Republican. It is a matter of caring enough to act.

Today, we lack true national unity. But America's citizens are powerful when committed. It's possible that they won't care, that they will opt for more of the same and the country will continue the descent of its ideals, institutions and democracy. But I think not.

Every writer sends words and thoughts out into the world to do their work. It is like sending your youth off to college. You know that, even if they come home, they will never be the same.

I do not know what kind of future my words and thoughts may find. Whatever their destiny, with publication words change from precious creations to carriers of content and intent.

I will miss them, but their DNA commands them to find and

inform others who will read and then act upon them. The latter are functions of our institutions, but they have failed. All that remains is the America citizen. America's risk is that there may not be enough of them or enough time for them to act. Volunteers are needed. "Uncle Sam wants you!"

Chapter One —— May 2008

Who Lost America?©

Who lost America? Or, more specifically, who replaced the America we were with what we have become? And, why? And, how? These questions and their answers provide the framework for coming chapters and, hopefully, will throw light on how, in a developed and functional democracy, a change of such transforming nature as we have experienced could occur without being formally acknowledged and framed as an expression of the public will.

The "lost" in the title does not refer to diplomacy, economics, militarism or any of the other many aspects of government which for a super power, or even an aspiring superpower, can automatically capture headlines and claim world attention. Rather, we are faced with an historical change that has occurred over an extended period.

History is an excellent teacher. To some degree it is infallible. It is both messenger and message and writes our records. In the end, it determines who survives and who doesn't and, more importantly, what is and what isn't. It leaves little room for argument when it is being written, and even less thereafter. It consists of innumerable events, actions and decisions many of which, when they occur, do not bear the sign of either present or future historical importance.

The historical process is far from perfect. Those whom it relegates to its dust bins may well have deserved better according to the moral or ethical values of their time, but the survivors of history's selection process are also keepers of the record with an audit and edit function that can dismiss as irrelevant the multitude of failed claims for inclusion.

For nations, their passage through history is one of self-definition with the ever present caveat that for the loser there awaits, not just defeat, but, in all probability, elimination. The opportunities for this definition, and the ways by which to achieve it, are complicated by nations' needs to defend or enlarge their borders, populations or properties. The latter are often designated as "national interests" and consist of mines, land, military bases, industrial plants and transportation facilities/services owned or leased by private or government entities.

Looking across a time span measured in centuries, it is easy to see how the way our nation defines itself could become separated from our individual ideals, as much is often lost in translation from the personal to the public condition. Humans, whether consciously or not, also undertake the task of self-definition in their lives where it is considerably less complicated, but far more fragile, than on a national scale.

In American politics on the cutting edge of the twenty-first century there is little evidence of unifying force. All the major issues — immigration, health care, taxes, Social Security, the environment, national security — reveal deep and difficult divisions over which and whose interests will be served. And in a nation as large, rich and powerful as we have become there are simply too many self-serving interests maneuvering for advantage. They act like a political virus, penetrating, entering and taking over the political DNA of its host and thereby altering our process of self-definition.

While unity may be impossible to discern in our major issues, there is one criticism of government and politics that has found broad backing and is leveled, with the assurance of certainty, by one and all against one and all. It is the charge of political polarization and its resulting paralysis of government.

And it is true. The legislative branch of our government, with the power and responsibility to create and pass our laws, is riven with so many divisions (both of substance and of style) that its 535 members in the House and Senate are more and more to be found at the far ends of the political spectrum without a refuge of reason at the center. In any government this poses a serious threat to political success. In our time and place it is a catastrophe. How did this happen and why do we permit it?

Polarization has occurred because it has become acceptable. This means that its political rewards are sure to outweigh the governmental risks that it poses. The amounts of money and power that flow through our government are so great that those who seek them have become increasingly willing to adopt extreme means to secure them. This includes adopting exaggerated positions and rhetoric which can gain greater attention and support as they move towards the ends of the political spectrum. This flight from sameness has had a remarkable effect on the range of our political thought, for, whereas the preponderance of opinion used to inhabit the political center, the latter is now seen as not offering the surest access to the benefits provided by more extreme positions. As a result, the political center, which often found consensus in moderation, compromise and, even collaboration, has been vacated by those intent upon victory and its spoils.

This new concentration of power toward the edges has been building for the last half century. Today it exists in a particularly virulent winner-take-all political exercise in which determined opposition is constant in Republican/Democrat, executive/

legislative, House/Senate and even Federal/State relations. The results of this continuing abrasion between essential moving parts of our system encourage our present polarization and paralysis which in turn prevent the passage of meaningful legislation to treat major issues of our time.

A less evident, but equally damaging, consequence of our shrinking center is that, as mass moves to the ends away from the center and balance is lost, our political mechanism suffers a loss of equilibrium whereby even small changes which had been tolerated at the center now produce wide or violent swings at its ends.

Strangely, although perhaps not by Washington's standards, while there is general agreement within Congress and the White House that polarization has reached an historically high and damaging level, there is no real consensus on how to reduce it. As congressional elections follow presidential contests by a brief two years and as campaigns have been stretched to fill the gap, America finds itself in a constant campaign cycle in which accusations of political and personal failure are readily available to tarnish the image of our democracy.

But politics are not the same as government; and the ways of the campaign do not lend themselves to legislation. The difference is both expanded and exploited by our new, 24/7 instant media coverage which every politician courts and none refuses. Within the Congress denial rules, as each party increasingly refers to its own policies and proposals as "bipartisan" and, therefore, to be accepted by the other.

This has been, and will continue to be, a highly unsuccessful tactic with the result that polarization will play a very real and limiting role in the quality of our self-governance until its underlying causes are recognized.

The processes of political self-definition whereby nations, parties and empires form and grow are publicly recorded and visible. Because of their visibility they are accepted as history's truth. They are not; they are real, but only contributory. Beneath them lie the many layers of human motivations, aspirations and needs whose impact, but generally not whose presence and power, are recorded in history's narrative. The special privacy of human development engenders personal self-definition without which its political/public accomplice could not exist. Understanding this role and reflection is the only way by which we can arrive at the new political enlightenment that will be necessary to change both the course and methods of our foreign and domestic policies.

Above the surface we can see violent storms make winds and waves that rage on the sea and batter the shore. Beneath the surface, silently and gently, unseen currents in continuous motion move enormous amounts of water around the world.

In the realm of self-definition, as in all others, its coin has two sides. They are self-validation and differentiation, and they occur so frequently and are so essential and dominant a part of the process that they transcend mere personal definition and are extended to many other areas of our lives — religious, commercial, political, social and others.

Self-validation is the process of outreach whereby we claim and apply to ourselves the values, symbols, actions, beliefs, manners, history and language which we think will establish a greater worth for us in our own sight and in the sight of others. This is a very powerful force and it is put to such constant use in our twenty-first century culture that, unlike most motivating forces, it is largely accepted without question. There are few things that have the power to sway as our need to establish ourselves as objects of worth; and, similarly, few things are as able to so effectively destroy or diminish our lives as failing this test.

Few. But there is one co-equal, undeniable companion that has been with us since our earliest days on the African plains in the mists between man and monkey. This is the need to differentiate ourselves, to separate us from the other. Nomadic man found it useful for hunting game to divide into smaller units of tribes, families, or councils maintaining a balance based on what size best served his needs for protection and food.

Postnomadic humans developed entirely different lives and institutions built around agriculture, property ownership/inheritance and settled communities. As life's scale and numbers grew, small communities expanded to villages, towns and cities that could better serve the needs for protection and commerce. However, even as man pursued this new way of communal life with specific functions, he insisted on the expression of differentiation in neighborhoods, clothing, language, religion and other means.

Most notable among these mechanisms was one which appeared early, has served every population group or government around the globe and endures today. It is the creation of borders. Whether made by man drawing lines on a map or by nature's rivers, seas and mountain ranges, borders made the same statement — that there is a difference between what is on one side and what is on the other. Many wars have been fought either to prove or to contest this thought, but history has so far supported the view that borders have a permanent place in our life.

The borders that describe our cultural, geographic or philosophic differences do so on a large scale. On a considerably smaller scale, at the human level, we make equally intense distinctions in order to define ourselves, to draw the borders of the self, and to say how and why our self differs from what lies beyond it.

Today the most popular metaphor in our American language is that which derives from football which dominates American sport to a far greater degree than baseball, our "national game". It is available in both professional and amateur forms and more people watch it and bet money on it than any other sport. From training camp to Super Bowl takes more than half of the year and on Friday night, which is high school football night in most of the country, small towns close down and move to the school stadium.

But watching and cheering are not enough. The commitment must be total! At any time during the season, and even off-season, adults and children wear sports clothing that recognizes their preferred team and even individual players' names and numerals. Nor is it unusual to see cars adorned with one or more flags bearing a team logo.

And there is more. In college communities across the country alumni pursue the ultimate in athletic boosterism by attending all practice sessions and games, home and away, for one or more teams. Usually it is football that commands the affection of these graduate groupies who often use expensive recreational vehicles with kitchen, bath and bedroom facilities to enable them to indulge their team passion both at home in stadium parking lots and on trips that may require a day or two on the road. These "land yachts" whose cost ranges from about one to five hundred thousand dollars are triumphs of space and convenience design/engineering and have elevated the basic "tailgate" picnic to an elaborate service of special menus. Their design can include furniture, fabrics, glassware, china, carpeting, etc. marked by the team logo, mascot and colors.

This is the way of life for the four month football and other seasons that fulfill the graduate groupies' dreams. But it is not merely attendance that measures this phenomenon. Groupies find and associate with their fellows with the result that their lives — their time, conversations, reading, finances and socializing — are dominated by this fixation.

What is taking place here? The over the top, out of proportion (and degree is key in these comments) sports booster, both college and professional, is creating an identity. And while it is an identity based on fantasy, it is nonetheless a reality for its creator. What is also very much a national reality is that these fantasy selves are being developed, encouraged and promoted throughout the country from little leagues to the professional sports leagues. This has become possible by the enormous increase in the amount of money spent on athletic facilities/programs and their marketing/promotion by corporate advertisers and the media.

And beneath the surface of the self, what is the real purpose of our fantasy identities? First, they provide validation because by claiming association with a team's history, geography, tradition, style, colors, heroes, etc. we are adding something to ourselves that, in our view and others, adds value or reason for notice to our lonely process of self-definition. Validation is internal and it is constantly at work. We borrow here and shed there and are so accustomed to these responses that we pay them little heed.

Secondly, the identification that underlies our sports mania is also a means of differentiation, for to choose one team is to reject the rest. It is an act of preference which establishes difference and distance between the one and the others. This is evident in sports fans' vocabulary in which words such as "the best" and "the greatest", and their opposites, are used with such frequency that they lose meaning.

The use of the sports metaphor to describe the function of validation and differentiation in self-definition taps into one of the main streams of our national, and even our global, culture. At first, this may appear an exaggeration, but consider the European football riots and the multiple occasions of drug use and boycotts and it comes into focus. So much for sports; there are other more fateful ways in which our self-definition process plays out in our national life.

Education is certainly one, for it is a process controlled by personal choice and action in which validation and differentiation are achieved by the acquisition of knowledge. Another widespread example is clearly and continually on display in the corporate world where validation and distinction are served by rewards of salary, perks, titles, responsibilities and powers. It is no accident that the ultimate corporate goal is a life described as being "lonely at the top."

But it is in our human expression of religious faith where validation and distinction work together most smoothly. For what better or more powerful means of validation can there be than to align and assign ourselves to the Deity? Validation by religion has appealed to mankind from its earliest origins, and often has been carried to the extreme levels presently used by militant Muslims. And, as with validation, so with differentiation have we put violence, cruelty and intolerance to use whether we distinguish between different faiths or, even more tragically, between different interpretations of the same faith, as in the conflict within the Christian church between Protestants and Catholics. The horrendous tortures employed by the Tudors and Stuarts in their English religious wars, as well as the methods of the Spanish Inquisition to abolish heresy, are joined in a direct line of descent to the recent bombings and assassinations of men, women and children in Northern Ireland. Lines of distinction are sometimes drawn by a sharp and bloody blade.

And then, of course, there's politics. Our present two-party political division can be traced back to our origins when two very different views of democracy and government emerged and fought for dominance. One was Jeffersonian democracy which favored full control and participation by the people. Its opposition was championed by Alexander Hamilton who saw Jefferson's model as unwieldy, and perhaps chaotic, and argued for restrictions that would concentrate power in fewer hands.

Jefferson prevailed with momentous consequences as we worked and fought our way through the nineteenth and twentieth centuries. Political labels changed over this time to reflect shifts in demographic and political issues, but we are now in a period of more than a century in which our American democracy has been channeled through our two-party, Republican/Democratic system.

The difference of concept expressed by Hamilton and Jefferson, however, has persisted in Republicans being seen as the party of "the few" and Democrats as that of "the many". This is an essential difference which can surface in many different forms and issues. It is not to be ignored. Throughout the turbulence of our late nineteenth century expansion of commerce, wealth, frontier, population and military power the line between Republicans and Democrats was broadly drawn in the policies they forged to accompany and control the nation's rapid development.

Republicans generally favored low taxes and wages, no labor unions, property rights and a laissez-faire economic environment that favored the accumulation of wealth. In the plants that constituted our burgeoning industrial capacity, where owners/managers were usually Republicans, the workers were mostly Democrats. Republican issues and policy gravitated towards the expanding and shifting economic circumstances of the time, while the Democratic party found its purpose and membership better defined by social aspects of labor and life in America.

Over time, as our political self-portrait was filled in, Republicans came to be seen as the party of privilege and Democrats as that of compassion. In politics one title very rarely fits all, and this was certainly true of emerging America. One crucial factor in our development had been our formation as a classless society whose openness permitted the acceptance and embrace of the different, and often divergent, Republican/Democrat policies.

This is a great quandary of our American democracy in which, although we attempt to disguise it, race and class have played their parts. The classless system pronounced by our founders was not exactly so. The country was small, concentrated, unified by its struggle for independence and flushed with the social success of the three dynamic revolutions of the time —French, Russian and our own.

But a classless society is not easily achieved, and time, technology and growth work against it. Money and power not only create differences, they magnify them; and often in government with such speed and secrecy that the moment for our evaluation comes and passes without our recognizing it. Without meaning to, perhaps, we have managed to reintroduce class to our classless society.

Small wonder, then, that, given the pronounced differences in their political values and goals, both parties offered their members ways to define themselves which seemed entirely consistent with the way the country was defining its national self. And only after the Civil War, when the slavery issue was finally determined, could the nation undertake its own definition with any sense of comfort and confidence.

Even in its earliest days, and increasingly thereafter, the G.O.P. offered its members validation by permitting them to claim and associate with its shared status of wealth, strength, independence, position — in short, advantage. On the other hand, Democrats could confirm themselves by their greater concern for the elemental needs of the greater number of our society.

One of the enduring miracles of our system has been that, in spite of their basic differences of concept and conscience, both parties offer meaningful ways for their members to experience validation. And when we find validation, can differentiation be far behind? Anyone professing support of one party must oppose the other, for, while there can be agreement forged on issues, our system does not encourage third or multiple party candidacies. The main streams of our political power, identity and motivation flow through Republican and Democrat channels. The advantage of this system has been its continuity for which, however, we have paid a price in flexibility.

People, when asked about their political beliefs or affiliations, can reply to the same question with a variety of responses that differ in phraseology, emotion, body language and intent, but which are remarkably similar in the degree to which they reflect the investment of our self-image in our political preference, and also the values, real or imagined, which we then draw from it to achieve self validation. Those who seek verification through independence, wealth, power and their special status have been the mainstay of the G.O.P. while the Democratic party offers its members the advantage of being seen to concern themselves more with social and community concerns that reach out to a larger, less affluent and historically less articulate electorate.

In politics this process of exchange is only intensified by the other part of self-definition — our distinguishing ourselves to the point of separation from others. We have put so much of our personal worth at risk that every vote, every election delivers a verdict as to our relevance that we are ill-prepared to accept. And therein lies the root of the pervasive polarization that grips our government.

Creating an identity is a constant process. At times it is the result of a conscious effort; at other times, it is a product of itself. And we can neither start it nor end it. It heeds without favor the commands of both our genetic code and our environment, often without our knowledge or consent. In its conscious mode, we give to or take from the variety of institutions that serve as way stations on our life path — schools, corporations, churches, clubs, communities, charities, etc. And, of course, also politics and the structure of government.

The confusion of ourselves with politics can make for worse, not better, government. Whether we invest too much in order to create identity, or take too much to validate it, we burden the political process with an unnecessary and incompatible force. Politics is the agency by which we create government's structure and policy. Our founders were seemingly aware of the danger posed by the fusion of political and personal identity, and by vision and wisdom designed a structure to resist their combination.

We have been tested many times in the past by the worst of demagogues from both parties. And today we face the persistent efforts of the Kennedy, Clinton and Bush families to maintain a political presence in the White House. This tendency of the American public to accept family as a dominant factor in its choice is a real departure from the past direction of our democracy. Moreover, the way in which it expands the values of these families to the national scale provides a clear example of mass self-validation.

Democracy is a delicacy, and not for everyone. It should be administered and received with trust and reverence. In the first decade of the last century, Theodore Roosevelt sent a group of naval ships, the "Great White Fleet", around the world to show the great European and Asian powers that the American democracy, while young, was strong. For this display we were accused of "gun boat diplomacy". Our more recent expression of our foreign policy in the mid-east might be labeled "gun barrel democracy"; and when democracy is imposed, its very meaning is challenged. The inability to understand this elemental aspect of our democracy is a primary cause of our predictable failure to rewrite the politics and culture of this region with one quick, light military venture.

As to being "received with trust and reverence", our civilian and military forces have introduced extensive corruption, waste, fraud, violence and hardship to the Iraqi people in the course of our occupation and the hoped for, but not yet accomplished, reconstruction of their country.

Looking back over the post WWII years, which include five major wars (Korea, Vietnam, "Cold" and Iraq twice) and some lesser ones as well, our greatest failure has been not trusting our democracy, with all its benefits and limitations, for what it is and can be, but instead yoking it to the "military/industrial complex" of which a frank and prescient President Eisenhower gave us clear warning. "Trusting our democracy" means trusting its ideals, not its riches or its power.

The latter is enormous, but not constant, and the edge that we have enjoyed since WWII is now shrinking. Flux is the only constant in world affairs and we are seeing it at work in the increasing authority of China, India and, most importantly, Russia with its great abundance of natural resources and smaller population. To protect ourselves, to the extent that we can, we must change our concept of power, and elect as president not someone who merely wants power, but someone who can wield it in a moral and balanced way. Only when we come to understand the larger demands that power makes upon all those who hold it in our twenty-first century will we be able to arrive at a truly effective foreign policy. The multiple failures of the last half-century culminating in the war in Iraq indicate that the next administration, whatever it is, will have some heavy lifting to do. More of the same will not provide the answers to the questions we must ask, nor the results that we seek

Polarization Redux

And back to polarization. The deep and divisive atmosphere that permeates our political life today is most prominently on display in the Congress and the White House, but is by no means confined to them. It extends to our state governments and also enjoys a presence throughout the many bureaucratic agencies and departments that have been created to administer and make functional our legislative intentions.

This division is more rooted in person than in political party. Our process of self-definition by validation and separation leads us to assume the values, characteristics, manners, goals, etc. of one of our political parties in order to create identity. With the passage of time, as tradition/money/power/status all increase, both the price of success and the cost of failure escalate. Whatever political issue is involved acts like a raging river that cuts an increasingly deeper chasm between its two sides. Yes, there is an old rope bridge at the top fraying and swaying in the wind. But who will dare to cross it? To risk all, including self?

This is the true nature and origin of our paralyzing polarization — in government; in our elections; and in the perceptions of our public media whose ability to present and to persuade have been vastly increased by their marketing reach, new technology and financial strength. From their humble beginnings of hand bills and newspapers in the taverns and coffee houses of colonial America our present media can deliver their product instantly at any time to any place of their choice. The greatest part of their product is entertainment in a variety of forms to a mass audience. It carries the power to create, and then to anoint, celebrities and those who seek public office. And, if this is not enough, by providing the essential link between marketer and consumer they stimulate the purchasing process for innumerable products upon which commercial success and our national prosperity depend.

A half century ago, in pre-television times, in most of the country the media covered local and national political campaigns in such detail as they deemed appropriate and usually, as elections neared, concluded with an editorial that identified the candidate of choice and their reasons. Today on a 24/7 schedule commentators, who can be equally as polarized as the politicians they cover, have become the active ingredient, not merely a bystander or reporter, in our political mix.

Like politicians, they define themselves by many of the same rewards which are found in most forms of public life — publicity, ratings, fame, money and power. This mirror image of the self-definition process shared by media and political personalities is an incestuous one, however. It has been said that incest is the last taboo remaining in our society, but to anyone who views what now pass for debates in our campaigns this is a taboo that's in trouble.

"Gotcha politics", personal attacks and "one mistake and you're out" are the order of the day. These are not the tools of issue-oriented candidates or reporters. They are the weapons of the ideologue and are designed to impart blunt force trauma. Ideology is the absolute antithesis of the political values favored by our founders. In politics it is the highest level of expression of the personal identity created by our self-validation and differentiation. It is such a stonewall, wagons-in-a-circle way of interaction that no objective argument, no suggestion of the national interest, no acceptance of compromise as the servant of both parties can penetrate it. We seem, as if mesmerized, unable to do away with it. It shouldn't be, but it is.

The next political generation will have to face the serious

financial, diplomatic, military and political circumstances that we are leaving behind us. Considering the opportunity that has been available to our country over the past half-century, ours is a tragic legacy. What can we do before we are gone that might offer even a hope of modest improvement for America and its government?

Those who follow us will take office at an earlier age than their predecessors. They will come equipped with every advanced technology form of management and communication and extensive experience in their use. But this should not convince us that they are whiz kids who can magically change who and what we have become. The two generations since WWII have benefited from unprecedented technological development, and yet our government is more corrupt, expensive, inefficient and unresponsive to the national interest than it was in 1945. But technology can challenge as well as benefit democracy. And, while the new generation may well be tempted to place its faith in the technological and economic super globalism required of a superpower, there is no reason to expect that the results will be any different than our recent experience.

The great fault of government in America today is that it is considered a means, not an end. It is a means to be elected (and reelected) to office, to find fame and power, to obtain contracts or subsidies, to borrow money and to fight wars with Communists, terrorists or any other of the targets du jour offered by our military/industrial complex. It is a means whereby our elected representatives connive in the distribution of our national political and material resources to favored areas or interests. We have badly abused our democracy and in the process have done ourselves a great disservice.

We must change our view and concept of our government. It must be viewed as an end, not a means. The end of government must once again, as it was when it was founded, be good government itself. We can do without the tiresome Republican vs. Democrat arguments in which both parties claim the support of God and the Constitution. Government is difficult work; big government is even more difficult, and ours has grown so large that it far surpasses in scope the intention of our origins.

Repeat: the purpose of government must be good government itself — not the wars of annihilation now fought for ideology and advantage that pervade our government. This is a thought that, if stated, would be well received by many Americans, but few can even imagine it.

And yet, it is at the heart of a simple, but far-reaching concept. Our fragile democracy must be treated with trust and reverence by those who receive its benefits. The other part of the contract is that democratic government, which depends on the opinion and funding of its citizens, must return the same trust and reverence by providing them with good government.

Today we show many of the signs of decline of the Roman model — cultural and economic as well as military. Every previous super power has used war to maintain its status, and has failed. We should be able to avoid this trap, but one of the candidates seeking presidential nomination has assured us there will be more wars ahead. Military men think that way. They are trained all their lives in military strategy, tactics and weaponry. It is what they do, what they are. But we live in a nuclear age of asymmetrical warfare against enemies without borders whose reasons for fighting are lost in the cultural and tribal arguments of prior centuries.

Warfare is just one aspect of our national life that requires new thought. There are many more that require our attention. Government is never a finished product. It is a continuous process and those who create it will never complete it. This is true of all government, but especially our democracy.

Over the last two centuries our American government has been obscured and burdened by the accretion of multiple layers of self-interest which we must now very carefully and fairly peel back and remove. This will require firmness and patience. It will not be easy and will cause both pain and frustration. But at the end we will see our government in its intended form and state. That is the prize, and, if we treat it with patient reverence, we will have a far better chance of surviving the next two centuries.

Most notably our democracy has been greatly wounded and weakened by our inability to maintain our legislative branch as an enlightened and fair proponent of the national interest. We are faced with a situation whereby Congress creates legislation piecemeal, seemingly on the assumption that if enough pieces of the pie are acceptable, then the pie, itself, will be good. This method has become such a common practice that a bill marked up in committee and running into hundreds of pages in length can be delivered to members of Congress only a few hours before it is to be voted on.

For far too long far too many Americans have been persuaded by our leaders to see our government as "the pie" from which they are entitled to receive their piece. They have been encouraged in this fallacy by our national abundance and by the boundless capacity of our elected representatives to subvert our system for their own political benefit.

Government is not "the pie". At any given time it is a menu of choices, each with its own moral and economic price shown. Restaurant menus limit our choice from all available foods to a smaller sample better suited to a single meal. Government should do the same, providing and making choices that are practical and disciplined to serve our truly national purposes.

To accomplish this, our national vision must change and we, as a people, must don some corrective lenses. We must establish that the only goal of government is good government itself — planning, balancing, managing and selecting from the many forces that confront us those that we hope will offer long term benefit. With our new, corrected vision we will have to redefine the meaning of being a sole superpower, and we should start with the realization that superpower status assures only one thing — its own impermanence.

Our redefinition must enable us to see that the superconsumption aspect of being a superpower is a trap we have set for ourselves which sets consumption against our environment and from which the Law of Limits will not allow us to escape. Similarly in commerce, it would be helpful to adjust our view of our national currency's value to reflect that of the world market. The fall in the dollar's value is one of several "key indicators" of decline and carries a message of danger which is all too easy to ignore.

And our new lenses must remind us that democracy is a delicate plant which can only be transplanted to a fertile soil where it can receive the constant care and encouragement it requires.

Man's ascendancy from the mix of species is due to his cranial development and use of three things — fire, words and numbers. Today these advantages face the threat of being lost to natural and/or human forces that could rearrange our planet's agricultural, chemical and physical patterns in ways that might favor another group in the way that mammals survived and prospered as the age of great reptiles came to its close.

We have dawdled too long listening to the music that carries across the water to us from the shore. We can no longer accept the causes and excuses of past governments as a viable way of envisioning our future. And we are challenged to alter the dimension of time in which we frame our future.

The problems we face at home and abroad are immense. To deal with them effectively will require a new, open and honest dialogue between our government and its people. Time is short and does not favor us as it did two hundred years ago, but we must try. And the time is now!

Who lost America? This is a question of real concern to all Americans which must be asked. Its answer is neither quick nor easy; in fact, just the opposite, as most of our political, cultural and commercial constituencies are at fault.

Starting at the top, the most obvious source of responsibility are the two major political parties, Republican and Democrat. Their most telling betrayal of our system has been their abuse of the public trust by accepting public opinion and then, instead of using it to shape a fair and efficient national government, putting it to use in inter-party ideological battles and to build and maintain a legislative structure with rewards of money and power for themselves and their contributors.

In America today the two parties consider themselves the ultimate goal for voters' opinions and have become an effective barrier to our participating in a higher level of national purpose which, of course, would diminish their importance and power.

The public must also share in the blame for this abuse of its constitutional power, as it has opted for the easy way of voting by party label, thereby allowing the Republican/Democrat electoral mechanism to so dominate the voting process that independent parties or other voices are simply not heard.

To be as indifferent and uninformed as our electorate can appear is a great tragedy for a democracy, but especially one which lacks the recall capability of a parliamentary system, for any error of perception or judgment is fixed in place for at least four, but more frequently eight, years.

Label loyalty is the preferred method at every voting level from local to presidential. It has achieved this dominance by the two major parties' commitment to the process of politics by emotion, identification and entertainment.

The latter introduces the media and its oversized role in our electoral procedure. This role has been formed and expanded in cooperation with the R/D organizations, and has been spectacularly successful in providing mass exposure to candidates and vast revenues to the media.

In keeping with other aspects of our society the messages provided by these entities to the public have been both dumbed down in content and sandwiched between endlessly repetitive commercials. With Washington's two, four and six year election cycles, with population and profits growing and with plenty of money available to back candidates who, when elected, will see that it is returned many times over there is little reason to expect that this cycle can be interrupted, and certainly not by means of the past.

Identity politics, whereby the voter bases his vote on an emotional bond with his party, play a larger part in our system than most of the parties involved are willing to admit. All too many people cite historical associations as the basis for their choice. The media recognize this, but try to keep it quiet as it acts against their argument that they can influence opinion. For the R/D parties, they are happy to have votes for any reason, but there is a distinct advantage in those who are "card carrying" members and whose support is pretty much assured regardless of the issues or candidates.

We must face the fact that we are at a crisis that will not correct itself. We face four issues — debt, immigration, health care/Social Security and the wars in Iraq and Afghanistan — that either individually or in concert have the ability to produce disastrous financial results for our country.

There is an unspoken hero in this mix and he is the American taxpayer. But there are limits to his resources, and probably to his patience. The idea that he/she will continue to pay an increasing tax burden to underwrite a deteriorating economic and social way of life is not realistic.

We are at a critical time in our history and we, the people, are the only ones who can effect the changes that are required to repair our government. There was a time when our institutions were strong enough to call for a change of course, but they have been dealt serious damage in recent years and are themselves in need of our care and attention.

From this mess emerge two truths that we must embrace. The first is that America, the America that we were, is worth saving. And the other is that we must accomplish our rescue outside the confines of the R/D structure through a genuine national effort.

Who lost america? The answer is that <u>we</u> did and, as a result, the course of our political thought and action have reached a point of decision. Are we to continue in our presently fragmented state in which government is only a magnifier and collection of personal self-interests? Or will we attempt to regroup around our original concept of democracy?

In the end we must refine and redefine national goals and character. We must be able to view our national strength in other terms than money, military or size and try to do away with the satisfaction we derive from referring to ourself as the richest, strongest, biggest,, etc. Our real strength should come from the government we create and its ability to present our values to others, as well as ourselves.

This is why our armed intervention in the Near East is such a nettle for us to grasp. Through torture, violence, corruption, martial law and destruction we put all the wrong values and methods on display. As these are the antithesis of our stated values, our nation destroys its credibility by having to defend them.

Character and credibility are key, but fragile, aspects of our democracy, and we abuse them as much at home as we do abroad. In Congress, at the legislative core of our government, the way of choice is often that of corruption, unenforced laws, corporate influence, lobbyists for special interests, lack of meaningful ethical standards and enforcement, abuse of seniority and the acceptance of "professional" elected representatives.

Money flows in almost unimaginable amounts throughout our political process and is constantly directed and redirected by the same people to the same places. Congress, by its profligate ways, gives the impression that our wealth is unlimited. It is not, and at this late stage only a concerted national effort can have a chance of bringing a measure of fiscal sanity to government.

Are we too indifferent, too uninformed, too rich, too "right" to even try?

Epilogue

When we commenced our study of the health care issue, it seemed that it was an intractable mess with no hope of solution, but as time passed and we became more familiar with its parts, the possibility of finding a solution grew more likely. And when we had completed our two issues, we were confident that a successful result could be achieved. We are beginning to engender some of the same sense of hope regarding the remaking of our government and its relationship with its citizens.

The truth is that we simply do not have another generation or two to devote to the same arguments — abortion/no abortion; private sector/government; black/white; high/low taxes; liberal/conservative; "cold"/hot wars, etc. We are very fortunate, however, that our time and technology have come together to present us with a real opportunity for the massive change in direction and methods that our current circumstances require.

The technology is that of the Internet. It is inexpensive, easy to use and highly efficient in reaching large numbers of people. And it is the medium of choice for all of the new generation and many of the old.

What seems called for now is for a small group of concerned private citizens with high personal and professional credibility and visibility to form a national group dedicated to the analysis and improvement of our government/policies. This group (let's call it American Renewal, or AR, for now) would issue comments on line on a variety of issues. Membership would be free, as initially minimal expenses would be covered by private donations. A key function would be maintaining a record of all votes cast by members of Congress and making them available on line.

With such an organization in place, it could announce the message of better government, call for reform and publicize current issues, as well as listing and grading Congressional votes. The general purpose of this group would be education, but it would be education with a specific and urgent message. It could resemble, only on a much broader scale, the Concord Coalition which has attempted to inform both government and the public of the severity of our country's fiscal position and its ever increasing amount of debt. Concord and AR would seem to be kindred spirits with the strong possibility that each one's presence would enhance and benefit the efforts of the other. Such symbiosis produces a magnifier effect whereby the sum of the parts far exceeds the whole.

It is likely that many of the new political generation would be drawn to AR because of its broad online access, but AR would not be served by being seen and characterized as a youth movement.

This is no easy task, but at this time in our history it seems with growing urgency to be a necessary one. The composition of the founding group is critical, as is the method by which it will expand the message and management from a standing start to the activity of a functioning national organization. The variety of issues that AR could confront is great, but it must not allow itself to be drawn into being all things to all people.

At any given moment it must select from our political menu that issue or information which it believes should be clarified or introduced to the public. AR's true value will not be determined by any one election result, but by its enabling the public to come to a greater understanding of our government and its issues beyond the limitations of the R/D worlds. One aspect of this larger view of government might be to exorcise the myth of eternal growth with endless benefits in our political, economic and social culture. This, of course, is holy ground, sacred to both political parties, but it must be repaired. We are paying an ever-higher price because we ignore the Law of Limits. We deserve a quality of leadership that can articulate this danger and can free us from the political demagoguery and clichés of the past.

There is wide disappointment across America over the results of previous administrations' leadership and policies. But there is no national, non-political voice that can express, unify and focus this discontent so that it becomes a strong and active ingredient of public opinion. The time is now.

"As superpower, our foreign policy is bound to be resented. It will also be mistrusted in varying degrees by other nations. The inherent danger of our position is that we will come to a time when our policies and our currency are equally mistrusted. Such a moment could develop spontaneously, perhaps from some seemingly minor origin, and without warning. It could cause disruption in other currencies and countries, and a significant alteration in our economy and way of life."

— Matters of Conscience
Issue 12 — May 2006

Chapter Two —— July 2008
Identity — Part I

This chapter discusses how humans and nations define themselves by the interacting processes of validation and differentiation, and how dangerous it becomes when they are applied to the conduct of policy in areas such as religion, agriculture and immigration.

In our first series we explored the institutional failures that have become more evident and frequent in our country over the past half-century. Why bother? Some of our institutions have been part of our country since its earliest times, and it is easy for all of us to take them for granted, but we shouldn't. Institutions provide structure and a framework for our government.

Policy is the application of government to a variety of purposes, and is often accomplished through institutions — i.e., through our Congress, our judiciary, our military forces or our Departments of Justice, Treasury, State, etc. As we have weakened and abused these institutions, we have altered our national identity politically and culturally and have created division along these lines of engagement in our society. The result is polarization at multiple levels which produces confusion in our domestic and foreign policies, as well as a blurred identity which it becomes increasingly difficult to honor and reflect.

And as institutional failures produce bad policies, so our flawed policies both here and abroad transform the way our society is seen by others and thwart our efforts to maintain our national purpose and identity. Many of the purposes which now make claims against our society (for example; capitalism, multiculturalism, security, diversity, unilateral militarism and even democracy, itself) are only achievable in varying degree, and often at the expense of unity.

We have embraced some policies over the past fifty years that yielded some very unintended results. Our thirty years of participation in the Cold War painted our world in two colors — black/white or capitalism/communism whereby a constant war of words and weapons dominated our thinking, with capitalism being transformed from a tool to a goal.

We were "the last man standing" and are fortunate that the Soviets' paranoia became a major factor in their collapse. The cost of this war imposed a substantial burden on our economy and greatly facilitated the rise of cynicism in our governmental process, as anything, no matter how tainted or suspect, could be argued and pursued in the either/or, capitalist vs. communist environment. Along with the Russians we achieved a pinnacle of unintended results as we undertook to fill both the political and the economic vacuums of the Third World. In tandem, we embarked upon a ruinous policy of backing, and even creating, local dictators to enforce our policies and presence, and paid them in arms and money.

While our political rhetoric at home portrayed our actions in lofty terms of resistance to world communism, the results in the Third World were often quite different. Most of the money we invested in Third World regimes was drawn off to private accounts of their elites and/or paid to American contractors for work specified under contracts, grants or loan agreements. As for the arms, they were often used to suppress the native population in the recipient countries or to fight wars with their neighbors. In some instances they were sold on the international arms market from which they found their way back to be used against their original owners. In the end neither we nor the Russians provided much in the way of benefits to the general publics of the countries we sought to control, and there was enough soul-searing cynicism in our actions to question our concept of superpower status.

With the collapse of the Soviet system and the end of the Cold War there came an ominous lull which immediately drew the attention of the corporate capitalists of the free world. Their rallying cry was one of globalism and free trade which could make use of much of the same machinery, equipment and investment techniques that we and the Russians had put in place to wage the Cold War. A few titles, phrases, laws and job descriptions were changed, but the essential capability of the private sector to make large sums of money from government's investment and policy did not.

The "A Train" To Armageddon

Of all the means by which humans have chosen to define themselves over the years none has been as pronounced and as constant as religion. For validation it has provided history, dogma, scripture, sacraments, music, clothing, rank, community and theology, and for differentiation there has been warfare (either secular or holy) salvation (or its opposite, eternal damnation), and the true faith, not just one of many shades.

The opportunities are endless and can be achieved in varying degrees depending upon the individual's effort. The results for the individual and the larger community can differ greatly so that what might seem reasonable and successful to the individual can threaten the larger group of which he is a part, as shown by Pastor John Hagee's efforts to fashion national military and foreign policy from his religions beliefs. Hagee is the founder and senior pastor of the Cornerstone Church of San Antonio, TX and has built a ministry of many thousands of members that he addresses both in person and by broadcasts. He is also founder of Christians United for Israel (CUFI) which provides assistance and unwavering support for Israel in both spiritual and political matters. Pastor Hagee is an extremely forceful and recognized Christian conservative whose comments draw notice even among his brethren of the Religious Right. In his many writings and sermons he emphasizes these themes, citing the Bible for their authority:

1) The land of Israel was given to the Jews by God.
2) Christians are linked historically and theologically to Israel.
3) The US and Israel are joined and an attack on one is an attack on the other.
4) God favors both countries, but if the US discontinues its protection of Israel, God will withdraw his blessing from America.

Throughout his writings Pastor Hagee so frequently and strongly cites this mutual relationship that they seem to emanate from the realm of policy rather than the pulpit.

In the fall of 2007 Pastor Hagee appeared on the PBS show, <u>Bill Moyers' Journal</u>, in which he stated that the US should "consider" a bombing attack on Iran. By using this word he can disclaim ever recommending it in definite terms, a tactic well known and regularly used in the political/policy arena. But in reality, anyone in public life addressing a TV audience of millions who makes such a suggestion does so with the knowledge that a message of positive action is being delivered.

When queried by Moyers as to the benefits and consequences of such an act, Hagee projected that an American attack would provoke an Iranian retaliation against Israel followed by an Israeli response that would ignite the whole Middle East and beyond. Hagee sees this as fulfillment of the Biblical prophesy of Armageddon's vast destruction from which, by His reappearance, Christ would rescue and draw to heaven the Israelis and the most devout and dedicated Christians as determined by Biblical standards. Evangelicals refer to this combination of final deliverance and destruction as The Rapture.

This scenario of coming events is nothing less than the Annihilation Express, the "A Train" to Armageddon, but it was presented as more than just a personal view of history to come. By placing it in the minds of the public and proposing it as a possible course of government action. Hagee is using his personal religious beliefs to create or influence national policy.

In our country, thankfully, everyone is entitled to his or her own choice and practice of religion, but that choice should not be extended to policies that impact the general public, and a resolution of the problem of good vs. evil such as his is not shared by many of Hagee's fellow Christian clergy. Are they to be bound by his view and policy? Or non-Christians of other faiths? Or even atheists? Are these to whom we guarantee freedom of religion to be tossed into the flames of nuclear conflict? Hagee's concept of how Biblical prophecy will be finally revealed may be true; or it may not be. But in either event it is a matter of personal belief, not government action or policy.

For many centuries humans on our planet have practiced a variety of religions that have differed in their deities, methods, and beliefs. They have also differed in their degrees of tolerance for other faiths which has led them to being responsible for persistent periods of war and peace. As a result, we not only validate ourselves by our choice of faith, and thereby differentiating ourselves from others, but we also introduce a quantitative element of having more or stronger faith than others and, therefore, being seen as "better". The Hagee theology with its emphasis on Israel and the US being joined as one makes for an interesting religious discussion, but falls far short of what is needed to formulate policy regarding nuclear war. Therein lies the danger of how we allow our process of self-definition to intrude upon government policy, but religion is not the only area of our life which human nature has chosen to put to this purpose. Others abound, and with generally negative consequences. *It is not "morning in America" yet; but it is time to wake up.*

What Is Our Role? What Is Right?

Pastor Hagee's message, while it may reflect a certainty of personal faith, raises some very difficult international policy questions that impact other nations and regions beyond the Near East. The spread of Marxist thought from mid-nineteenth century Germany to its global presence today was accomplished by its appeal to disaffected populations. In its early years its primary target was the vast concentration of agricultural and industrial poverty found in the monarchical societies spread across Europe from Russia to the Atlantic from which it was then exported to the US. For over a century the anger of the disaffected was directed to the political and economic circumstances into which they were born and which, in their view, offered them neither justice, a fair wage, nor a means of exit.

This disaffection carried different labels for different groups such as conservative/liberal or state/individual in politics; and wages, housing or management/labor in economic issues. Its lack of fairness, along with the many military and social disruptions it caused, were at the heart of the lengthy socio-economic polarization that extended from Marx until the collapse of the Soviet Union and the end of the Cold War.

Today a new polarization grips the world. With the growing wealth of Russia, China and India and the financial unification of Europe the old economic polarization no longer commands the attention it once did. But the disaffection is still there and now finds an outlet for its claims in the religious polarization born of Islam's determined expansion. The latter is now truly a global religion that has had the ability to tap into the world's ever present disaffection, capture it and convert it to fuel Islamic expansion.

Unfortunately, in the process the Muslim faith became a tempting target for extremist elements who have combined Islamic spiritual fervor with a Marxist overlay, and have created a message with irresistible appeal to the millions around the world who know no life other than the hopelessness of unanswered anger, envy and isolation. This merging of Marx and Mohammed yielded a marketing miracle for Islam.

But there were two other timely circumstances that enabled our present global religious polarization. The first, with centuries of prior success, was improved weaponry which for the extremist sects' purpose translates into smaller, lighter, more powerful explosive devices that can be carried on the body or detonated remotely.

The other technology, of course, is broadcast TV. Think back, for a moment, to the nineteenth century labor union organizer whose effectiveness in pitching his message was limited by the time, space and schedule of the workplace. Meetings were not encouraged and often prohibited at the plant, and the organizer was frequently beaten, arrested or both. Additionally, the local newspapers' interests were usually aligned with the companies that made and advertised products so that press coverage of labor issues tended to be brief and occasional unless distinguished by violence or other newsworthy events.

Fast forward to today when mass murder or mayhem on land, sea or in the air is almost instantly available on TV screens throughout the world via Muslim or western news broadcasts. The impetus and hope that this public exposure gives to the faceless, but faithful, Muslim poor are incalculable, but can be sensed in the images of their mass demonstrations where emotion and fervor rule. The best way to counter the benefits of technology for the extremists would be to put it to our own advantage, but therein may lie a problem. Our own media with their extensive skills may treat global Islam's growing reach as an ethnic or religious issue to be given "soft" treatment. *In a situation that calls for hard objectivity soft bias is not an answer.*

Policy is rarely an easy task, as conflicts are many and solutions few. But two questions, if asked, can eliminate a lot of early error. What is our role? And what is right? These are questions to which Pastor Hagee fails to provide persuasive answers. He advises government to engage in an act that will bring about the agony of nuclear war based on his personal religious beliefs. We should note here the extent to which individual interest is placed before that of the country. This is scary, but very much part of our time.

Evangelism is not the only way we use religion to define ourselves. Others, involving a less literal reading of the Bible, are not as extreme, but can be equally useful. Religion, like language, in its varying intensity can either join or separate us. At its center lies the historical debate between its communitarian potential for unity and the deep divisions that arise from individual dedication to dogma.

Today the Christian west is a secular society in which "the good life" dominates the afterlife. In the pop culture language of the Internet Mammon can be seen to get more 'hits' than God. This is a relatively recent turnaround, as for most of its existence Christianity embraced the concept of human life as a daily struggle with Satan over whom only Christ and his followers could triumph. The battle with Satan may take place on earth, but its penalties or rewards are not dispensed until after death.

Outside the spiritual realm, religion in our time continues to be the source of prolonged and bloody conflict. The Protestant/Catholic wars in Europe reached their zenith in the horrendous cruelty of the carnage in 17th and 16th century England. At that time the process of self-definition by validation and differentiation was spread through all levels of the English and Scottish populations and was very much a matter of life or death. Religion and life (both here and hereafter) were dominated by fear of unreasonable and extreme violence which only began to moderate in the 18th century Age of Enlightenment.

This moderation of Protestant/Catholic opposition was able to continue until the last century when violence flared up again in Ireland. This was the same war, the same words about substance and form; only the weapons changed. They are now quicker, more powerful and are designed for use against the general public. Such a relapse into intrafaith hostilities should not have happened, but it did.

On the broader, interfaith scale we also find the Christian west embroiled in a war against Muslim opponents in Iraq, and there are other conflicts in Africa and Asia in which the Muslim faith and its agenda for expansion play a dominant role. It has been useful for Western governments and their leaders to describe these Muslim engagements as limited to small and extreme groups on the far edge of Muslim life and worship, but in the Muslim world they seem to have a somewhat wider acceptance which increases as the result of our extended occupation in Iraq. The message of the Quran is a mixed one and can be taken as a call to religious arms and warfare. Those who hear that call, and then add to it the Marxist overlay of repression and resentment, come readily to the cause of a global insurgency that will bring them spiritual, economic and political respect. While Iraq has served as a flash point, basic Muslim/Judeo-Christian differences have gone unchanged since the Crusades, and, as in the Protestant/Catholic divide in Ireland, have now reappeared in a highly explosive form that combines old anger with new weapons.

There can be no clearer example of our need to define ourselves by validation and differentiation than in these two controversies. In Ireland this need is so powerful that the overarching linkage of Christianity is diminished and its details used as the basis for differentiation and conflict.

Our invasion of Iraq which was sure to have repercussions beyond its borders into the extended Muslim community was the handiwork of G. W. Bush, an evangelical Christian whose process of self-definition depends heavily upon his conservative religious and political beliefs. At a time when the loss of life in Iraq and the public's dissatisfaction with his presidency were at very high levels he was asked whether he had consulted his father. The president's reply indicated that his conversations were with a higher father than his earthly parent. Here is the textbook, lab test proof of self-definition by validation and differentiation, as in one brief answer he simultaneously elevates himself by association with God and distinguishes himself from all others who lack his special status and ability. The problem with Pres. Bush's self-definition, as with Pastor Hagee's, is that he fails to separate it from his policy decisions.

Looking back to the Crusades of the 11th, 12th and 13th

centuries when advanced weaponry consisted of swords, spears and maces, both Christian and Muslim forces engaged in acts of extreme barbarism and cruelty with neither having an advantage. Since then we have progressed to the pike, longbow, rifle, machine gun, tank, submarine, rocket, etc.- — an impressive development program with no shortage of testing opportunities. *In our nuclear age reality suggests that the next test will be the last,* and yet those nations, or groups, with the ability to do so continue to produce or obtain improved weapons technology. The years since the Crusades provide a sense that the Christian West has mellowed and will not revert to its former violence, but it is by no means certain that others will share our restraint.

Islam is generally a more committed religious force today than Christianity. It requires worship five times a day and projects images of earthly satisfaction in the afterlife (i.e., 72 virgins in heaven await the martyr). Much as our founding Puritans did almost four centuries ago, Islam dictates cultural expression such as justice, dress, music, visual arts, architecture, diet etc. And whereas we have moved away from these restrictions, Islam has not only rigidly maintained them, but has combined them with Marxist victimization theory.

We may seek safety in citing that we only conflict with Islam's extreme minority, but that minority has a global political action capability far beyond its numbers that derives from both religion and repression with the potential for instant ignition. These facts seem very clear, and yet they do not seem to be sufficiently reflected in our foreign policy.

The use of public institutions in pursuit of personal definition has a long history which societies in the future should be able to forgo, as more often than not it becomes just another way by which we abuse our institutions. These abuses are not imagined. They are real and are readily found in our media, schools, courts, Congress,

Dept of Justice and other areas that constantly mold our society. The end result of this abuse is that it contaminates, weakens and misdirects the force of these institutions in a way that can blunt their purpose or even render them useless.

Cultures are validating mechanisms and people coalesce around them. Lines of distinction are formed and provide a sense of us and the other which encourages the formation of social, political and economic power centers. These lines of distinction then create, magnify and multiply both group and individual differences. Religion has been a prime example throughout our recorded history, as we have noted in the protracted Christian/Muslim and Protestant/Catholic struggles, but it is only one of many. Other validating sources and techniques have played out in uncountable tribes, nations, empires and communes in the course of our cultural and social development.

Our form of democracy poses a difficult challenge in this area. Because it lacks the pervasive conformity of more authoritarian systems it tolerates a much greater exercise of the validation/differentiation function. And the current state of our democratic government only compounds the problem. Our democracy began with the philosophic values cited and claimed in the Declaration of Independence. Then, in our Constitution, we established a governmental structure of institutions and laws designed to deliver these values, one of which was our bicameral legislative Congress, to the people. In the process we portrayed ourselves as "a nation of laws" and have continued to do so ever since.

Today we are anything but "a nation of laws". It is not that there is a shortage of laws. There are plenty, but they are often not enforced or funded, and we have come to allow local laws to take precedence over national ones. The idea that we might look to Congress for either philosophical or legislative leadership is one whose time no longer exists. Public opinion can be expressed to and can reach members of Congress, but then it hits a kind legislative ceiling, and becomes mixed and mangled by the war of words and ideological battles that dominate Congress. Public access is more concept than fact, and not even a very successful one. There are messages that can penetrate the legislative ceiling and do so routinely, but they are those of the special interests who know that entry fees open doors and permit access to the currents of money and power that flow through and around the Congress.

"Other Voices, Other Rooms"[1]

At this moment in our political history an objective look at issues other than religion will reveal the extent to which personal definition is used to further policy which then creates a problematic or negative consequence. Pastor Hagee does not stand alone.

In agriculture, Congress has passed legislation that provides rich crop support and subsidy programs for farmers throughout America. With a very recent sensitivity the White House has threatened a veto, not because of its agricultural provisions, but because it contains too many earmarks for non-agricultural local projects. Members of Congress and President Bush who support this bill have claimed that it protects our small farmers, but, in fact, their benefits from it are minor, as by far the greatest part of its funding provided by American taxpayers goes to farms with incomes over $250,000, and some that are measured in the millions.

These mega farms operate with many types of new and expensive equipment including tractors that cost over $500,000, computer systems and a 24/7 capability to irrigate hundreds or thousands of acres of leased or owned land. *The small "family farmer" does not live here*. His role is to clap, if he has the time and energy, when the heroes drive by. Our large-scale agriculture is an extension of corporate America where we find the same values and techniques employed in the pursuit of profit. Farming is a tough business, but the cushion provided by the capital of mega farms greatly reduces the risk. Capital can perform its transformative magic equally as well on the farm as in the executive suite.

And there's another striking similarity between these two worlds. Both the mega farm and the mega corporation are enabled in their growth and success by government programs that provide lending sources, subsidies, tax relief, price/production supports, etc. Where money and power congregate, criticism of government is often long and strong, and yet government can be a useful partner, especially if silent.

The roads taken to money/power by politicians and corporate leaders are quite different, primarily because politicians have to be elected by public process, but they both clearly share the enjoyment of the chase and its rewards. And there's no need to go much further than the next fund raising campaign at a wealthy donor's home to observe how easily politicians validate and differentiate themselves by their association with those who inhabit the highest level of corporate success. The ease and frequency with which politicians transfer to foundation or corporate work after leaving electoral politics is yet another reflector of these ties that bind.

Every presidential campaign provides occasional moments which, although they may not be significant, can offer interesting insights. For Sen. John McCain such a moment occurred early in his campaign when he stated both that we may have a military presence in Iraq for the next hundred years and that in the near future there will be other wars of American involvement for which his military experience could offer the best leadership.

Sen. McCain deserves high praise for his military service and his ability to endure and survive his captivity in Vietnam. The latter was an incredible achievement of great character and strength. He now finds, however, that his campaign is restricted in many areas by his and Pres. Bush's previous voting records, and he must seek areas of comment that do not conflict with their past. In the two statements above he is saying "Elect me because I am a warrior; I've spent my life in military service." And so he has. The military, much like the clergy, is a calling in which one starts early and generally stays late, and demands a high degree of commitment.

Sen. McCain by word and attitude leaves no doubt that he defines himself by military service and values which pose no problem for him as a one-vote member of the senate. However, in the White House as Commander-in-Chief, or at some other high policy level where determinations are by decree, not by vote, the totality of military identification and definition may lessen policy options and results.

The military's planning and execution functions are far different from those of foreign policy. In the latter, nuance, and its effect upon friend and foe alike, is everything, and often delivers the true message not found in public statements. Sen. McCain's statement that we may have a military presence in Iraq for many years seems to offer a military judgement that such a presence could assure the US of meeting its current goals, but fails as realistic foreign policy which has to operate within much shorter time frames and must consider the thrust and parry, trust but verify, carrot and stick and other dual action techniques that will be called for in dealing with Iraq's neighbors.

The six Neocon architects of the Iraq occupation all seem likely to have viewed their policy in terms of self-definition and validation. To some extent that may always be true in those who seek the role of public leadership. Within limits it can be tolerated, but in extremis can be fatal. It is a flaw rarely subject to self-correction, and in a democracy its ultimate control lies in the electoral process.

Any effort to answer the question "Who Lost America?" must examine the vastly changed role of the media over the past half century during which both its content and its reach have greatly altered our culture. In content, it has provided a parallel track to the dumbing down of our education system with a relentless focus on sex and violence and multiple combinations thereof. Its reach now enables a 24/7 assault by TV broadcast, newspapers, magazines, internet, mobile electronic systems, cable, etc. directed to every segment of our population. And there is another way by which our media can influence and control our political destiny. *The media is the flame for the political moth.* The attraction of media exposure to politicians is a powerful, addictive and sometimes fatal force that must be pursued. Some politicians are better than others at controlling and directing it, but its use is a must and has become by far the most efficient way of getting their message out and bringing money in.

Not surprisingly, it has become a means of self-definition. For politicians with the weakest intellect, psychological profile, values structure, grasp of leadership, commitment to objective truth or other inner resources it offers a refuge where these weaknesses can be concealed behind the crowds, the hoopla, the canned applause and laughter, the "soft lob" questions and the carefully scripted and rehearsed dialogue and answers. Easily and cheaply purchased media coverage, mostly notably TV, now offers substandard candidates a form of political sleight of hand which in too many instances has deceived or confused the nation's voters. Unless the latter begin to pay more attention and demand more from better candidates the quality of our government will continue to decline.

The immigration issue is like Kudzu. It appears quietly, spreads quickly and provides a "handle" for a variety of legal, social, political and economic objections many of which derive from the objectors' need for self-definition. Perhaps the most obvious example is the choice of religious groups to offer sanctuary to illegals in opposition to our federal law. This act of civil defiance is based on the moral superiority of God's law as put forth in Christ's teachings, and those who join in sanctuary efforts define themselves by their commitment to compassion, even to the extent of resistance to the law of the land.

But again, the personal values that demand validation are not universal and the popularity of sanctuary as a social or political policy is not as evident in non-Christian groups and even less among the irreligious. It is almost impossible to overestimate the number and ways by which the many facets of the immigration issue provide receptors for the self-definition process. They act as a sort of psychological magnetic force capable of bonding individual emotion to difficult political choice. This plays out very dangerously in open immigration's impact on our population. Of all immigration's negative effects population is the most numbers specific and, in addition, has given hard evidence of its social and economic potential for dislocation. Keep Kudzu in mind.

Population is the umbilical cord that feeds politics, and for a couple of centuries now we have had the benefit of knowing that it increases geometrically at a much faster rate than that of resources that are fixed or only increase arithmetically. Today, estimates from both government and private sources indicate that, if immigration continues in its present form, we can expect a population increase over the next fifty years of over 150 million. Enter the Kudzu curve! Extend it for another fifty years and *our America will join the Easter Island sculptures looking for help that will not come.*

Any such increase would create a new political reality in the country, as in twenty-first century America assimilation of the kind we have experienced in the past is no longer the recognized goal. Without it multiple political constituencies will form that will lack a national perspective and may push for self-serving legislation such as the return of our southwestern states (Aztlan) to Mexico, or retroactive reparations for the period since we acquired them in 1848. In all likelihood, we should expect these constituencies of mostly third world origin to find other ways to direct more of the nation's wealth and favor to them.

Can this come to pass? And why is it considered a very real possibility by many Americans? For an answer it is only necessary to turn east to Europe. We have seats, front and center, to observe the deadly results of unchecked immigration in France, Germany, England, Denmark, the Netherlands and Italy where the former colonial powers are being swamped by constant third world arrivals, mostly from Africa or the Near East, and mostly Muslims.

The result has been extreme violence in the streets with random acts of murder, rape, torture and extensive property damage. To look at the European history, to listen to the arguments on both sides, to observe the results and then to think that "it can't happen here" is sheer folly. But history can only teach us, if we let it! Europe and America have managed to share some significant historical events— the almost twin revolutions here and in France, the industrial revolution, and WWs I & II. And, with almost eerily simultaneous timing, Congress in 1965 passed the Immigration Reform Act that totally transformed our process while Germany initiated legislation that invited large numbers of Turkish Muslims to enter, work and become citizens. Now almost fifty years later, the results of these two related and fateful efforts to accommodate third world demographic problems without consideration of long term damage to their own societies are playing out in our full view. The European narrative has run ahead of us, but our numbers are great and growing. This gap will be closed. The only question is "When?"

Is our government, are we ourselves, so anesthetized that the pain of the events in Europe does not register here? Time passes, and not to our advantage. Unless we change our policy we will confront the question of our own survival with progressively fewer opportunities and means to secure it. That we should reach such a point is unthinkable, but certainly possible, and perhaps even probable, as our national policy has been controlled by the personal beliefs and identification mechanisms of the elites in the White House and Congress from the Reagan administration to the present. And, most importantly, in spite of the expressed will of the American people.

Recap

Pastor Hagee, the media, the providers of sanctuary, and our elected representatives are joined. They are threads that make up an intricately interconnected web of cause and effect that has been formed over the last half century and which now dominates the exercise and policies of our government, and threatens its existence as a democratic republic constructed on a base of Anglo-Saxon law, religion, history, ethnicity and identity. In the beginning some of these were elements of choice; others of chance. Today, they are all challenged by a variety of forces that make claims to impose multiculturalism, to expand Mexico's territory at the expense of ours and to swing our national course so that an ever increasing share of our economic and political benefits is directed to the non-native, third world constituencies to which we have assigned special privileges.

This web is circular which provides equal strength to all parts. As with most problems of our current world, population is a key factor and a good starting point. At the end of WWII our population was 150 million and consistent with the carrying capacity of our habitat. Today it is around 300 million and challenges our ecological stability. Much of this recent growth has been due to the influx of immigrants from high fertility cultures.

During these same years we experienced an unusual technological explosion that enabled us to make and sell an array of newly developed products both here and to foreign markets. The third element that combined with population and technology to complete our economic growth capability was marketing in general, and the media in particular. It has a multiplier effect and was able to generate the steady growth in consumer purchasing that accounts for about 70% of our GDP. From their efforts our media were able to create enormous wealth and power — and to retain a healthy share for themselves.

Our prolonged postwar economic boom was largely the result of these three factors — more consumers from more population; new technology from government, academia and the private sector; and the miracle of modern media marketing.

Two capabilities within the media industry appeared almost simultaneously, and dramatically changed its ability to serve its users. The first was the arrival of TV as a national, color medium for advertising around the clock. This was a natural evolution from prewar pioneer efforts and it provided the broadcast media with a profitability explosion that had not been available from radio. But there was a catch. And it was that in order to derive revenues from 24/7 commercials there also had to be 24/7 programming — i.e. product, and 24/7 product meant there would be a lot of cheap, "quick and dirty" programs. It was instantly recognized, but rarely acknowledged, that to have a constant and ready source of such product would require a massive "dumbing down" of the medium. Slam dunk! Done; no further questions; meeting adjourned.

The second media industry capability of enormous consequence was technological and had its greatest impact on direct mail and print media activities. This was the adoption of our zip code system which has made it possible to target and reach ever smaller groups to the extent that individual office buildings or other destinations can now have their own zip codes. This ability of zip codes to provide demographic distinction has revolutionized the value and reach of market research which can now create more specific messages designed to motivate these smaller and more distinctive areas of purchasing power.

The end result of these combined forces of population, technology and marketing growth was the sustained economic advance of the postwar period which elevated our national and personal wealth/power to new levels.

Looking at the new media/marketing techniques, could there be a more inviting stage set for the arrival of millions of ethnically, culturally, and geographically mixed immigrants? As the pursuits of politics and commerce adapted to the limited language (mostly Spanish) of the new arrivals, the goal of assimilation receded. Specific groups in specific areas could be easily reached with culturally and/or politically specific messages.

Communities differed substantially in their ability to attract or absorb the growing immigrant population, but in those areas where circumstance encouraged concentration it was only a matter of brief time before politicians (often former immigration attorneys) appeared to represent the new constituencies in their mother tongue and to build their representation on the issues of the immigrant agenda. As these communities grew in number and in size they became able to engage in and benefit from our "gerrymandering" process, which is practiced nationally by both major parties, even though it opposes democracy in spirit and practice and makes possible the existence of "safe seats".

The Connection

This chapter touches upon some very sensitive subjects — religion, immigration and war among them — but, as important as they are, it is not about them. It is about government and how far our present system and practice have fallen from their original intention and function.

The goal of government must be good government itself. This can be achieved and kept in balance only by enlightened policy which must serve both our lesser and larger interests here and abroad. In our present circumstance, policy is rarely anything other than a frequently exchanged hostage in our political wars. In these, the decisive component is often revealed, when the ideological curtain is lifted as in The Wizard of Oz[2], to be our own bumbling need for recognition, definition and identification.

These may explain some of our personal, political and cultural failures, but they cannot serve as the foundation of good government. For that, we must undertake a national renewal, although we may no longer have the will, or the time, or the means to accomplish such an effort. But, if we don't, we will be faced with more war, more debt, more population, more immigration, more environmental degradation, more polarization, more climate change, more drugs, more gangs, etc. The list goes on. This is not summer beach reading, but it is our real image, our Portrait of Dorian Gray.[3]

There is a choice to be made, but, to have any chance of success, it must be a national choice, and in our current condition that means the process of renewal must be initiated by the people. Those who look to the November elections for answers will be disappointed, as the real problem is one of institutionalized failure by Republicans and Democrats alike, and the only force not bound by their area of failure and yet powerful enough to reform our system is the vox populi.

End Notes

[1] Truman Capote
[2] Frank Baum
[3] Oscar Wilde

ECD 6/28/08

Chapter Three —— October 2008
Identity — Part II

We continue to explore how the ways we have failed our institutions have played out in our politics and policies and have separated us from the original intentions and character of our democracy. Future chapters will concern themselves with different perspectives and aspects of this new America.

In this and the previous chapter we show how we have embarked upon a way of disguising our country by actions and values that are of recent origin and which stand in contrast to how Americans saw and conducted themselves until they assumed the authority and title of sole superpower.

Disguise, like definition, is very much part of the human condition which regularly asserts itself in matters of history, government or politics. Fraught as it is with inconsistency, frailty and error, the human condition must be recognized for what it is — the only one we have.

It does not reduce easily to jingles, slogans or bar graphs. These can reveal the results of human nature, but not the mysteries of its essence, its origins or even the way or the why of its many forms. The human condition can create wonderful institutions which serve as centers for our expression of language, law, justice, religion and politics, and which in our country have mostly spoken with one voice for many people. This is important, for speaking is language in action, and language is one of humanity's oldest and most necessary institutions with the power to unite or to divide.

Our institutions can be fragile. To serve their purpose they must be honored, energized, nourished and maintained. If they are allowed to become contaminated by, or put to, petty purposes, they will fail, and in doing so will offer a very credible answer to "Who Lost America?"

In our society, human nature and politics make strange bedfellows. One or the other regularly delivers a poke in the eye, a jab in the ribs or suffers a leg spasm. They seem to have shared our time and trust too long.

GOOD GOVERNMENT SHOULD PRODUCE AN ATMOSPHERE OF NATIONAL RESPONSIBILITY AND OPPORTUNITY CREATED FOR THE PEOPLE BY THE COMBINED EFFORTS OF THEIR ELECTED REPRE-SENTATIVES. DIVISIONS WILL ALWAYS EXIST AS TO GOVERNMENT'S DIRECTION, AND DECISIONS MUST BE RESOLVED BY THE OBJECTIVE APPLICATION OF BOTH PERSONAL AND POLITICAL INTEGRITY. THE STRUCTURE OF GOVERNMENT SHOULD BE FIRM AND OPEN AND SHOULD NOT BE BURDENED BY BECOMING A PROVING GROUND FOR EITHER IN-DIVIDUAL OR PARTY IDEOLOGY.

Many people, especially those in politics and other forms of public life, like to give the impression that their actions result from an elaborate or noble thought process. This is usually wrong, the truth being that they are subject to the same search for self-definition as anybody else. The most notable difference is that their self-deluding perspective provides an effective disguise of their true purpose and capability

We live in a time and place of continuing ideological trench warfare in which politics and identity are so joined that each easily passes for the other and their true form is unknowable. In this warfare, at the heart of our government, broad claims and accusations such as "tax and spend", "support our troops", "the best health (or school) system in the world", "fiscal responsibility", etc. are lobbed back and forth by both parties in a punch/counter punch process designed to provide cover in capsule form. *There is no effort to define the national interest, nor how we, or they, can serve it.*

Nowhere is this more evident than in the complex issue of health care where its meaning, and perhaps future, is regularly condensed into two phrases, "socialized medicine" and "universal health care", that appeal to opposite emotional responses and have become favored weapons of both parties. While these phrases may well catch the emotions of the moment, they do not carry the force of truth, for reality is that in our health care issue the lines of unyielding division follow economic, not medical or political, contours.

It has become increasingly difficult over the past half century for our government and our society to define the difference between the national and the public interest. For instance, the Republican Party has steadfastly, in good times and bad, advocated "lower taxes" in any election in which it participates. And yet, in our present, almost thirty year, period of overspending and going into a "guns and butter" debt, what is in the national interest? And in projecting Republican ideology to government policy, which has greater resonance and authority — "lower taxes" or "fiscal responsibility"?

Similarly, it can be argued that the Democrats' historical commitment to spending for broad social goals should be restrained in deference to our steadily increasing deficits and debt. These kinds of conflict in matters of health and finance are all too frequent and clear, and the inability of our elected representatives to resolve them is key to answering the question "Who Lost America?"

Religion's impact on our Near Eastern policy was accorded specific and prominent mention in the previous chapter. Freedom of religion is one of the most basic freedoms guaranteed by members of the free world and was enshrined in the UN charter at the time of its founding. However, sixty years later Muslim/Christian conflict is more intense and widespread than ever.

Our founding fathers' intent was to allow every person to make a religious choice, or no choice, thereby granting the individual citizen the greatest possible spiritual freedom. Today this freedom is attacked and confined by those on the far left who oppose all religion (i.e., socialists and communists) as well as those mostly Christian evangelicals on the far right who want others to conform to their beliefs and ways, with the result that our religious landscape today is a far more troubled one than our founders faced. But true freedom of religion is not merely a matter of government policy, as it must succeed at the community level to reach beyond policy and achieve reality.

And it is at our neighborhood level that we define ourselves religiously by validation and differentiation. So far, most of the religious conflict in our country has resulted from Roman Catholic/Protestant differences within the Christian faith. It has ill prepared us for the new mosque across town with its different architecture and dogma, and the dress and appearance of those who worship there. In the end, our acceptance of the Muslim religious presence in America will depend upon whether the Muslim community allows its mosques to act as political centers as has happened in England. *Here, as there, if they do, violence will likely result.*

The European colonial powers after WWII were morally compelled to accept immigrants from their colonies who had served in the allied forces, and this moral element was politically expanded by the presence of the UN's forum and the diplomatic center it provided to its growing post-colonial membership.

Within a decade, the grand-scale economies in England, France, Germany and Italy began to show signs that the influx from their former colonies was creating economic and social problems. These have multiplied and intensified to the point where deep social and judicial divisions now are widespread and have the ability to damage, and even dominate, the political process.

We, of course, were able to observe the European course of events without learning from them and, as we had no colonial immigration source, set out to construct an immigrant inflow of our own without bothering to distinguish between legal and illegal arrivals. Not surprisingly, in a short time we were #1. Today both political parties agree that the system is broken, but not how to fix it. In this instance "Who Lost America?" is a question that answers itself.

Throughout the self-definition process, wheth-er by validation or differentiation, we make decisions with almost the speed of light that present ourselves to others in a way that indicates we are right, what we do is good and/or we are the best. These are powerful motivators all of which carry elements designed to create approval of our actions. Societies differ in how they emphasize these values, and, unfortunately, in present-day America laying claim to being the best, "We're #1", has become our national mantra.

Rather than enhance our image, its obvious note of bravado diminishes it and, more importantly, obscures the immense corrective effort we must undertake to recapture our abandoned principles.

Nations define themselves, as individuals do, and seek the approval of other nations through foreign policy. This is not easy because in foreign affairs there are always games within games, circles within circles and mazes within mazes. The Cold War permitted most international confrontations of its time to be identified with one or the other side, thereby simplifying what would otherwise have been more difficult political and emotional choices. As the Cold War extended its reach and its risk/reward, it is not surprising that both parties ratcheted up their assertions that they would bring truth, strength and benefits to all.

Since the Cold War's end, America has experienced a growing loss of respect in its foreign relations culminating in the military and other related contradictions of our principles that have resulted from our invasion/occupation of Iraq. The face that we reveal to our fellow nations may permit us to wear a mask for a while, but in foreign relations truth is accelerated by the interplay of interests, and can only be held in check temporarily by the spin, hype and artifice that are on immediate call to the modern state.

IN ORDER TO POSITIVELY ALTER OUR IMAGE AND REGAIN OUR CREDIBILITY ABROAD WE MUST DECLARE AND HONOR OUR HISTORICAL PRINCIPLES AT HOME. THIS WILL REQUIRE US TO RECOGNIZE AND RESTORE OUR IMAGE OF OURSELVES AND OUR ORIGINAL VALUES, AND THEN TO RESTRUCTURE GOVERNMENT SO THAT IT SERVES THEM. ONCE THIS IS IN PROCESS, GOVERNMENT CAN AGAIN ACT IN OUR NATIONAL INTEREST.

Our judiciary is an area of our national life that has undergone significant change in recent years, including self-definition by judges. We live in a time that has witnessed a pronounced alteration of the role of our courts. Some view this as judicial activism, while others regard it as a contemporary interpretation of not only the language of the Constitution, but also its intent, whether specified or not.

We can both define ourselves, and be defined, by our careers. Notable examples are doctors, the clergy and the military and, of course, the judiciary's attachment to the law. In the latter, sometimes the need is so strong that judges ignore or contradict actual fact, cite non-existent precedent or refute established law, thereby inviting an appeal process. Still, it happens, as judges have a uniquely powerful advantage in pushing their personal beliefs in that they can write them into the law under which we all must live.

There is a strong body of legal, and non-legal, opinion today that views the Constitution as being written on rubber that can be stretched to deal with almost any social or human problem that appears in court. That our Constitution was not designed to resolve contemporary social issues was clearly stated by Chief Justice Warren Burger in 1982 when he wrote:

> "the Constitution does not provide a cure for every
> social ill or vest judges with a mandate... to remedy
> every social problem"[1]

And yet, in the language of local, appellate and even Supreme Court decisions one can find ready acceptance of this broader purpose.

This expansion of the courts' role may well be the result of our society's vastly increased use of litigation as, with a growing number of lawyers filing more and more cases, it is only natural that they will reach out for whatever theories will support their representation of their clients.

The Supreme Court has long been seen as the ultimate arbiter in our system of government — in effect, "the court of last resort", but that lofty position was attained by its acting as interpreter of the law. If it finds itself attracted to making law, as some recent decisions can seem to suggest, and veers off in that direction, it will come into conflict with the Congress which enjoys the sole and specific authority to make law. If Congress concludes that the Court's actions and their consequences threaten its assigned role in government, it could either legislate around the Supreme Court or undertake to amend the Constitution.

Our presently highly polarized Congress might find these actions beyond their reach, especially amending the Constitution which is usually a long and slow process involving the concurrence of two thirds of both houses of Congress and then ratification by three-fourths of the states' legislatures.

Of greater concern is the effect that such a divisive issue might have on the public at a time of deep division over other major issues such as health, debt, immigration, war, the economy, etc. To add a constitutional crisis derived from argument over the function and identity of our branches of government might just be more, in our present political circumstance, than our government could endure.

This is not a tomorrow's headline issue, but it is real and serious. The Court has been infected with the same political polarization virus that demeans the Congress, as evidenced by the frequency of 5-4 decisions. Should we continue in this pattern, we are liable to find ourselves facing a stalemate as to much of the work and many of the issues that confront all three branches of our government. We might yearn for the return of 7-2 or 8-1 decisions that offer more hope of consensus and stability, but at the crux of the matter is both the Court's and the general judiciary's defining view of themselves.

There is nothing more pernicious to democratic government than selective law enforcement. It strikes at the very foundation of the democratic concept of the relation between government and citizens. For the last half century this discrepancy between what government says and what it actually does is most evident in its broad failure to enforce the letter or the intent of its own immigration laws. This has been explored in detail in previous issues and it is not necessary to revisit it here.

But immigration is not the only area of our government that skillfully forms and alters our laws. We need look no further than the Federal Election Commission (FEC) to find "the good, the bad and the ugly" at work. The good is its intended function to enforce our campaign finance laws after which "the bad and the ugly" take over.

The FEC is a six-member body supposed to include both Republicans and Democrats. Today it has only 2 members and, as 4 votes are necessary to have a quorum, it is unable to function in a presidential election year which is considered to be especially important and in which enormous sums of money will be spent on a variety of techniques and tactics, some of which may not comply with the requirements of our campaign laws. As it is, the FEC can neither render decisions nor impose fines and exists pretty much in name only. Enforcement is <u>not</u> an option.

This has come about because Senate Republicans have not confirmed proposed nominations by Democrats and the latter have opposed a controversial Republican nominee. If Washington holds true to form, then sometime after the November elections the matter may be resolved, but until that happens it will be "no holds barred" business as usual on the campaign trail.

In addition to the obvious way in which the public interest is being ignored, there is a growing "fox in charge of the hen house" feeling that comes from having members of the FEC determined by a political process centered in the Congress!

Another cause for public concern is that the more the Congress tries to rewrite our election law, the more ideological interests have to be served. The result is that it then must be subjected to judicial review and exposed to further recrafting according to the judiciary's view of its role and responsibility. The chances are that the end result is more confusing than the earlier version and may restart the process by opening new avenues of ideological attack.

Recently the Department of Transportation granted permission to Mexican truck drivers who cannot read or understand English to use our highways. While actions such as this that give preferential treatment to Mexican interests are not unusual in the Bush administration, the DOT order opposed the Federal Motor Carrier Safety Administration (FMCSA) rules for interstate motor carriers which require drivers to:

> "Read and speak the English language sufficiently to converse with the general public, to understand highway traffic signs and signals in the English language, to respond to official inquiries and to make entries on reports and records."[2]

The DOT's ruling has been protested by members of America's Independent Trucker's Association (AITA) and thousands of other truck drivers who clearly recognize the danger to the public and to themselves of tractor-trailer rigs weighing up to 80,000 pounds and moving at high speeds being operated by drivers who can neither read nor understand highway signs, vehicle identification of loads/limits and other information important to maximizing highway safety.

Selective enforcement becomes more apparent in this matter by DOT Secretary Mary Peters' admission that the Mexican drivers covered by the Bush administration's border demonstration project are classified as "proficient in English" even if they need to use their native Spanish to convey the meaning of our traffic signs.[3]

Accidents involving multiple fatalities that were directly attributable to lack of language comprehension have occurred in IL, MA and PA and have been called to the DOT's attention, but from the point of view of selective law enforcement, the most galling aspect of the DOT's position is that it permits "Mexican drivers to flout the very same safety regulations that it requires American truck drivers to follow."[4]

Our founders created a system based on fluid tension — pull here and snap back there. It is constantly in motion and has done a reasonably good job of protecting the nation from excesses of all kinds, from sudden transfers of power and from the demagoguery from which no democracy is spared. This is no small accomplishment and we have been very fortunate.

In the normal stretching and straining of our system reasonable men with the nation's best interest at heart have striven for an historic balance between our three branches, realizing that from time to time advantage may move from one to another.

This does not seem to be the intent of the Bush administration which seems to seek not just an unusually strong executive branch, but rather its permanent dominance over the other two. This direction has been aided by presidential power exerted against Congress via Republican control, by the placement of proponents of executive dominance in key positions at the Justice, State, Defense and Treasury departments, and by initiating the practice of signing statements by which, when he signs a bill to which he objects, the President identifies those parts which fail to meet his goals and which he will, therefore, not enforce. This is selective law enforcement at the top!

President Bush frequently identifies and refers to himself as "the Decider". Unfortunately for our government much of his deciding has to do with which laws he will or will not enforce.

While the Bush administration determinedly expanded the force and reach of the executive function, it simultaneously restricted access to a wide range of information in no way tied to national security by the public, the press, scholars and other individuals and institutions.

Much of this information had never been previously classified and was generally available by simple request or under the Freedom of Information Act (FOIA). But at the inception of his presidency, Bush declared that no external review of extensive records of his and his father's terms of office would thereafter be permitted. In effect, this removed the presidency from the scope of the FOIA which was certainly neither contemplated nor intended at the time of its passage.

The elder Bush could have neutralized the situation and supported open government had he made a quiet, even casual, statement that he had no personal objection to his records remaining open. Sadly, no such statement was made and another battle was won by those in government who favor selective law enforcement.

Almost certainly, Bush, Cheney and their Neocon cohorts view their transformation of executive authority as a "win". For our nation and our historic democratic system, however, it constitutes a serious loss and breach of faith.

In our society we find numerous occupations that require their practitioners to wear uniforms — merchant marine, airlines and passenger ships, postal employees, judges, fire and police, Salvation Army, concierges and other hotel personnel, athletic teams, symphony orchestras, etc. And, most prominently, there are what we refer to as our uniformed services — Army, Navy, Air Force, Coast Guard and Marines. What they all have in common is that, for one reason or another, they want their members to dress the same way, to appear uniform — in one form.

The first use of group uniforms probably dates back to the earliest national cultures that employed standing armies such as China and Egypt. For these forces a uniform provided cohesiveness via visual equality and a ready means of identification that was critical in hand-to-hand combat. In our missile age, cohesion/equality is the dominant factor and is basic to the discipline structure that must be developed and maintained.

But, not surprisingly, some people in the military, as in other callings, are more "equal" than others. Variations in skills, intelligence, attitude and character appear and are noted by promotion in rank, pay and authority. Such recognition is institutional, but we are not institutes. We are individuals and we define ourselves throughout our lifetimes in one way or another, the most obvious and persistent of which is by differentiation. As our modern military is committed to the plain brown, blue or olive green colors of its branches' uniforms, the only way to indicate change of status, to differentiate, is to add to the basic uniform.

This process has its origins in the awarding of medals for conspicuous battle action. In time, as more decorations were created to reflect more wars, battles, and casualties, a small piece of ribbon that could easily be attached to the uniforms came into everyday use as evidence of an award. At this point emphasis seems to have shifted from individual ribbons to their accumulation. Today badges and other insignia representing skills such as marksmanship, a geographical area of service, completion of a training course and others have been added to further distinguish the wearer.

Not long ago, shortly following Gen. Petraeus' appearance before Congress, Chief of Staff Admiral Mike Mullen appeared on TV. Both of these high-ranking officers carried an array of perhaps twenty-five or more ribbons on their chests and other insignia on their shoulders, sleeves, collars, etc. and one can wonder how and how frequently they are transferred from one uniform to another.

The element of differentiation seemed particularly evident in Admiral Mullen's case. On each shoulder he wore in gold braid the four stars of his rank, and then within a space of six inches or less the four star rank reappeared on his shirt collar tabs in the form of a metallic bar.

In the military every possible symbol is displayed. Some reflect valor or sacrifice, but others don't. Why? Businessmen don't wear insignia indicating their salaries, or the number of contracts they've closed, or the number of bridges or buildings they've built. Is the military's broad use of distinguishing insignia tied to its authoritarianism? *As individuality is suppressed in military life and dress code, does the display of insignia provide an alternative way to express individuality, to be recognized, to achieve distinction?*

The military is not the only occupation to require uniform dress and then to offer embellishments that depart from uniformity as rewards. The Christian clergy wear mostly black or, more recently, gray during their ordinary daily duties, but during worship services change to mostly white with the addition of other elements in bright and rich colors and fabrics which are keyed to the iconography of the church's dogma and calendar. Although the church may see its variety of dress as another way to celebrate the glory of God, it also serves the more mundane purpose of indicating religious rank.

Academia is another area of powerful distinction, although, again like clergy, not on a daily basis. At any of our universities, public or private, the faculty goes about its daily routine of lectures, laboratories and conferences in the usual campus dress of jacket and trousers. The teaching role calls for most academics' time to be spent in class with students or in research, and there is little opportunity or reason for differentiation, even though there may be wide differences in pay scale. But on formal occasions, most evidently commencement, when the entire faculty is called together, the long, black robes emerge from academic closets and appear in public. While the basic color is black, it is accompanied by many other colors applied to cowls, linings and trim. These colors are clear markers of distinction that proclaim the wearer's rank, degrees and even his/her particular area of study and expertise. The casual observer is not versed in this language, but to those who are it offers dramatic proof of self-definition by distinction.

In the various occupations mentioned at the beginning of this section such as hotel employees or the Salvation Army it is necessary to be able to readily identify employees from the people that surround them. The uniform is a quick and economic way to do this, but identification is not enough, as the human element surfaces in the appearance and use of insignia that indicate rank, length of service and specific activity.

And, finally, a most discreet, and yet revealing, instance comes from our Supreme Court where its nine judges, when in session, don the elegant, but simple, black judicial robe. A few years ago then Chief Justice Rehnquist appeared after a summer break with the addition to his robe of a modest, but very visible, line of gold thread trim that encircled both sleeves between the wrist and elbow. As the court's size (9) is small, personal identification is precluded as motivation. But there is no doubt that Justice Rehnquist intended to let his fellow judges and those outside the court know that there was only one chief justice. He took some ribbing, mostly good-natured, from the press, but the ground-breaking stripes stayed.

There can be no doubt that a uniform offers advantages of economy, efficiency, morale, identification and cohesion in mixed amounts, but human distinctions must be served too. *Any totally bland and plain uniform imposes more equality than we can probably tolerate.*

The two major revolutions of the twentieth century imposed the regimentation of communist thought and dress on the largest countries in the world. Think back to the public demonstrations under Mao and Stalin when the participants wore either the military or the worker's uniform. Today, images of public life in these countries are much more varied in costume, as the Communist leaderships have recognized that, while still maintaining total control of government, making some room for individual distinctions can relax the tension between the people and the state.

Self-definition under authoritarian regimes is more difficult than it is in a democracy. The validation process is entirely engaged with the state apparatus, with the opportunity for individual differentiation severely limited, and yet it is silently and surely at work — while the leadership sleeps, gives speeches, turns its back, goes to war or attends world conferences. It is part of the human condition which we must recognize. Thankfully, it is not a matter of politics; *it is what we are; it is found in everything we achieve and much that we don't; and it is inseparable from us.*

Two interesting political efforts toward uniformity are now taking place. The first is the European Union with its immense bureaucracy established in Brussels to administer all of Europe's commercial, judicial, and economic processes. Over the half century of its growing presence and acceptance it has been mostly successful in simplifying the many social, currency, travel and trade problems that marked life in multi-national Europe, and yet a single vote by Ireland earlier this year prevented its full confirmation and implementation.

Ireland is an island, as is England which joined the EU but has refused to adopt the Euro as its currency. These two island states differ in one very significant way from the EU's continental membership in that they have not been washed over by the wars of territorial extension that have formed Europe's history over the past millenium. Every major power — Russia, Rome, Austro-Hungary, Germany, France & Spain — have served as initiators or partners in these repetitive and bloody attempts to tilt the balance of power to the point of dominance over the land, the people and the destiny of the European continent, and beyond.

After each wave has been challenged, beaten back and forced to recede, many of the old, seemingly timeless distinctions drawn from Europe's origins in many small hereditary entities have re-emerged to reclaim their pride of place in a process that might gain strength through repetition.

The map of Europe shows fewer countries than it did two, or even one, hundred years ago. In the next one or two centuries will it reduce itself to the ultimate one — the EU? Will the EU's members, over time, surrender their national and cultural distinctions and loyalties to Brussels' administrative center? In the past, the many European states have found the way to restore their individual status after each consolidation. Will the way of the future be from baron to bureaucrat?

The other instance of political regionalism is the nascent North American Union (NAU) that was initiated by the leaders of Canada, Mexico and the US in 2005. The NAU is an example of selective law enforcement on the grandest scale possible, as it has been secretly put in place only by executive order, and has been stealthily expanded within our presently existing government structure (i.e., mostly in the Department of Commerce) without congressional or public debate. Selective law enforcement comes into play because the NAU concept and regulations conflict with our historic sovereignty and existing law. Because they do, the NAU's structure has been designed so that it circumvents present law and operates through newly formed departments, committees and tribunals whose identities need not be made public.

The NAU differs from the EU in that it lacks the latter's growing base now in excess of twenty-five members. There will only be 3 members of the NAU and two of them will probably draw very substantial political, security and economic nourishment from the third. Loss of sovereignty is an obvious result of this projected merger, but just as important to us as Americans is whether we will be willing to do away with those many cultural and historic identifying distinctions which we have simply accumulated or passionately embraced in the course of our remarkable journey.

There is nothing wrong with a mutual cooperation agreement, but the NAU far exceeds any such framework and envisions a merger of our territory and laws. There is an enormous loophole that hangs over a future under the NAU. It requires that any NAU-related issue be resolved in special NAU courts presided over by NAU appointed judges. This would allow almost any civil or criminal matter directly or indirectly associated with NAU to bypass our courts and juries. This parallel system of surreal bureaucracy would seriously compromise our own judiciary, dilute our justice and damage the legal foundations of many parts of our democratic government.

If alerted, if given the chance, one must assume that the American people would gather themselves and turn this threat away. But the alarm has already sounded, the night is long and our sentries are nowhere to be seen.

Why have we devoted these two chapters to the process of self-definition? Is it that important? There are reasons to think it is, although it will not in any direct way produce legislation. And yet it informs our knowledge of people, and people are the only means by which we create and conduct government.

Our world is crossed and recrossed by many lines of differentiation — genetic, ethnic, national, racial, geographical, climatic, economic, social, cultural, religious, topographical, political and others. These differences allow humans, and their lives, to take different forms in different places. Consciously or unconsciously, it is difficult to ignore them and it would be impossible to eliminate or significantly reduce them because people and their circumstances are engaged in a process of multiplication that brings about more change and more distinctions.

America is at a crossroads and it must redefine itself to its own people and to others. We cannot logically argue that the results that most Americans want our policies to yield can be accomplished by more of the same — more wars, more debt, more immigration, more population, more pollution and more rhetoric, for example. *This means that we must change our government and its way of thinking.*

Today both presidential candidates freely admit and state that Washington is broken. This is true and appears to be one of very few things upon which both parties can agree. That's about as far as they go, however, for no reason is given as to how and why our government came to its present state. The reason is that our two-party system now functions only as an electoral system. After their election our elected representatives are unable to represent because they have no real sense of government as an instrument for serving the public interest as fairly, justly and efficiently as possible.

There is a glass ceiling in the Congress which limits public involvement. Opinion is expressed to or through our elected representatives, but goes no further. It is deflected by the invisible barrier and relegated to be used by the members of Congress in their endless Republican/Democrat battles for political advantage. That there are many personal "perks" involved only serves to intensify their efforts to further diminish any concept of the national interest.

What has played out in the halls of our government over the last fifty years is a strange mix of human thought and failure of which we were warned by Orwell, Kafka and Beckett, but we paid no heed. The mess is so extensive that only a "new" way of thinking offers the possibility of a remedy. And that way of thinking must view government as a way of expressing and achieving our truly national interest.

But where will we find those capable of this new paradigm? It is unlikely that they will emerge from the ranks of the two major parties who dominate access to the ballots in most states and localities. In our system the people have the right to elect, although that right is often clouded by party control of the local nominating process.

Still, it is the people that have the power, and it will only be through them that government will be able to change itself sufficiently to return to a form consistent with its historic and constitutional values. Today, for the first time in our history we have available to us a technology that can inject the vox populi back into our government process without it being hijacked and put to the use of the two major parties.

That technology is the internet. It can provide a platform by which reasoned people seeking to define the national interest by objective truth and open review can reach millions of citizens who, in turn, will enjoy instant access to this new entity. The initiators of such an internet presence could manage its growth and channel its popularity by keeping faith with their commitment to new government. Their control of the website's content can refuse access to it by the wacko/wahoo demagogue element with its relentless pursuit of audience manipulation and personal publicity.

As a matter of policy, it would be useful to severely restrict personal visual images, but rather to offer articles, analysis, reporting, interpretation, evaluation and clarification of important issues and how they can be resolved in the nation's interest. This should be the primary purpose after which the next, asking for comment and responding to it, should logically follow. We are at a moment when technological progress serves its highest purpose in being able to reach into and improve the lives of the nation's citizens at a modest cost and great benefit to our system of government.

Nothing less than new methods and thinking can repair the many kinds of damage which we have leveled against our form of government in recent years. The old ways will no longer work, as they and their sponsors have become mired in the mud of ideological trench warfare. Self-definition is important because members of two of our three branches of government define themselves by ideology, and the third is not far behind. Attitudes vary. Some see it as a game; others as a life-or-death issue; and some shift from one to the other. But their commitment to the struggle never wavers. In war, peace cannot come until the fighting stops. There is little chance that political peace will break out in Washington and bring an end to our war of ideology and polarization.

There would be enormous honor in being able to reform our ways of government and realign them more closely with our origins and Constitution. The term "peace with honor" is used frequently in referring to our various military ventures, but it has different meanings for different people. If we could end our ideological war of attrition and provide our government with a new form and direction fueled by dedicated and broad public involvement, we could achieve a real "peace with honor".

Election Year Notes

We are only just past the political conventions at a time when a seemingly endless nominating process has finally concluded. It has been an agonizing two years since the first candidacies and exploratory committees were announced during which we have been subjected to a constant mixture of hype, cliché, opinion, comment, speculation, rumor, suggestion, innuendo, etc. This makes for a ruinous process which can anesthetize the public and diminish the credibility and stature of the candidate. From a marketing view, it is overexposure on steroids.

Mark Sullivan, director of the Secret Service, puts the cost of protection for Obama and McCain at $40,000/day and estimates that the cost for the presidential nomination and electoral campaigns will exceed $100 million.[5] With other expenses by the two major political parties and other groups certain to run into billions of dollars, the excess and waste of our system becomes ever more clear.

It is time to change our procedure, to reduce its length to something more reasonable. British elections are conducted in a matter of a month or two. Allowing for our larger size and population, *we should aim for a four-month nominating period followed by two months of electoral campaigning in September and October.*

Besides the ennui and cost factors, there is the matter of diminished job performance. Most of the candidates for nominations were members of Congress who, for about a year accorded priority of their time and effort to campaigning. As they receive their regular compensation during this period, the government is in effect subsidizing their campaigns. Preferably, they should resign, but that would open the job to a new appointment with the possibility of altering the political balance. At the least, a leave of absence without compensation or retirement benefits would be appropriate.

The chances are almost assured that no such changes will take place. The media thrives on campaign revenue much as politicians do on public appearances and media coverage with the result that only new thinking will bring about change. And yet, there's something truly unconscionable about government paying legislators during their prolonged absences for personal reasons and then paying again to protect them while they run for another office. This is double dipping on a scale and by reason that could only come to us from Washington.

On the plus side, the vast amount of money and press coverage being applied to this year's campaigns may have the effect of reversing the longstanding trend in lowered voter participation which had been predicted to dip below 50% of those eligible. Both parties have spared neither money nor effort to attract new, and especially younger, voters, and it will be interesting to see which has been more successful and what the final figures will be.

Another serious trend with mostly negative consequences has been the exceptionally high percentage, around 90% of congressional incumbents that are reelected. Republicans are now experiencing more vacancies by retirement than usual which may obscure somewhat the overall impact of the national mood for change, but even with Democrats expected to pick up seats in both houses, our incumbency reelection rates testify to something other than an open and vibrant democracy.

Lastly, we may have arrived at a time that represents the end of one era and the beginning of another. Throughout the lengthy nominating process and debates both parties shifted the time frames of their references to former presidents. For the Democrats, the old description as being the party of Jackson, FDR or Truman gave way overwhelmingly to association with JFK. Similarly, Republicans cast themselves as the party of Ronald Reagan far more frequently than calling upon Lincoln or Eisenhower.

This is a quantum leap in political role modeling, made perhaps because JFK and Reagan have appeared as the stars of the post-WWII TV age who worked the medium better than others and were, accordingly, able to obtain from it the benefits of far greater coverage and exposure. We will miss FDR, Honest Abe and the others. They were with us for many years and their lessened visibility marks a major shift in our political culture.

Can we be at some new cultural divide that is shifting everything pre-television back into a more distant and less accessible past now beginning to be out of mind and beyond memory? Any such process is by its nature slow and subtle and one of which we should be aware. Changes in our political, or even historical, perspectives suggest that our history can be rewritten by both conscious and unintentional means. It can be reasonably viewed that Presidents Reagan and Kennedy are figures of lesser leadership and accomplishments than Lincoln and FDR. If they are to be the new standard of political descent, have we lost something in the exchange?

And finally, we combine the self-definition and political processes in the stunning displays of our recent political conventions. As if designed specifically for it, the conventions served as the theatre in which to showcase our self-definition.

Fix your attention on the speaker on the podium as he differentiates his/her candidate or party by creating and applying lines of distinction that include ethics, economics, voting records, leadership, character, origins, marriage, offspring, religion, the public welfare, diplomacy, and on and on. *Nothing is out of bounds because there are no bounds. There is one end and all means are justified.* No difference, it seems, is so small that it can be ignored and none so large that it cannot be claimed. Indeed, the success of the party, the election and the nation will be determined by these differences and the roles they play in our lives.

But differentiation is only part of the process. The speaker faces and addresses thousands of the party faithful who have come from all across the country. Why? To wear outlandish clothes and to party? No, not really; they can do those at home. They have come to bond, to be associated in very demonstrable ways with their party, with others like themselves so that they can cheer and scream and applaud and wave signs and nod their heads in knowing agreement; and validate themselves by the interaction of group personalities, characteristics and goals. Watch closely. Look at their body movements and listen to their voices. They are at a different level than they would be at home listening to the same speeches. They are intensely committed to seeing themselves, and being seen, as bearers of Republican and/or Democratic truth and values. They are no longer individuals from Louisville, Albany or Tacoma. Having been transformed by truth as they see it, they can share it with others whom they can elevate and enlighten. *They have become leaders!*

Both conventions revealed the art of audience manipulation at its highest form. Small numbers of organizers spread throughout the crowds were able to start a chant, a stomp, a cheer, applause, sign waving, marching etc. and literally within a few seconds it would become a mass movement that would mostly continue until it was terminated from the podium.

Applause was the most frequent and evident object of manipulation as if sustained length or louder volume conferred greater validation on those who could offer the most. The extent of this manipulation showed itself repeatedly in the audience's interjection of applause on demand whenever the speaker paused for emphasis or even punctuation.

There was an amusing instance at the Republican convention when the speaker momentarily lost his place or concentration and then quickly resumed, but not before some in the audience were able to mount a round of inappropriate applause. Although flustered, the speaker had the good sense to continue and keep control at the podium.

We are not at our best at our political conventions. What elements of political theatre they used to provide now seem more like old vaudeville acts lacking in suspense and originality. Their failures extend to delegates, speakers, the media and the parties' leaderships. Tedium, parochialism and repetition are rampant, and one can even sympathize with the broadcast commentators who have to be on camera for many hours of continuous coverage.

These conventions should be seen for what they are — a confluence of political and emotional forces by which the delegates and the parties attempt to define themselves. At many levels banality rules, and insecurity is everywhere. As a nation we deserve better, but self-definition is not an easy process.

There is an important human dynamic very visibly at work in our conventions. It is the age-old, seemingly endless process whereby individuals (delegates), seeking greater strength, and especially recognition, bind themselves together into a group (the audience) and then, both within and without its confines, draw deeply emotional lines of distinction. It is a process of harmony gained and harmony lost and has played out over our evolutionary millennia in the record of war, religion, politics, economics, diplomacy, empire and other ways in which our human, and even animal, natures have been expressed.

It can only be changed if it is recognized and if we apply the light of reason to it. In another two years, our electoral mechanism will crank up, restart itself and again climax in conventions. While we can hope and look for something better, it is unlikely that they will vary much from our present model. It is worth noting that planned obsolescence, which is a dominant element in our commercial life, is shunned "like the plague" in politics.

End Notes

[1] Justice Warren Burger, dissenting opinion, Plyler v. Doe 457 U.S. 202 (1982)
[2] McAlpin, Pro English, 6/20/08 Letter
[3] Ibid
[4] Ibid
[5] Parade Magazine - 8/10/08

ECD 9/20/08

Chapter Four —— January 2009

The True Crisis in America

"Good government should produce an atmosphere of national responsibility and opportunity created for the people by the combined efforts of their elected representatives. Divisions will always exist as to government's direction, and decisions must be resolved by the objective application of both personal and political integrity. The structure of government should be firm and open and should not be burdened by becoming a proving ground for either individual or party ideology." Politics is one thing. Good government is quite another!

Matters of Conscience,
Issue 21, 10/08

M any people reading the above paragraph from the previous chapter would dismiss it in its entirety as being impossibly optimistic. Actually, we have achieved all of these criteria at one time or another in our history, but rarely all at once. Nevertheless, this short, simple purpose statement, were the nation's people and politicians to commit themselves to it, could create a new and better form of government.

The choice is really a relatively simple one because, if we persist in our present practices and principles, although the American entity may survive in some form, our great democratic experiment will fail and/or be replaced.

Today, our country faces multiple, serious issues each of which is referred to from time to time as a crisis. These include the environment, immigration, Social Security, health care, energy, our economy/national debt and, of course, population. There are a host of others such as nuclear proliferation, education, taxation, foreign policy and a variety of real and imagined constitutional issues that are encouraged and exploited by the political and social perspectives of our time.

The seven primary issues that we cited above are ones that we have emphasized. They vie for our attention from time to time and seem to maintain a constant political presence regardless of efforts by both parties to provide legislative solutions.

These issues endure as crises because of their potential impact and their very real urgency. And they also have in common certain elements of enormous risk that seem to go unnoticed by those in Washington charged with conducting our government and creating its policies.

Accordingly, we must come to realize that America's true crisis, that transcends all of these issues, is *the appalling and pervasive incompetence and intellectual isolation of the executive and legislative branches of our government* over the past three decades and, with regard to some matters, notably longer.

This incompetence does not reveal itself in the minutiae of writing tax codes, seemingly endless debates and photo ops, campaigning for office or raising funds. These are all activities which consume a large part of our legislative time and which the Congress has come to undertake and perform quite easily.

No, the incompetence that threatens our nation exists at another level. It is embedded in a failure of vision which seems to have a local focal length that stops at states' borders. Beyond them there seems to be only a blankness which obscures the national interest. And it consists of refusing, or not being able, to recognize major forces that are at work around our world. In the age of globalism, which we have been instrumental in constructing, there can be no more certain assurance of disaster. These forces all have tipping points with the capability, when exceeded, to overwhelm us.

Tipping points are unique events that can break completely with what took place before them, and can create both new directions for the future and the need for new ways of thinking to accommodate their consequences. If they are moderate in their form and efforts, we can count ourselves fortunate, as, more typically, they can produce severe and surprising results.

A tipping point is an event which alters the behavior of a force, usually because of a gradual accumulation of stress within or upon it. Common to most tipping points are that they occur suddenly and sometimes violently; that they free the force that produces them from its original constraints; and that they can overwhelm our normal management and control functions.

Minor tipping points are often easily managed in our early activities and surroundings, but with larger forces and their consequences we either fail to recognize, or we deny, their reality. Nowhere has this dangerous, and possibly fatal, lack of vision been more evident than in the upper levels of our government and its enabling bureaucracy.

Major tipping points in our economy, our environment, our population or other vital areas of life can produce change, pain or chaos on a grand scale. Not only do we fail to see these threats in their true light, but we also seemingly cannot grasp that most tipping points are irrevocable.

Here are the primary issues which our government must address in a meaningful way:

1) Our real and perilous debt level.
2) Social Security
3) Energy
4) Immigration/Population
5) The Environment — including climate change/global warming, species loss, air and sea pollution, and arable land and aquifer depletion.
6) Health Care

All of these problems are subject to the Law of Limits (LOL) — some sooner and more severely than others. This law, states, without exception, that within the confines of any space or system there is a limit as to how much of any element can be added or subtracted without causing its destruction. This failure is often triggered suddenly by silent and/or invisible tipping points which identify themselves only in retrospect. The urgency of our present circumstance is that in all of the major problem areas cited we are approaching tipping points of one kind or another which our past policies have failed to recognize.

The current state of our government is perilous because its primary focus is on Republican/Democrat ideology and conflict. Our system is rich, large, inefficient and lacking in fairness. The latter, because it involves a state of mind, may be the most difficult challenge to correct, but it must be done, as any effort to recreate a government of principle must be based on fairness.

We have vast, although diminished, resources of will and wealth which we can draw upon to correct our course, but our success, both nationally and globally, will require us to place greater emphasis on cooperation; and to realize that our past policies of endless growth are not realistic and carry the risk of accelerating all tipping points.

One great fault of present governments throughout the world today is that they convince their people that they are more than they actually are. At no time has this been more evident than in our present economic meltdown when we were treated to a menu of solutions, proposals, clichés, arguments/counter arguments and rhetoric that changed with disconcerting speed.

This ability of governments to overstate their value is a direct result of the enormous growth in our media. Media coverage of today's reach and frequency gives government a bigger bullhorn, more opportunity to portray itself, and a larger political presence, but when we turn the volume down, or the set off, we come close to the moment of truth in Frank Baum's <u>The Wizard of Oz</u>[1] when the Wizard is revealed to be a somewhat confused, bumbling, ordinary man without any magical powers.

<u>Debt</u>

The word "model" is one that has shown a wide increase in usage in our time. We are frequently exposed to references to models for business, weather, architecture, archaeology, computers, electoral results and many more. Models are representations of what we think is, or is to be.

Consider this model and its application. On a flat surface such as a table or desk, place a cloth cover. On this we will erect three structures — a house of cards, a tower of toothpicks and a column of single, empty beer cans. Each structure is inherently unstable because their parts are joined in such a way that the slightest movement of one must impact its neighbor, and any force is transmitted through the entire system. Also key to their common instability is the fact that at some point the addition of the next piece will cause the structures' collapse.

Such points are tipping points which most of us first experience in childhood playing with blocks. They are messengers for the physical laws of gravity and balance, and are shared by our three structures because they are common to all structures. The instability of tipping points is an internal risk that commences with the addition of the second piece to the first. Eventually, although at different times, as the building process proceeds, each structure will succumb to this risk.

There is another external risk unrelated to intentional construction. A passerby could nudge the table/desk or a seated observer could move his body in a way that causes the cloth cover to also move in which case collapse will also occur. We have just described a model of our national debt structure.

In two prior reports in 2004 and 2005 we dealt in detail with our national debt and the variety of perils it poses to our country and way of life, in view of which we felt a day of reckoning was bound to come. America is awash in debt today, and not just its federal debt. There are also untenable levels of state and local government debt as well as credit card, mortgage, margin, corporate, installment and personal debt. All these are interrelated to such a degree that in times of stress the sum of the parts may be greater than the whole.

From our view four years ago there was no way to anticipate which card, toothpick or can (i.e., — housing, securities or credit market) might be dislodged first, but it was readily apparent that the course we have followed was no longer tenable and would self-correct if we took no action. Writing in our April, 2005 issue, we offered:

> "We must be aware of the scale and seriousness
> of our true debt. Its accumulation has become a
> narcotic to which both political parties are now
> addicted. It has the power to overwhelm our

government and way of life, and will surely do so if
we do nothing"

Today we still do not know the true dimensions of our financial
crisis other than to say with absolute certainty that they will be
measured by extreme pain and hardship for many Americans most
of whom are bystanders caught up in someone else's mess.

Again, there is a larger scale at work. It is international in scope
and involves our relations and policies with other countries, and
these are as intricately bound together in the world markets as the
cards, toothpicks and cans of our model.

Our government and our corporate and financial sectors have
been prime movers of our embrace of economic globalism; and yet
they seem to have missed one of its more evident aspects — that its
interconnections which can spread great rewards under favorable
conditions can also cause enormous losses and pain when political
and/or market circumstances deteriorate.

There is no pleasure to be had from labeling our government
incompetent or inept, but for weeks last fall it had the look of a
deer caught in headlights. The immobilization of our domestic
and international financial markets and the losses that resulted are
direct results of mismanagement and laxity by our Congress and
White House over a prolonged period, but most notably during
the G.W. Bush administrations.

The job ahead will require us to cut spending, to start saving,
to reduce our debt, and to return the value we have lost to our
currency. It will not be easy and will take a long time. To do
it right it must be done with fairness and determination — no
returning to business as usual in a year or two.

We have suffered a severe stroke and our rehab program will
be long and hard.

Social Security

This issue is unique in that frequent public discussion of its changing demographics invariably includes prediction of a tipping point at which time the system will no longer be able to honor its present commitments. Increasing population and longevity will translate into greater costs that will not be offset by larger revenues. This imbalance is worsened by previous administrations having spent years of accumulated surplus with the result that SS is no longer sustainable under its original form and concept.

This financial sleight of hand, performed by both Republican and Democratic administrations, reveals political cynicism at its worst and how badly our government has been compromised, for, although SS drew early criticism as being socialistic, it gained steadily in popularity. *More importantly, it completely altered the way most Americans viewed the living of their lives after age 65 by giving them the assurance that their destiny need not be one of destitution, that some funds would be available on a regular and continuing basis.*

The early promise of SS's concept has been so badly tarnished by its mismanagement that its continuation as a viable program is now questionable. Private and public sources alike now make frequent predictions that in the span of a few decades it will slip into negative revenues at which time its payments to beneficiaries will fall far behind rising costs, and the charges to new participants will be insufficient to maintain the successful mathematics of the past.

Here is a threat to one of our key economic and social programs in which a tipping point is generally acknowledged and publicized. And yet, "government" (i.e., successive administrations of both parties) has continued to raid SS funds for other purposes and has limited its corrective efforts to tweaking at the edges.

It is this kind of failure that occasions public outrage and charges of ineptness and incompetence. While there is ample evidence of the latter in SS's management, the overriding dereliction of our elected representatives has been their treatment of SS as a political issue rather than one requiring a vision of our national interest.

Energy

Our energy crisis, unlike SS, has several tipping points, which, either singly or in combination, can face us with disaster. There is the point at which our carbon-based natural resources first become scarce and then are exhausted. There is the time when our population has increased so much that it surpasses the carrying capacities of our supplies of arable land and clean air/water. And there are possibilities that our enlarging efforts to develop new and "greener" fuels will alter the basic natural or economic relations between ourselves and our protective cover of plant life.

For example, consider our pursuit of ethanol made from corn as a replacement for gasoline. The ethanol fuel production process has serious environmental drawbacks, and its need for corn as a feedstock has put pressure on our corn supply and caused a substantial increase in its price.

Similarly, efforts are now underway to develop a gasoline replacement from cellulosic plant fibre. Any significant success and expansion of this technology would require the harvesting of vast numbers of plants/trees. As the latter absorb carbon dioxide (CO_2) and give off oxygen, their disappearance would have an offsetting, negative, energy consequence.

The larger focus is that new technology, increased population and more persistent marketing practices have greatly expanded our use of energy products/services. Air conditioning is, perhaps, most notable, but there are many others.

All these are easily visible patterns of our life. What remains far more difficult for elected government to see is the inevitability of their tipping points.

Immigration/Population

These two issues are so closely bound together in their threats and consequences that we treat them in tandem. They often appear as different sides of the same coin — but are not, in reality, all that different.

In both, the critical element is what is sometimes referred to as a unit of population — i.e., a person with no distinguishing features such as wealth, religion, race, location, intelligence or political preference added. In the best of all possible demographic worlds this unit would provide us with the means to measure, study and report its movements unhampered by the blind curves, trip wires and pitfalls of human emotion, but, as we will see later, that is not presently possible. And it has probably not been so since we surrendered our nomadic way of life in favor of permanent communities.

The basic unit with which we are concerned in the twenty-first century is the human being found in decidedly different numbers, forms and circumstances around our world. Over time, since its nomadic origins, it has become a person or, in plural, people or peoples. And this added humanity has become very much a complicating factor.

Whether units, persons or people, their needs, ambitions and movements translate into consequences that are measured in money, violence, bloodshed, identity, faith, war, sovereignty, health and other areas that determine the form and strength of the ever changing social fabric that is necessary to hold us together in a viable society. Such is immigration/population at its primal level.

Fast forward to our twenty-first century America where immigration/population emotion runs on high, and when differing thought processes, interests and ethnicities constantly challenge each other. And again the unit of population, with its ability to reach into all areas of our life, is the basic measurement which maintains a free translatability into others.

Last August the Census Bureau released its revised population projections predicting that our population will increase by 135 million by mid-century. As Steven Camarota points out[2], such an increase "is equivalent to the entire populations of Mexico and Canada moving here." And, Camerota further states, if we assume our present ratio of population to infrastructure is maintained, we would need 36,000 more schools, 52 million new housing units and additional highway capacity for 106 million more vehicles.

Not to be forgotten is that schools, housing and roads all require adjacent land to accommodate their uses and users. America's carrying capacity[3] has been estimated at 150 million which was our population at the end of WWII. Today our population is 300 million and will increase to 435 million before mid-century according to Census Bureau projections.

Any effort to comprehend the effect of such rapid growth upon our society must include the realization that for every added unit of population we lose one acre of land to the various development projects such growth requires:

$2 + 4 + 8 = 14$ is an arithmetic progression
$2 \times 4 \times 8 = 64$ is an geometric progression

Population is a process of silent and powerful geometric increase.

History provides us with a way to look backwards and see the effects of our and others' actions. It can also provide the necessary scale and perspective to reveal the actions of forces that create tipping points and the exact moments in time when they occur.

Because populations and natural forces are in constant flux around the earth, it would be difficult to isolate the exact event and moment which might cause a major tipping point that would alter our relationship to our environment from one which sustains us to one that destroys us.

Still, as we move ahead on our present course, we must know that at some point just one more birth, one more species destroyed, one more aquifer depleted, one more barrel of oil produced, one more inch of rising sea level, or one more degree of average temperature increase could irrevocably modify, or even destroy, the balance between our environment and ourselves.

Our view in America is mostly of immigration/population as a national argument. It is more than that. It is one aspect of a global migrant problem marked by the movement of increasing numbers from poor to richer zones. In Latin America, Hispanic natives move north and join the Mexican exodus to quietly accomplish the Reconquista (reconquest) of our southwestern states by population.

In southeast Asia the economically and politically weak try to enter Australia; and Europe is the target of choice for all of Africa and the Near East. There are three important learning opportunities for the US in the way these patterns are playing out:

1) The European powers who admitted large numbers of immigrants from their former colonies are being repaid with violence and unrest, as major civil disturbances causing extensive damage have taken place in Spain, France, Italy, Germany and the Netherlands.

2) These wealthy countries are the center of the EU and are chosen by migrants for their proximity of wealth, jobs and services. There is not a significant migrant flow to Albania, Switzerland, Latvia, etc. But, unlike their predecessors of a century ago, money and employment are not all they seek, as they now more frequently and stridently call for substantive change, not to just political parties, but to basic constitutional systems.

This push towards widespread upheaval is fueled by an accumulation of political and economic anger and envy, and, while the causes of these volatile emotions lie in the home countries, their effects are felt in the migrants' new host countries where they create a very difficult Catch-22 in that the more migrants that are admitted in order to resolve human, social and economic problems in the emigrating areas, the greater will be the cost of social, economic and political turbulence in the new host nations.

Our country has not experienced the scale of property damage and loss of life that Europe has. For that good fortune, we can be grateful, but it doesn't mean that it can't happen here. In fact, given the state of our present immigration policy, it is almost inevitable.

3) If we look at immigration/population as the global problem it is, we find that Europe and Asia, are zones where most developed (i.e., target) nations make an effort to control their borders. Nowhere are there extensive borders (like our northern and southern) where thousands of new arrivals daily walk across and start the process of obtaining benefits and exercising "rights".

In immigration/population, as in physics, any exerted force will follow the path of least resistance. As population, and with it poverty, increases in the desperate zones, so will the flow of migrants to developed areas. There, efforts to maintain or increase their border controls will serve to move migrants to those areas of least border control where access is favored — i.e., to Canada and the US.

Immigration and population are two parts of the same issue, each of which has its own tipping point. Merely because of its smaller size the immigration tipping point will be more readily discernible. There is good reason to believe that this point may have already been reached in Europe, but we cannot yet determine whether events there are irrevocable and beyond control. That is an historical judgement for which more time is needed.

But we do know that we Americans are an integral part of this global problem. And yet there is no evidence from anyone in the Congress or the executive branch that it is more than a local issue.

Today our country annually accepts more immigrants than almost all the other developed nations of the world combined, and the percentage of immigrant vs. native-born Americans has doubled since 1970[4]. We stand-alone among developed nations[5] in continuing open borders policies, which may bring us to a tipping point before others. And yet there is no vision, no recognition of this as a realistic threat to our society. Admittedly immigration/population is an issue that rubs raw so many local political nerves that most nations do not choose to reveal or share the pain.

Nevertheless, it is there; and we have a government. And any concept of good government would view this as a risk to be engaged.

The Environment
Earth, Air And Water —
The Fire Will Come Later

In using the term "environment" we are referring collectively to a combination of natural issues that have the ability to define how we live (or die) from something as immediate as breathing to as distant as evolutionary change. We include climate change/global warning (CC/GW), species loss, air and sea pollution and our persistent depletion of our arable land and aquifers.

We are not alone in putting economic concerns ahead of caring for the natural resources that sustain us. Other countries and populations do the same, but our position as sole superpower provided us with a brief moment of leadership which we have let pass because it posed a challenge to basic Bush/Cheney ideology. In the latter's failure to understand the science and the urgency of our time, we have assumed enormous risk for others and ourselves.

With the exception of a handful of scientists and academics, CC/GW has been an issue of note for only about twenty-five years. Today, due to rapidly increasing evidence of its accelerating effects, scientists around the world recognize that our response time is shrinking and that we may well have passed one or more tipping points to which we may never be able to return.

CC/GW, like many other aspects of our environment, is a global issue. The tide that floods South Florida is the same one that floods South Africa and we can no more separate it and package it for local treatment that we can clean the air over Brooklyn, but not Manhattan.

Here is what we must understand about CC/GW for ourselves and others. It has the power and the means to permanently change, and perhaps destroy, much of our planet's food and water supply.

This would disrupt our global systems for their production and distribution.

Such a dislocation, whether quick or slow, would lead to a time when governments would not be able to assure that food would be available for their people. Along the way, of course, such mechanisms as markets, contracts, prices and currencies which function only by maintaining an element of shared stability, will have also been subjected to stresses and changes to which they will not be able to respond in an efficient and profitable way.

This process is one of emerging chaos in which the consequences of our planet's abuse of our environment are felt by all countries, all people. There will be many voices that will deflect any mention of tipping points and the notion that we can lose control of our natural systems and resources. We have heard this siren song before.

And remember Pilottown, Burrwood and Port Eads, three thriving towns below New Orleans on the Mississippi delta in 1950 which were reclaimed by the sea and no longer exist. That was then and this is now, and our environmental clock runs much faster.

The Bird And The Bear

Canaries, those ever-singing, seemingly joyful birds, are used in coal mines to detect the presence of odorless, invisible poison gas. Birds are placed at the front of work crews and are the first to encounter the lethal gas. When they do, they die. By their silence they warn and save others.

The polar bear is one of nature's most magnificent creatures and the result of heroic evolutionary change over its specie's lifetime. At some point, probably millions of years ago, climate change or catastrophe may have isolated a group of bears in the arctic region, forcing them to adapt to their new environment or die. Following their separation from their brown, black and grizzly cousins, they changed their coat color to white and their diet from terrestrial to mostly aquatic sources. Swimming became equally important for locomotion as walking and, to facilitate it, several physiological changes were made. The rear end and legs were raised and the torso and the skull were both narrowed. The result of this streamlining was a smooth and silent swimmer, and an efficient and fearsome predator in arctic areas.

Today, the polar bear population is in rapid decline and will soon face extinction due to global warming. The latter, acting upon both sea and air, melts the ice flows, sheets and bergs which provide necessary shelter, rest and hibernation habitats. As this ice grows smaller in area, it also becomes softer, weaker and unable to support the weight of bears at its edges. To watch these beautiful creatures attempt to climb out of the sea onto ice which repeatedly crumbles is a sad and painful sight. As the bear cannot stay afloat forever, it must eventually weaken and drown.

Arctic waters are now known to contain substantial oil reserves and the oil industry pushes strongly for their development. Any such effort would further deteriorate the polar bear's environment and its chance of survival.

"Big oil" continues its "drill more, drill now, drill deeper" approach to our energy/environment crisis. In the past, in the corporate vs. species (ours and others) argument "Big Oil" had the full support of the Bush/Cheney government, but this seems likely to change under President Obama. If our policies and process do not change, the polar bear will most likely be extinct by mid-century and perhaps even as soon as twenty years from now. The bear is our canary, but will we heed its warning? The silence is deafening.

The black (oil) and white (bear, ice) distinctions of the polar bear's predicament are easy to visualize, but such clarity is the exception, not the rule, in species' loss. There are probably millions of species, known and unknown, which must face the changes in air, temperature, precipitation, light and food supply that are now taking place on our planet.

These species exist in swamps, rain forests, deserts, lakes, oceans and rivers; the topsoil of our lawns, gardens and agricultural fields; and on the tops and sides of our highest and steepest mountains. We know neither their full extent, nor their numbers. We do know that they are both prey and predator and are joined in a food chain that does a surprisingly capable job of supporting all.

Like our toothpick tower, can column and house of cards they exist in a fine state of balance and interrelation which, if disturbed, can collapse into chaos. Because our knowledge of this structure is incomplete, our measurement of cause and effect is often faulty. And yet we know enough to know that we have been given notice of vast change much of which will be beyond our control.

Species loss is not just about the beautiful polar bear that we can see or the elusive, as yet unidentified, butterfly deep in the Amazon rain forest. It is also about us. To think otherwise is a risk, a hubris, so great that it must challenge our belief in human intelligence.

The Kyoto conference was a first step towards proposing an international response to global environmental concerns. Our refusal to view and frame it as anything other than a threat to our economy has lost us the benefits of almost a decade of participation and the significant credibility required of a sole superpower.

We must start over; we must try to retrieve what we ignored; we must catch up with others and with the clock, realizing that we are not the timekeeper.

Land And Water

The two most vital elements of life on our planet over which we exercise a meaningful degree of control are the land that feeds us and the fresh water we drink. As much of these in our society are under private ownership, we have failed to establish a policy to maximize their public benefits. Individual owners in different areas, all with their specific needs and concerns, do not form a ready policy base.

The truth we have not faced is that our supplies of land and water are limited and that the rate at which we have used them in the past is no longer sustainable. This is not just a matter of philosophy or way of thinking. We are well along the way to exhausting our natural aquifers; and by our practice of expansionist economic and population policies we have greatly reduced the amount of arable land available to us.

Our country and our planet are finite spaces with a variety of resources capable of supporting human life. The uses of these resources, many of which are in limited supply and under human control, are often interrelated. Some are renewable; others are not. But this distinction is not apparent in our embrace of unlimited and constant growth

We have tended to take for granted the great abundance of our American landscape, but that is no more a sustainable attitude than constant growth. Our land and water resources both have tipping points and, at such time when we reach or pass them, these essential resources will pass from our control. Life on planet earth will take on a new form. *Playing catch-up will no longer be an option.*

Health Care

Another issue of prime concern to our country is its health care program. The one we now have, and have been tinkering with for several decades, fails in many ways, although its original premise could have produced a workable result.

Today, our per capita health care cost is approximately twice that of Canada, France, Australia & Britain, and we have allowed to be included in our annual health care expenses approximately $100 billion each for administrative costs and fraud. Again, "we're number 1."

Why do we permit these unnecessary and excessive costs? The answer is that our health care system is designed to produce profits for some of its participants at each and every operational step. Over time, the profit motive has become dominant with the result that benefits for patients and doctors have been reduced while those for insurance companies and medical/pharmaceutical providers have increased. This shift from health to wealth has, of course, been accomplished with congressional approval.

There is one other critical factor that is now threatening our health system. Its costs are rising at a rate far greater than those of our economy in general. As it becomes increasingly expensive for its participants, they will shrink in number and per capita costs will, therefore, rise even further. The Congressional Budget Office estimated in 2005 the growth of Medicare/Medicaid's share of our national budget from 2% in 1966 to an estimated 22% in 2006 and 35% in 2046. This last increase amounts to over 50% and, in order to take place, will require the reduction or elimination of other budget items.

There are many determined bureaucrats and/or other constituencies, some at the Pentagon, who would resist any such realignment of budgetary shares. This is only one of our health care system's tipping points. Others lie in waiting while members of Congress claim "we have the best system in the world".

The closure of community hospitals due to the financial drain of having to treat uninsured (and often undocumented) patients is another concern. Add the cost of having to provide medical care in the language of the patient. And there is continuing evidence that insurance companies have stepped up their efforts to limit both doctors' determination of patient charges and the payment of their claims. This has established an ongoing confrontation between our medical and legal professions.

Our system can be repaired, but broad changes are necessary which the Congress can be counted on to avoid. Meanwhile the prospect of escalating costs, diminishing care, and expanding population assures us that our health care system can provide its share of tipping points.

In Summary

We have called attention to key issues facing our country all of which have tipping points, and we have been highly critical of our government's lack of attention to them. Our criticism is not of the snipe and gripe, cocktail party type most people engage in because of a specific act or ruling with which they disagree. Rather, these issues can surely be considered as or among the most serious we face, and yet there is an absolute, collective failure on the part of our government to be able to view them as essential elements of our national interest.

The process of failing to understand our relationship to our environment is one of long standing, but the seriousness of its consequences only began to be noted in the scientific community in the last half century and has greatly accelerated in recent years.

There are many elements in constant motion that, like

subatomic particles, push, pull and collide with each other so that their actions and reactions become undistinguishable. This mix is composed of dollars, population units, fisheries, agricultural crops, temperatures, precipitation, flooding, forest fires, desertification, industrial pollution, contagious diseases, contamination of our oceans, rivers and livestock, and other forms of degradation.

They are the tower of toothpicks, the column of cans and the house of cards. They are all physically measurable and identifiable, and they all have tipping points.

For example, our national population is now just over 300 million. If we increase at the rate of 1% a year, as we are now doing, at some future time the added population will overwhelm the available resources, the system will collapse and pass from our control. If we increase the population growth to 10%, the tipping point and collapse will be reached much sooner. The same holds true for the other toothpicks, cans and cards that form our environmental structure. No great leap of reason or vision is needed to recognize this truth.

And yet, strain and hope as we may to hear a voice from our 537 elected representatives in the House, Senate and White House make this connection, there is only silence.

It would be fitting if there was a special circle in political hell reserved for those who have been given great power and, by putting it only to petty use, mock the whole concept of representation on which our government is based. Delay seems endless. Opportunity is not. And somewhere between the two, tipping points await us.

And there is another tipping point which we may well have passed and which may claim as casualties some of our republic's most valuable elements and aspirations. Unlike our previous ones, it does not involve money, population units or measurements of sea level or temperature. It is one of spirit, truly a "matter of conscience".

We refer to the massive, almost pervasive, reach of corruption throughout our political system and governmental bureaucracy. As we have pointed out before, our national corruption has increased in direct proportion to the growth of money and power that we have experienced in our pursuit of the role of sole superpower.

As with other departures from our historical tradition, corruption expanded in the recent G. W. Bush administration. It appeared in a variety of forms and enabled many others. This corruption of money, power and spirit works in several ways, mostly silently and beneath the surface until it can no longer be contained. Then it erupts in a media frenzy (i.e., Jack Abramoff) after which the political ranks are closed more tightly than they were before, and it's back to business as usual.

The prime sources of corruption in our government in twenty-first century America are our legislative and executive branches, and it is because of their acceptance and complicity that corruption has been able to thrive in spite of the fact that most Americans prefer higher ethical standards. Although corruption can take many forms, it generally fits this profile:

1) <u>Legislative</u> — the normal course of political progress in our country starts with election or appointment to a local board or office, then to the state legislature and finally to national office in the Congress. By the time the latter is reached, the newly elected member of Congress can look back upon a period of perhaps ten to twenty years in which the critical element of persuasion was not the thought, language or philosophy by which we usually present high purpose, but rather the ability of money and power to bring together separate, and often different, interests and to be shared by them.

With more money and more power at hand in Washington, the flow of power continues and accelerates. Sometimes it is referred to as "compromise", and sometimes as "the art of the deal", but what it amounts to is a "go along to get along" method of legislation mostly designed to provide specific benefits to small groups of local interests usually identified as "constituents" or "the American people".

This crafting of our national legislation in a way that keeps it captive to local interests/contributors is corruption in its most lethal form. The essence of representative government is that the people have access through their elected representatives to the nation's laws and policies. With wide-scale corruption in Congress, that access is effectively deflected or denied.

In our Congress there are two kinds of corruption at work. The first is the usual quid pro quo, bridge-to-nowhere (or bridges-to-everywhere) kind of legislation. The other is much different and more lethal. It is the corruption of individual and collective legislative minds so that they are unable to form a true vision of the national interest. In a state, composed of as many differing elements as ours, it may be difficult, but absolutely essential, to be able to have a national vision.

2) <u>Executive</u> — the power of this branch can be used in tandem with the Congress to move the machinery of government. Unfortunately, since the Nixon presidency the tension between the two branches has increased, mostly as a result of various presidents' efforts to extend and strengthen executive power. This is accomplished both through outright executive orders and the less obvious, but equally destructive, toleration and expansion of executive

power and political ideology throughout the government structure. As with other failures, these have reached new heights in the second Bush administration in its efforts to edit, dictate and/or restate scientific opinion to meet White House ideological criteria.

3) <u>Bureaucratic</u> — The Washington bureaucracy is host to many governmental departments, as well as private and public institutions and associations, all of which to some degree reflect the political character of government.

In recent years, however, the practice of tying staff employment and promotion to political ideology has had a stultifying effect upon employee performance, thereby reducing efficiency, has narrowed or eliminated their national vision and rendered them incapable of serving those whom they are charged to protect — for example, the Bureau of Indian Affairs and our Native American population.

Perhaps nowhere has this imposition of the ideological imperative been practiced with such determination and devastating results as in our Department of Justice under Attorney General Alberto Gonzales. Today, the DOJ remains very much a flawed institution divided by serious morale and personnel problems, and unable to perform its role as the people's lawyer. To rebuild it to a level of professional respect will require considerable time and effort by the Obama administration. The DOJ is not alone, as there are other dark corners and corridors of our government where the light of our Constitution does not reach.

Our spiritual corruption and loss of national vision are an ongoing process in which we may have passed the tipping point, meaning that we may never again be able to have or aspire to an ethical government and national vision. Spirit is not easy to regain, and, as in nature, ours may have been irrevocably changed or damaged. Nothing short of a concerted public/private effort will recapture what we had.

Post-Election Political Notes

The 2008 presidential election broke new ground in several ways — some, perhaps, welcome signs of what's to come, and others not. With regard to the former, the gradual erosion of voter turnout over the past half-century was emphatically reversed.

As states completed their electoral certifica-tion process in mid-December, it was revealed that somewhat over 131 million people voted as compared to 122 million in 2004. In terms of percentage of eligible voters, 2008 was 61.6 to 60.1 for 2004.[6] These percentages are significantly larger than the almost 50% level of past elections.

And on the dark side we have estimates that the cost of our '08 elections have also risen appreciably. For the two-year period of 2007 and 2008 the Center for Responsive Politics has concluded that $2.4 billion was spent on our presidential campaigns and $2.9 billion on House and Senate candidacies, for an eye (and wallet) opening total of $5.3 billion.[7]

Further focus on the presidential election is irresistible and shows that the per capita presidential expenditure ($2.4 billion for 131 million votes) was $18.32. As we may tend to take excess for granted in America, the shock value of such an amount may not be readily recognized. We lack statistics for other countries, but suspect they would be much lower.

Almost certainly a new, two year high was reached for the tedium level of the presidential nominating and electoral campaigns. Endlessly repetitive rhetoric by all designed to avoid making an error which could be turned back upon the speaker left viewers/listeners with the feeling (mostly justifiable) that what they were being offered was stale, not newsworthy and lacking the specificity necessary to make an informed decision.

Ours is not now a good system for making serious choices. It depends too much on spin, hoopla, trivia, money and the manipulation of the voter, but, as any change would have to have congressional approval, it is unlikely that it will occur. Still, we can dream of a time when the public might call for something better.

For this to happen, and be successful, our elected representatives in Congress and the White House will have to be able to see themselves and their roles in a new light focused on the greater benefit for the nation — not political parties, or local special interests or the election cycle. *These work better as the by-product, not the purpose, of government.* And, given such a transformation, we might once again be able to view our members of government as leaders.

Caroline Kennedy, who to date has shown no evidence of interest in or aptitude for public life, has announced that she wants to be appointed to succeed Hillary Clinton as one of New York's senators. As there is certainly nothing like starting at the top to assure success, she has chosen to eschew the hurly-burly of electoral politics and is now interviewing, or being interviewed, for this very powerful and important position.

We have not been informed as to the reasons for this move at this time, but perhaps she was galvanized into action by the prospect of our Senate without a Kennedy due to her uncle Ted's failing health.

Jeb Bush, George's younger brother, was thought by many people with a political view and interest, prior to George's becoming governor of TX, to be the Bush family member most likely to enter politics and continue the family's participation at the national level (i.e., final destination — the presidency). This progression suffered a slowdown due to George's gubernatorial success in TX and then his running for president. Jeb stepped back and settled for Florida's governorship.

Jeb has a Hispanic wife and a young son who speaks fluent Spanish and who has already been pointed towards politics and mentioned as the means for continuing the Bush political presence into the next generation.

The Bush and Kennedy families certainly throw a bright light on the American public's embrace of politics by genetic descent, perhaps a modern echo from our monarchical ancestry.

Dynastic politics are dangerous in many ways. They are alien to our origins and yet they have captivated many levels of our political process. Why? How?

First, they are a form of arrogance which appears as a sense of entitlement — actually two entitlements. The first is that of the dynastic family's candidate who assumes an office should be his/hers because other family members had previously held it. I am; therefore, I serve.

This is not strong enough to stand by itself and must be accompanied by the belief that the country's need for the candidate is as strong as vice-versa. This is the second entitlement, which of course, is bogus, but it establishes the perception of a need that serves the country's interest. Underlying the arrogance of these two entitlements that operate in tandem is condescension towards the American voter that says, in effect, out of over 300 million people "only this family will do."

And why do Americans accept this national put-down? It is because their first function — that of determining who shall represent them in government — has largely been taken over, with their consent, by the relentless spin machines of our mass media whose wealth, technology and reach dominate the political process, and both parties as well.

President Eisenhower was the last president of the old system which came to its end with the Nixon-Kennedy debates after which all things political changed.

The American people have lulled themselves into a state of political suspension in which they fail to do the hard work of attempting to decide the merits and/or faults within serious and complicated national issues. It is easier to consult polls, listen to 24/7 talk radio or TV or read the proliferating sources of home-delivered direct mail, all of which create a state of dependency which the mass media and our elected representatives are all too happy to put to the service of their own, rather than the national, interest.

As the prospects ahead are those of greater numbers, more technology, more money and more spin, it is unlikely that we will be able to take back our electoral process without enormous and dedicated effort. But is there the will to overcome the media's momentum?

There seems to be an unsettling, inverse correlation between money/media and the quality of our government over the past two hundred years. As we turned from the eighteenth to the nineteenth century, our primary medium was the printed newspaper in a form that seems primitive by today's capabilities. Our government was purposeful and surprisingly responsive considering the limited communications technology available.

By the next turn into the twentieth century, the media/money factor had expanded considerably due to growing population, railroads and the telegraph. The whistle-stop campaign was a marvel of efficiency for candidates — train pulls into small town and blows whistle; people stop what they're doing and run to railroad station; candidate gives speech from train's rear car and moves on to the next stop with the speech's length, more often than not, being determined by the size of the audience. The unaided human voice did the work, as there were no microphones. Meanwhile, government had become more money oriented, and we had undertaken to assume our place as an international power — our "manifest destiny".

Today the media/money element is dominant in both the election and functioning of government. Candidates can address millions from a studio, stadium or auditorium. Microphones are pinned discreetly to lapels and the messages they carry are instantly combined with colored visual images. We have achieved instant campaigning, instant reporting and instant politics.

But our government has not fared so well. The bargain it has made with our multi-media forums bears a Faustian imprint. The debt that our elected representatives owe the media for their election can never be repaid because they will always need and want more. What's worse is that the eye of the media, the camera, knows all and can be persuaded to tell. This combination of obligation and threat has brought us to our present point of having a government that has been driven to irresponsibility and fear of engaging issues that go beyond local and ideological concerns. Even when forced by circumstance into obvious instances of national interest, government may offer only lip, not real, service.

America will not be able to deal effectively with the many problems it faces at home and abroad until its government can take a close look at itself and find a voice and identity of national purpose.

It should put aside its policy of avoidance of increasingly grave issues, as this will only bring us more quickly to the moment when we must face its consequences.

While bearing the greater burden, government is not alone in needing to be changed. The electorate must also be able to see and feel the need for a national vision, and the media must be able to take full advantage of their unique license and opportunity to press those who hold or seek office for specific answers and commitments.

Our past strategy of avoidance is doomed to failure. For example we have only to revisit our political corruption problem. We are burdened by two forms — that of the individual and that of the process. These are closely joined — each one feeding on and breeding with the other. Listening to President Obama's early statements, we sense that he would like to be able to confront this problem, but recognizes the enormous amount of political capital that would have to be spent to attract support. And at this time we think it doubtful that our political system could generate sufficient capital to mount a corrective effort.

The question before the nation is whether all its parts, but with government leading, can join in vision, find the will, make the effort and return us to the methods and purposes that we once saw as fundamental to our national character.

This is just one of many challenges that face our new president, but if he can start us on our way to rediscovery, he will also have made our other problems significantly more manageable.

End Notes

[1] L. Frank Baum, The Wizard of Oz, 1900

[2] How Many Americans? By Steven A Camarota, The Washington Post, 9/2/08, p A15. Mr. Camarota is director of research at the Center for Immigration Studies in Washington

[3] "Carrying capacity refers to the number of individuals who can be supported in a given area within natural resource limits, and without degrading the natural social, cultural and economic environment for present and future generations. The carrying capacity for any given area is not fixed. It can be altered by improved technology, but mostly it is changed for the worse by pressures which accompany a population increase. As the environment is degraded, carrying capacity actually

shrinks, leaving the environment no longer able to support even the number of people who could formerly have lived in the area on sustainable basis. No population can live beyond the environment's carrying capacity for very long. The average American's "ecological footprint" (the demands an individual endowed with average amounts of resources, i.e., land, water, food, fiber, waste assimilation and disposal, etc. puts on the environment) is about 12 acres, an area far greater than that taken up by one's residence and place of school or work and other places where he or she is. We must think in terms of "carrying capacity" not land area. The effects of unfettered population growth drastically reduce the carrying capacity in the United States." Source: Carrying Capacity Network, 2000 P Street NW, Washington, DC 20036 Tel: 202-296- 4548.

[4] Bob Goldsborough, President; Americans for Immigration Control; letter, 1/09

[5] Canada pursues a similar policy, but its population does not exceed its carrying capacity as ours does. Much of its land mass is available for further development, but the severity of its climate has inhibited habitation.

[6] Associated Press via Palm Beach Post, 12/15/08

[7] Palm Beach Post – 10/31/08. George F. Will

[8] Palm Beach Post – 1/7/09 – by Michael C. Bender, Capital Bureau

[9] Ibid

[10] Ibid

ECD 1/20/09

Chapter Five —— April 2009

This chapter explores past and present circumstances that inform the economic crisis which America now faces, and why, as the result of our embrace of globalism, its remedies will prove far more challenging than previous combinations of economic downturns and financial debacles.

A Time Like No Other?

According to numerous voices from the White House, the Congress and our top government agencies and departments, our economic system arrived at a point of near collapse last fall which called for massive injections of new capital that only the federal government could provide.

History, tradition and ideology all caved and, despite contrary assurances, our country committed itself to a course unlike we had ever undertaken before. Although the end results could not then, nor cannot now, be known, our economic system, and especially the face and form of American capitalism, has been irrevocably altered.

We do not argue with those who have described our situation in dire terms. We must hope for the "best", although there is no real "best", while recognizing that the elements we face and the stark choices they may impose are of our own making.

How did we get here? What were the legislative, ethical, managerial, political and human failures that produced this meltdown? Today we can provide only a few answers. There will be more, as time releases them, but even now it is evident that we are surrounded by tragedy, folly, arrogance, power and greed that would have intrigued Shakespeare had he been able to imagine them.

History, as always, is a great teacher and can provide answers. As for solutions, they're something else, and for them we have to go elsewhere, but let's start with history.

As far back as our colonial period there was a common bond between our politics and our economics which expressed itself in preference for minimal intrusion by government in either area. Our resentment of England's monarchical power was the basis both for our revolution and the continuing embrace and emphasis of independence thereafter in our lives, culture and government.

Our economic persona was no different. It was marked by independence from birth, and this imprint was a guiding force in its early growth and later excess. Our colonial period was not an economically easy one. With the exception of expensive imports from Europe (mostly English) everything — food, clothing, housing, furnishings, and transportation — was either home grown or homemade.

And yet a level of commerce developed that could sustain the operation of an elemental banking system. Our earliest step towards a production based economy was the manufacturing and marketing of textiles centered on the free source of waterpower offered by New England's rivers.

Waterways could provide transportation as well as hydropower and grew from early local usage to the completion in 1825 of the 352-mile long Erie Canal which joined Lake Erie and the Hudson River. But canals required relatively flat terrain, water availability and either man or horse for motive power. As the country and its travel distances grew, however, their role diminished.

The answer to America's transportation needs (the silver bullet in more ways than one) came in the form of the railroad. Trains moved people and goods safely, economically, profitably, quickly and mostly directly from one point to another across our continent.

Originally invented in England to accommodate travel over much shorter distances, trains proved to be able to provide travel benefits of cost and comfort on our larger scale. They bound the country together socially, psychologically and politically, provided the beginning of a distribution system for a production based economy and became the first and, perhaps, most essential step in moving our country from agriculture to industry.

Our age of the railroads lasted for just about 100 years until auto and air travel appeared. In this railroad century we closed our geographical frontiers and established the structure for a mixed agricultural/industrial economy that has been able to continue to compete and grow so that it can now serve our vast twenty-first century highly technical consumer markets.

The framework within which our economic growth occurred was that of laissez-faire capitalism, the natural heir of the economic/political independence which attended our birth and early growth.

Our 19th century economic and territorial expansion called forth an economic system that provided very rich rewards and just as harsh penalties. In addition, laissez-faire capitalism avoided any regulation, elevated competition, both corporate and individual, and was relentless in its pursuit of maximum profit and efficiency.

These goals were considered as equally appropriate for both corporate production and financing.

And nowhere was this more evident than in the golden age of railroads. While routes were obtained, labor hired, fed and housed and miles of track laid as fast as possible, an equally determined game was being played out on Wall Street and in other financial centers.

There, lacking any meaningful regulation until the Sherman Anti-Trust Act of 1890, highly competitive efforts raised capital in amounts large enough to build the nation's railroads and some of its largest personal fortunes. Bond and stock issues were often floated by bogus boards of directors for companies lacking both rolling stock and rights of way. Many engaged in these financial battles failed; others such as Morgan, Harriman, Gould, Vanderbilt and Hill prevailed.

In this century of dominant laissez-faire capitalism other industries engaged in financing activities similar to those of the railroads, but the latter remained the "gold standard". During the early part of the twentieth century the emergence of our labor union movement and the income tax, along with the elevated unity and patriotism of WWI, dented our capitalistic image, but its considerable political and psychological momentum was able to deflect these challenges.

With the stock market crash of 1929 and the Great Depression of the 1930s, however, it was clear that our capitalistic system would have to be modified. Quite simply, laissez-faire capitalism, which had enjoyed a century of supremacy and withstood every challenge of its time and place, could not stand shoulder to shoulder, nor eyeball to eyeball, with the jobless poor who moved from production to bread lines.

FDR unleashed a barrage of legislation which extended government's reach into areas previously considered private of which the economy was clearly one. But another enormous change was underway. It was technological development and, with radio, the first step towards our modern consumer society. Radio, as television would later, bound the country together. *It enabled us to have a national conversation between ourselves and our government.*

With WWII the call of patriotism tied us even more closely to each other and to our government. The latter, by honor rolls, bond drives, rationing, new taxes, travel restrictions, production priorities and both civilian and military mobilization, entered into our lives in many new and unexpected ways.

1939 was a line in time that changed the world and WWII was fought to determine who would make its changes — democratic or totalitarian forces. Russia fought with the former, but in the postwar period revealed its true intention to achieve global domination for communism. It took another generation of the Cold War before the USSR succumbed to its own internal failures.

It is against this backdrop of our capitalistic history that we must view our present economic circumstances and the various methods and attitudes now emanating from Washington that seek to provide remedies.

Then And Now

The situation that our nation now faces is as dangerous as any we have experienced in the past with the exception of Pearl Harbor and the Civil War both of which involved military struggle for survival. The closest non-military threat to which our present circumstance is compared is the Great Depression (GD), although official sources of both political parties now prefer the milder "recession" and even held off its use until as late as possible.

Before proceeding there is one note of warning to sound. Our western culture concerns itself with and makes use of the past in many ways — "those who ignore the past are condemned to repeat it", for example. And yet, in this study we find and cite instances where, in forming policy for future actions, the conditions are so different that our past will not apply.

The tendency to use the GD as a standard of measurement for our current problems is one of these instances as it implies that these two events have more in common than they actually do. In fact, there are some very significant differences which we must recognize and understand.

At the most basic level, the numbers are entirely different. We are dealing in trillions, not millions, or perhaps billions, of dollars, and our population is more than twice what it was in the 30s. Scale-ups, whether economic or industrial, do not always perform as intended, especially if the human factor is present. In economics money can be a commodity. It can also be a weapon. We are challenged to employ trillions of dollars to achieve a first effort success. The possibility of unintended consequences is very real.

In a prior issue we commented on the difficulty of visualizing large numbers. Kathleen Parker of the Washington Post provides help by stating that a million dollars in one thousand dollar bills would form a four-inch high stack, whereas a trillion dollars would reach a height of 67.9 miles. [1]

This is the first of two visual challenges that face us. A stack of currency 68 miles high creates perspective. It helps us to comprehend fiscal enormity. Our second visualization problem is somewhat different in that it involves events as well as numbers. It appears later in our text.

In listening to people talk about the GD, especially those who did not live through it, there is often the sense that its ten-year life was controlled and that it ended as the result of the Roosevelt administration's efforts. This is only partially true, as it was the economic improvement wrought by our preparation for and participation in WWII that ended the GD without which it might have continued.

Our tendency to see it as a neat ten year event carries over into references to our present recession that include arbitrary time lines for policy success. This poses both a psychological and a practical threat. In our situation nothing is assured, and false hope is worse than none.

But the most striking, and perhaps telling, difference between our times and the GD lies in our level of private, commercial and governmental debt. Any effort to relate these two events to each other must fail on this account.

Prior to WWII and FDR's kick-start spending programs the country still aimed to create budgetary surpluses. Commercial debt was moderate and consumer debt was minor and tightly controlled. It would have been impossible for anyone, within or without government, to imagine the trillion dollar scale of our present debt structure for private and public debt alike. We face an economic musket-to-missile discrepancy between these two times and yet somehow we must develop enough coherence to bring relief to our own and other economies around the world.

This will be a formidable undertaking. We will need an enormous amount of good fortune, the understanding and fairness of the American people and the ability of our elected government to cooperate in the nation's interest, none of which is guaranteed.

Our present economic crisis is made of several parts. They go by different names, strike at different times and targets, but they are interrelated and their cumulative effect could alter our attitudes about our government, our future, our society and ourselves. We are at one of those perilous moments in history when the old controls may fail and the new ones are not yet in place.

The first is the credit crunch in which banks find themselves unable and/or unwilling to conduct their usual lending function. This has been blamed on the "toxic" securities marketed by the mortgage industry and the associated failure of the housing market, but equally important was our general high level of debt that seems to know no boundaries.

Credit crunches, formerly known as "panics", are not new to our economic life. In our nineteenth century period of homage to laissez-faire capitalism they occurred frequently, striking large banks and communities as well as small ones. Cash was king; credit was mostly local and personal; and many people and businesses slipped from prosperity to insolvency. Surviving these sudden "panics" required being wary and alert.

In those times, as communications and bank records keeping were primitive, panics could form and spread without warning. The causes of these painful disruptions were not clearly understood, although their effects most certainly were. This helped to foster a view that the "market" was an omniscient force with its own unnerving rhythm and regulation best served by lack of human interference.

The economic and psychological pain of the GD was so severe and extensive that FDR was convinced that government intervention was necessary to save the country. His were the first real steps for our government on the path of economic macro management, and they encountered bitter resistance from those who considered our "free market system" one of the pillars of our form of government.

Today, the "free market" is one of the conserva-tive right's most frequently used mantras, although our "free market" has become considerably less free. It is allowed to function freely only up to the point when it causes political pain for one party or the other. Then intervention is permitted. Currently, intervention is undergoing a severe test, not philosophically but because of the enormity of the numbers involved. Even President Bush, viewing Wall Street's systemic failure last fall, felt it necessary to scrap the "free market" mantra and weigh in with massive government funding to avoid a complete collapse of our financial system.

As this drama continues to play out, it becomes increasingly clear that we are embarked upon a game we have never played before. We no longer speak in terms of billions, or hundreds of billions, but trillions. We do not know what the effect of government intervention on this scale will be. Henry Paulsen's attempts were ill-fated. Will Secretary Geithner's be any better? Why? He has not told us. Is there any reason to believe that a few cabinet officers can produce results that will cure our malady? Witness our newspaper and auto industries where "top" management now presides over their collapse.

In any activity, when we abandon the comfort of our human scale in pursuit of the gigantic, we incur greater risk. This is true in weaponry, transportation, architecture, investments, etc., and there is every reason to believe it will apply also to the distribution of trillions of dollars to various states, authorities, localities, agencies and contractors. We have not dealt in these numbers before and it is suspect to conclude that a very few people, just recently elected or appointed, will get it right on the first try. And at a cost in trillions, our remedial resources are limited.

We can hope for the country's sake that our programs succeed, but the numbers are daunting and we may encounter problems of scale as difficult as visualizing a stack of thousand dollar bills almost 68 miles high.

The element of time is important in attempting to repair our broken economy. Certainly, any remedy that would take ten years, as with the GD, would not be deemed a success. And yet, various comments from administration sources, suggesting that we may begin to see evidence of a turnabout in the next year or two seem highly unrealistic to us. Larry Summers and Tim Geithner are intelligent and successful economic managers, but we run the risk that some of the major forces they face, which have been gathering for years, may prove beyond their rescue capability. Or they may provide improvement in some sectors and further problems in others; or perhaps short term benefits followed by long term penalties. Here again, the image of our three major automobile companies and their failure to deal with the political and economic problems of their industry offers some insight.

But the economic challenge is not all that the new administration and congress must face. There is also the parallel problem of our national psychology which is now in a seriously troubled state. As the number of our people that are unemployed, in pain, insolvent or in poor health increases, so does their disbelief in encouraging statements from Washington. For, as they listen, they recall the lies from the past and the multiple failures of other programs such as "the war on drugs", immigration and energy which give the sense that we are not in control of our own destiny.

In the past, wars have often served to provide unity and improve our psychological state. That option is no longer available due to our depleted financial and military resources. The war in Afghanistan is an important economic and psychological factor in how we survive our current crisis. At the worst, its conduct and outcome could become another negative; at best, it might be neutral. As always, we must hope for the best.

With regard to our national spending policies we are in a "damned if we do and damned if we don't" situation, and our present purpose seems to require us to mortgage our future. We cannot foretell with assurance what will result from our massive spending programs, but can be certain that their impact on our nation and way of life will be long and deep.

Globalism

The roots of globalism extend back to the postwar period when America, with its currency and production capability intact, was able to create export markets throughout the world. This put pressure on foreign producers to design and build innovative products that could compete with ours.

Our increased exposure to foreign cultures during and after WWII led Americans to seek the products they offered, and we used our strong dollar to increase imports.

The auto industry shows quite clearly how imports, which were originally limited to luxury models, were able to compete with our higher priced cars and become successful enough to establish their own production plants in this country.

Over time, our high standard of living with its built-in high labor cost made American manufacturers vulnerable to the new designs, engineering and consumer benefits that foreign manufacturers developed and marketed.

Not surprisingly, our corporate sector came up with a way to increase profits by "offshoring" — i.e. moving our homegrown, high labor cost production and services to lower labor cost areas such as India, China, Eastern Europe, Latin America, etc.

Globalism is essentially a continuous effort to combine available capital and labor in such a way, time and place that profit is maximized. Any number can play, and do so instantly, thanks to the 24/7 trading and managing capability of our global markets.

Offshoring is one globalistic technique which has proved profitable for its corporate sector sponsors but damaging to our country's economic base. Here is how, more often than not, it works:

1) Ajax Inc. is a manufacturer of a line of consumer products faced with growing foreign competition and a high labor

cost per unit. In spite of having taken a series of cost-cutting actions, profits continue to erode.

2) It relocates its manufacturing operation to India where it can take advantage of lower priced Indian steel and labor. Encouraged by the results of its manufacturing move, it also relocates its customer service function and then its design and engineering department.

3) For the US this results in job losses which translate into reduced tax receipts and increased unemployment expense at three different, but important, levels of our economy. Net effect for the US is a minus.

4) For the exiting corporation, the move is a plus, as it accomplishes savings in raw materials and labor. It can dispose of its US plant, and operations will benefit from the elimination of both its property taxes and employee health and retirement plans. Profitability is restored; shareholders are pleased; and management can logically argue for increased compensation.

5) The goods newly manufactured in India are sold back into the US as imports which provides a profit opportunity for the manufacturer and calls for expense by the US. Again, the net effect is corporate/positive and US/negative. Nor should we forget that the sales revenues generated in India may be put to use there or elsewhere and not repatriated in which case they can qualify for special US tax treatment substantially less than what would have been due under domestic manufacture.

6) In each direction, exiting and entering, revenues and savings are enhanced for the corporation and diminished for the US.

Globalism's goal to align the elements of the world's economies in the most profitable way possible attracted the participation of many international financial institutions that recognized the opportunities for new and larger fees and interest payments. With governmental and private institutional acceptance in place, the corporate sector did not want to be left out. The necessary pieces of the puzzle were in place and globalism developed a surging momentum that overcame most doubts and defied opposition.

But here, again, the matter of human scale arises. The combined trade figures of the world's economies measure in trillions and it is not easy for bureaucrats in Beijing, Brussels or Boston to fully understand at all times the effect of the movement and relation of these vast numbers.

Their interrelatedness made for a cohesive market in the expansion phase which most participants viewed as permanent. But as error or instability, at first locally and then more widely, began to appear, the mass and reach of this interrelatedness proved to have unforeseen and dangerous consequences. Shared benefits could quickly become shared penalties. And nowhere was this more apparent than in the closeness of the international banking community.

At first this may sound like nothing more than another comment on human greed which, of course, it is. But it may be more, if negative results persist and governments are called upon to make real changes in their international financial structures. Presently, this appears to be both highly possible, and perhaps probable, as recession increases and we contemplate the deeper pain of a major depression.

"As Far As The Eye Can See"

In 2001, when G. W. Bush took office this was his forecast of budget surpluses. Today, it is accepted by both political parties as a reasonable prediction of <u>deficits.</u> That's a 180° reversal! Such a result does not come easily. What happened? Do we need new lenses, or values or measurement techniques? Probably some of each.

Our budget deficit future appears beyond bleak and reaches almost to impossible. To further complicate the situation, while Pres. Obama has tried to correct some of the less than transparent accounting methods of his predecessor, the view ahead that we are now given by the administration and Congress seems both incomplete and optimistic.

The annual budget deficits of the Reagan, Bush I and Clinton's first term years <u>averaged</u> $134 billion. There were three years of surplus in Clinton's second term and then under G.W. Bush one year of first term surplus followed by seven years of deficits. The annual average of budget deficits under Bush II was $253 billion which did not include off-budget items, most notably the war in Iraq[2].

Looking ahead, the same source predicts deficits totaling just over $6 trillion, or an average of $864.3 billion for an Obama presidency expected to last for two terms. Another government source[3] carries its projections out through 2019 and estimates total deficits of $6.35 trillion with an annual average of $577.3 billion. Although their time frames differ both sources arrive at a total deficit figure around $6 trillion.

All such projections represent fantasy of one kind or another. The possibility of accuracy with numbers of this size with which we have no experience is slim, indeed. Add that these funds are to be distributed to a mix of locations and projects selected at the national political level but administered locally, and the expectation that they can be controlled and applied effectively grows less realistic.

As a consequence, our own estimate of the task ahead to repair our economy is that it will take longer and be more costly by another $2 trillion than what is now proposed. If this is the case we can expect our official national debt to approach $20 trillion in the next decade, and our total, or true, debt to increase from our present $56 trillion[4] to $64 trillion.

These are sobering figures. And yet, more than dollars are involved. Even if we are able to withstand their arithmetic, they will have a profound effect upon how we and the rest of the world experience and define the different America that they will produce.

Everybody will keep their own count --— Bin Laden his, the EU its, the Chinese theirs. But there will be shifts in perception. We will be seen as less of a leader and certainly no longer all powerful. Our foreign policy initiatives will not be delivered with the assumption of unopposed success. They may well, along with our dollars, show signs of weakness and of age — of being less than before and everyone knowing it.

And, if we can summon the truth from our trial, we must realize that our own identity has suffered a significant change. We will no longer be #1, the sole superpower. We may have to share privilege, authority and power with others and have to test and address our concept of international leadership. Such a shift would reflect the political and diplomatic realities of our changed status. To ignore or deny them would only make our way and future far more difficult.

Our government has deceived us, and we have deceived ourselves, for far too long. And it is unlikely that our friends and enemies throughout the world will join in this deception as our fortunes change. The real truth and beauty of America are found in our Declaration of Independence and Constitution. Without them the American people are not better or worse than many others.

We, and others, have been widely misled by the hollow hype of our media age. We, and they, deserve better. We could redeem ourselves by leading the way. Will we learn? Will we lead?

The Banking Crisis

In 1933, a senatorial inquiry into the stock market crash of '29 chaired by federal judge Ferdinand J. Pecora conducted hearings and took testimony from the heads of Wall Street's leading banks and brokerage houses[5]. This was an occasion of great public interest, as throughout it there appeared a common thread of denial and deflection which, although artfully presented, was unable to prevent any conclusion other than that those questioned comprised a tightly joined community whose interests enjoyed precedence over those of its customers or the public.

Last fall, seventy-five years later, Wall Street again almost engineered its own destruction. The practices in which it engaged and the defenses it put forth were eerily similar to what had been disclosed to Judge Pecora's investigating committee, but the present circumstances carry with them the threat of far greater future risk — both financial and psychological.

Following the Pecora committee's revelations, Congress passed legislation that separated the brokerage and investment banking functions from commercial banks. But breeding will out, and our political DNA is formed of tightly wound strands of money and power.

Chafing under this unnecessarily restrictive rules change, the financial services industry through elected representatives, media, trade groups and lobbyists undertook a campaign to rescind what it regarded as an onerous burden. Eventually, it succeed-ed and embarked upon a new round of marketing "I win, you lose", increasingly arcane products for which even their originators could not provide convincing evaluation.

America entering the Great Depression had little in common with America today. We were still on the gold standard. There was little consumer or national debt. Government played a lesser role in the lives of the people, and there were no retirement benefits of any significance to be had from either the public or private sectors. Those too old or ill to work depended upon savings, annuities, family support or taking residence in a "home" with others who shared their plight and where life could be described as "spare" at best. In general, there was the sense that the country had suffered a very bad turn of events from which everyone should do their share to recover.

To many Americans today those times and ways seem distant and quaint compared to ours. We have become dependent upon retirement benefits from both private and government sources and through them, especially Social Security, have provided a measure of independence for those at the end of their working lives. And a new care providing industry has grown rapidly into one of our largest. In making these changes, which most people see as improvements, we have become more used to and tolerant of a larger role for government in our lives.

This, of course, is neither all bad nor all good and requires constant tuning to maintain a reasonable balance between the extremes of more and less. And, although over the years we have developed a different psychology, solutions to large social problems do not come easily in our contentious, contemporary America.

As Americans look upon our present wreckage and feel the effects of destroyed credit, greatly diminished home and securities values and job losses, they tend to try to make sense of it all by likening it to the 1930s. Except in a most general way this is not valid, and the fact that we are laboring under new circumstances increases the possibility that our government will not be able to provide the answers.

We have a bitterly divided two party political structure that draws strength from the extreme positions of both. We have within our economy an element of consumer debt of $2.5 trillion. More than a third of those with credit card debt of $10,000 or more earn less than $50,000 a year[6]. We have an official national debt of about $11 trillion moving towards $20 trillion; and total obligations of $56 trillion, also increasing. These realities today were not even imaginable in 1930.

The end result is that, while studying the history of the GD may offer us some comfort, we have been dealt a very different hand to play. By several measures one can make the argument that our country's reckless overspending and irresponsibility over the past half century has rendered us insolvent. This may sound shocking, but it is difficult to view our enormous levels of national, state, local, corporate, mortgage and personal debt with a realistic belief that we have the means to repay it.

We have found out and now must accept that economic "growth" of the Reagan through Bush II years was based on an expansion of credit, not production, in which there were many players. There has been a painful sorting out, and what's left are those "too big to fail" and those "too small to bail".

The dollar is still the world's reserve currency, but already we can hear arguments against this status. Should these voices grow to the point where the dollar has to prove its value and/or its status in the face of actions by central banks to reduce their dollar holdings, our economy's reliance upon debt could prove very hazardous to us and our currency.

As the world's reserve currency, our dollar finds support not available to lesser currencies, even though we erode its value by our increasing level of debt. Were another currency to appear that could challenge the dollar, the latter would quickly lose value, causing dollar owners to reduce their holdings and thereby putting further pressure on its value.

International currency markets are delicate mechanisms. They are highly interrelated and hostage to both internal and external events whereby minor actions can produce major movements.

There is one other important difference between the GD and today. It is the extreme outrage felt and expressed by people towards Wall Street for its role in our national disaster. This has been a story that has replayed itself with increasing frequency primarily because the financial services industry's immense political force is able to deflect any appropriate regulation by government.

Like any industry, Wall Street strives to create growth opportunities by developing new products, but today Wall Street's products all too often are designed to generate fee opportunities rather than to fulfill a genuine consumer need. This was not always the case. Our great age of railroad construction in the nineteenth century was made possible by the funds obtained from Wall Street's issuance of bonds and shares. And its role was repeated in the electric utility combinations and construction of the early twentieth century.

In both instances, Wall Street's skills and people generated "products" that well served the interests of our nation and people and tied them more closely together. In the process, of course, large fees were paid and profits made which were justified by the results. Not so today when, quite reasonably, the public is outraged that it has been duped again.

There is deep resentment over the obscenely excessive amounts of money that Wall Street managements paid themselves as the bubble was clearly bursting and the equity markets in almost free fall. In the final months of last year the total of bonuses paid reached $18.4 billion[7] some of which were paid while, and even after, the government undertook its bailout program to avoid total financial collapse.

More recently, in March, it was revealed that AIG paid out $165 million of bonuses to traders in its Financial Products division after receiving over $180 billion in bailout funds. Up until the last minute before its passage, the stimulus bill had contained a provision that limited executive compensation to bailout recipients, but it was removed by Sen. Chris Dodd (D. CT), Chairman of the Senate Banking Committee[8]. Dodd, who ran for the Democratic nomination, received over $850,000 during the 2008 election cycle,[9] from corporations that received TARP bailout funds. There is no quid pro quo evident or suggested, but political giving of that magnitude inevitably produces close relationships and the potential for bias, whether conscious or not. Duped is one thing; arrogance on a scale such as this is another and will not be soon forgotten or forgiven.

The sub prime loan mess suggests persistent fraud at every stage. In its initial lending phase there was widespread collusive fraud between lenders and borrowers which was continued when these toxic loans were bundled and presented to the rating agencies. The latter committed their own brand of outrageous fraud by assigning to them their highest ratings. The deception continued when the toxic loans, now rated triple-A, were presented to investment banks and again in the final stage when the investment bankers sold them to their clients. Wall Street is a numbers game in which the present players ran out of bounds. Its recent show of greed and incompetence may well impose upon it the effective regulation it has so determinedly tried to avoid.

Market Mayhem

While Wall Street puts its numbers to use in "Mickey Mouse" games, beyond the tip of lower Manhattan the rest of the country must deal with a mass of constantly changing numbers upon which our country's future may well depend. These are the economic forecasts, projections, analyses, models and business plans that we hope will resolve our current uncertainties as painlessly as possible.

They are subject to interpretation, discussion and argument by the public and by "experts" who speak for the broadcast media from early morning to late at night, and sometimes around the clock. Although some of them may turn out to be accurate, at this point they all compete for credibility.

Eventually a few of these numbers will emerge from the efforts, legislation, hearings, conferences and proposals of governments here and abroad as truth. They will be seen as results, not forecasts; they may still be subject to debate as to whether they are "right" or "wrong", but they are more fixed; they have established their place and time. They are fact, or as near to it as we can come in the present moment.

But, unfortunately we are not there yet. We struggle to imagine, to see with clarity, to choose wisely, desperate to put our own imprint on reality. But, of course, there are always other voices dedicated to other goals — "But what about...?"; "On the other hand...?"; "What if...?"; "We must remember... "; "Don't forget..." One by one, on the road to reality, they will drop away, but for the time they are very much with us, and we must use them as best we can.

First, however, we must confront our second visualization challenge. We must ask ourselves and our elected government to imagine the circumstances that must take place to permit us to create meaningful surpluses by which we can <u>realistically</u> expect to <u>reduce our debt.</u> We do not refer to minor or occasional reductions of our annual deficit. We must recognize our problem in its entirety, and that means creating policies and programs that make a persuasive argument for serious and continuing debt reduction.

Our past and present budgetary deficits are not sustainable. The arithmetic of their accumulation is cause enough for concern, but they also have the capability to threaten and erode our dollar's value and our social contract between the people and their government.

This last is critical. Congress and the executive branch seem to operate on the basis that there is no amount of expense that the American taxpayer will not accept. They are wrong. Governments and political systems have their tipping points when unrest grows to the point where law and order fail and the spirit of the mob is let loose among the people.

The Obama administration's budgetary forecasts make for bleak reading in themselves. Congress' failure to identify or propose any debt reduction mechanisms suggests that our economic future will be marked by as much folly as our past, and that the burden is expected to be added to that already carried by the tax paying public.

In a time when both population and major expense categories such as health care, Social Security, education and infrastructure are expected to increase incrementally, the taxpayer's load may well prove too heavy to bear. At that time his/her sense of abandonment by government may reach the point where the pain is so great that the economic, political and social threads of our people/government tapestry must be rewoven with different fabrics and from different patterns in order to survive.

All of which raises another vital question. In nature, in physics and chemistry, elements can change their values according to the temperature, altitude, light, pressure, etc. of their environment. We face an economic environment with laws which we do not fully understand. Our question is whether, as major changes are wrought in our public/government relations, we will be able to retain our historical political and economic values. This should be a matter of open debate by the public, the media and government in considering programs as vast as those we now undertake. Sadly, no such expression of national interest has occurred.

Much mention has been made in our recent discussions of stimulus spending of our need to repair our infrastructure with primary emphasis on the roads and bridges of our interstate highway system. The latter received spectacular attention last year when a key bridge in Minneapolis collapsed without warning. "Without warning" is not quite correct, however. The American Society of Civil Engineers (ASCE) has claimed that we must spend $1.6 trillion over the next five years for infrastructure repairs and maintenance[10], and the truth is that we have had ample warning going back about twenty-five years when a large section of I-95 collapsed into Long Island Sound at Byram, CT. Other isolated signs of deterioration, often attributed to local circumstances, began to follow.

President Eisenhower initiated our interstate system in 1956 which gives it a 'shelf life' of about fifty years measured to today, but only about twenty-five years to the Byram collapse. As maintenance work lacks the appeal of new construction, local/state agencies and voters find various ways to defer it, even though the federal government normally pays 90% of the cost.

The question that these failures raise and that few people ask, and even fewer attempt to answer, is — "What is the real cost of present and future infrastructure expense?"

Our present interstate highway system of 47,000 miles[11] differs greatly from the original 1956 program which was designed mainly for passenger cars. Today, the mix runs more to commercial traffic with its heavy trucks and trailers and the wear and tear they cause. More telling, the number of vehicles on our interstate highways is now four times what it was in 1956[12].

The recent stimulus bill assigns $30 billion[13] to highway infrastructure over the next two years, but we think our continuing growth in population and vehicles would prove this amount insufficient to meet future market and safety demands.

The escalating cost of taxes, tolls and fuel poses a negative for our popular commercial trucking industry and may offer new opportunities for our railroad freight system.

The Eisenhower system's cost ran to billions of dollars and its "shelf life" seems to be about one generation. Now, as we undertake repairs, we are speaking in trillions! That is an enormous difference. Looking ahead to increasing raw materials/labor costs and more population/cars/travel when the next round of maintenance will be necessary, the costs will be significantly greater and the "shelf life" will probably have shrunk.

As we go down this road, paying both more and more often, what is our real cost? It would be most revealing to measure the dollar cost per mile of US highway construction from 1956 to the present and also for what is planned under the current stimulus legislation. How do we get our elected representatives to employ a budgetary system that recognizes these realities? In effect, this is one aspect of the task of creating good government in which we have been sadly negligent and unsuccessful. New numbers are needed.

One of the absolutely critical elements of the present economic circumstance is our rapidly increasing national debt. Recent

Congressional Budget Office estimates anticipate $9.3 trillion of budget deficits over the next decade will result from the Obama stimulus program[14]. Any such projections involving massive numbers over a lengthy period defy reality.

And yet their impact will be felt. There will be results with which our government and our fellow citizens will have to deal as best they can. Some of these consequences will be domestic; others will be put to us by friends and enemies abroad.

In recent memory we were the world's largest creditor. Today our role is reversed and we are its largest debtor. As debt increases, debtors find it more difficult to determine their own destiny and, while we still enjoy exceptional status throughout the world, we will not be an exception to this rule.

Both the dollar amount of our debt and its percentage of our gross domestic product[15] have reached levels that are viewed by many economists as unsustainable. Similarly, as interest on our "official" national debt may come close to an increase of 100% in the next decade, it will put real pressure on the amounts available to other expense categories, as the "pie" cannot always expand to accommodate the appetites it must feed.

This interest in the fiscal year ending 9/08 amounted to $457 billion and was the third largest item in our national budget[16], exceeded only by our spending on Social Security and defense. Anyone who has experienced excessive debt will recognize the irresistible force that it will apply to our future budgets were it to double by 2019.

Federal spending on Medicare, military/defense and Social Security over the past decade has shown persistent increases and reached record levels. In the case of Medicare and SS they enjoy wide social, human and political support.

The biggest shock to our system is finding out that things are not as we have been told by Wall St, the media, and our elected government. We have experienced an enormous loss of confidence which is reinforced locally and painfully by friends, family and neighbors losing jobs.

Rot is strong and deep. It shows up in Bernie Madoff, Allen Stanford, local political corruption, and flagrant misuse of church funds for Las Vegas junkets by Florida Catholic clergy not burdened by diocesan supervision, accountability or punishment.

Our federal debt having grown from $5.7 to $10.6 trillion during the Bush II presidency[17] its limit was extended in the recent stimulus bill to $12.1 trillion, a 10% increase in one year. Our total true debt is now seen as $56 trillion by Concord Coalition, an increase of $5 or $6 trillion from the figure we used in our 4/05 issue.

These are not just numbers. They carry with them a message of human pain and fear in a society whose claims, character and values are being revealed as less than what we have been told and have believed. Prominent in this process of societal downgrading is the failure of many of our institutions to protect those for whom they were created.

In the course of our financial meltdown we are exposed to much false rhetoric — now is the time to buy stocks, go shopping, etc. Our current situation shows how dangerous these attempts to manipulate public behavior for personal profit have become.

But there is another looming threat on a far larger scale which we must recognize. Again, it has to do with our enormous debt load. Listening to our political representatives from both parties, we are given the impression that our stimulus measures will create near term debt which, as the stimulus kicks in and the economy improves, will be retired by rising revenues and their receipts.

This is another trap! It is simply not possible that the accumulation of spending and debt that we have built into our system can be eliminated by a few years of improved circumstances even if they are accompanied by budgetary surpluses.

Consider that the interest on our debt will show a large increase. Consider that health care is expected to continue to claim a growing share of our budget. And there are the unavoidable consequences of expansionist immigration/population policies that translate into higher service and maintenance costs at all levels of government. All these claims upon our budget will continue to alter its percentages. And they will be paid.

The Ever Present, Uninvited Guest

There is an uninvited guest that has a seat at our economic table. He is of our own blood and yet we do not acknowledge him. He attempts to avoid notice and yet he takes a share of everything that is served. Whether we eat with our hands or use implements, he does the same. Occasionally, we move against him. We ask him to leave, or say that he will no longer be served. But he pays no heed. He has friends in high places. His name is 'fraud'.

How did he come to our table? Why can we not expel him? What claim has he upon us? Again, we may look to history for answers, but not for solutions.

In early America law was created, not imposed by royalty or invasion. Our creation borrowed heavily from the body of English law that had developed since Magna Carta, but bore our own distinctive American imprint. And, as with finance and politics, as we moved our borders westward, the circumstances of that expansion were reflected in "the law of the land".

From the earliest days of our westward migration certain patterns repeated themselves. The first communities were small and composed mostly of a few families and/or friends. If they were successful in establishing an economic and social base, they grew to become towns, counties, territories and, finally, states.

At the leading edge of this process, law was mostly of the basic criminal variety and was delivered by sheriffs, marshalls and enraged citizens. There were many more firearms and "hanging trees" than courtrooms and justices. In time, this mix would change and, as population and trade increased, the niceties of commercial law took their place alongside the criminal code.

With statehood and admission to the union our law enforcement and judicial systems entered a more mature phase which established a variety of restrictions, benefits, regulations, penalties and procedures that had not existed before. Life (and law) became more settled, more formal, more fashionable and less violent. The frontier was replaced by "civilization".

However, our legal DNA has carried down for generations some of our early frontier legal code. As in finance and politics, we engaged in a highly competitive, independent and often arbitrary form of co-existence that rejected intervention as much as possible. To the extent that we could make it so, financial law was seen to be as laissez-faire as capitalism.

The relationship between the two was symbiotic and the result was that our economic and political systems have historically tolerated a high level of fraud. It has been in the past, and continues to be, a growth industry. It is there, like the guest at the table, and shows no sign of voluntary departure.

Earlier we pointed out the various stages of the "toxic" mortgage debacle during which massive fraud was perpetrated by the Wall Street lending, rating and marketing sectors. Backed into a corner by their own cupidity, they warned of total collapse if they were not rescued and, putting aside their usual objection to intervention, opted to accept the balm of taxpayer billions, and perhaps as much as a trillion. There is no telling when "more" will become "enough".

But even then the guest will not excuse himself and leave our table. He hears the political argument revolving around the proposed stimulus package, knows that it will pass and that he will play an important role in it. For fraud it will be a "slam dunk", a golden moment not to be missed.

We have dealt with massive fraud before — in the Iraq war, in Medicare, in Social Security, in FEMA and elsewhere — but the potential here is far greater, and will probably be achieved.

In a previous report devoted to healthcare we cited an FBI estimate of $60 to $100 billion for annual Medicare fraud. This is a shocking amount and yet it applies to only one of our key government programs. There are others such as SS and our agricultural subsidies; and there are many smaller programs tucked into the dark corners of our budgetary legislation.

But they pale beside the opportunities for fraud that will be created and realized at local, state and national levels by the immense and prolonged stimulus funding upon which we are about to embark. What's more, as with most federal programs, it will lack meaningful safeguards and enforcement procedures which increase the cost and time of implementation.

As the amount and reach of stimulus fraud are revealed, Congress will feign surprise, but by that time all the necessary state and local power structures will have been activated and reformed around the new money from Washington. The truth of Tip O'Neill's defining statement, "All politics are local.", reaches far beyond the voting booth.

We tend not to think of our historical insistence upon independence in our political and financial pursuits as encouraging anything illegal. And yet it is in our DNA and marks our economy in ways and places large and small.

As he contemplates the future, the guest at our table allows himself a wry smile of anticipation. In due time we will know why. The proof will be in the pudding.

Conclusions

The greatest peril from our present crisis that our nation faces is the long term effect of its vast increase of our indebtedness. Unemployment may decrease and sales may increase, but annual deficits of a trillion dollars have a force all their own and are not manageable.

We are fortunate in a way in that, because our dollar is the world's reserve currency, we can print, rather than purchase, the funds we need to pay our debts. But there are unwanted consequences there, too, as any cheapening of the dollar would invite challenges to its reserve currency status. Such a challenge would accelerate its loss of value and, were it to succeed, would cause considerable instability in international economic markets.

Historically, printing more money has appealed to politicians and offered them, for the moment, the least painful course of action. Like all addictions it is dangerous and possessed of harmful side effects. We should not undertake it, but all indications are that we will, as it is a quiet and time-tested way of "kicking the can down the road".

We may find that globalism's ties are ones that bind and we will not be able to act with the same economic insouciance and independence as we have in the past. Such a realization by us and others would most likely result in a realignment of the international financial structure.

But there is more to be concerned about — more than our federal debt. Our states, too, face budget deficits that emit a disturbing signal. Over the four year period from '02 thru '05 total state budget deficits averaged $60 billion. In the projected '09 thru '11 period their shortfall is anticipated to average $115 billion. Only eight states are expected to break even or show surpluses.[18]

Why is this significant? Because states must seek their funds from the same source as the federal government — the American taxpayer — and will increase the load that he/she must carry.

We exist in a time of great peril from natural, political, social, military and population forces that we can neither anticipate with accuracy nor, with any certainty, control. All of these have the power to impose sudden and major change upon our economy and society.

How do we propose to deal with the heretofore-unimaginable numbers and unknowable challenges that lie in wait for us? Our primary line of defense is an inept Congress so given over to achieving ideological and political advantage that it has become a portrait of paralysis. Given the magnitude of our problems, it would be unrealistic for us to expect it to readily come up with solutions. But, solutions aside, the Congress does not seem able to aim itself in the right direction, to align itself with the increasingly beleaguered public's need for good government.

What comfort can we take from what we face? The stimulus package and the recovery effort needed to implement it are immense and the problems seem even larger. The dollars envisioned are vast and seem destined to reach all levels of our economic structure. Their successful application will require fairness and a deft touch.

The numbers of everything — dollars, forms, regulations, applications, recipients, projects, and possibilities for failure or success — form a scale with which we are unfamiliar. They travel along lines, more often of imagination than experience, and intersect at inconvenient and painful places in our national political and social life that do not adapt easily to government intervention.

Our present situation is not one of chance. The fact that it has been self-made over an extended period of time lessens the possibility of self-correction. And the dollars required preclude any significant additional funding if flaws or failure result. The money and, perhaps, the time will not be available. If it is to work, we must get it right the first time. There will not be time, or money or patience for tinkering and a long learning curve.

This is a time when our past theories and efforts may not be able to provide solutions. There are so many unknown and unpredictable elements that we will need a large measure of good fortune in order to succeed.

The most damaging ingredient in this mix of money could well be our own government, those in our agencies and the Congress who are empowered to form and implement our economic policy.

From the beginning of the meltdown last September through last month they have engaged in their usual ideological conflict. This is marked by personal accusations and attacks, by votes and non-votes and media exploitation. There is little evidence that this atmosphere can change, but what's far worse than this behavior is the dead-end realization that our government cannot function in any other way, as most of those involved, whether elected or appointed, cannot envision a national interest, or debate, or effort without a strong ideological component.

There are some, but few positives. One may be the realization that our economy is not a real-life board game played for fun by those on Wall Street. It is likely that our present pain will bring about meaningful changes and improvements in our capitalist system. These are long overdue and need not limit its opportunities.

Of one thing we can be certain. Spending close to $10 trillion will bring about many unforeseeable changes in our national and individual lives. There is the strong probability that they will be of such size and immediacy that they will require us to think more clearly and closely about our world and government. That would be a real plus.

The American people have a shared sense of fairness which they have allowed to be abused by their political representatives. Quite simply, the public's fairness is more advanced, more effective and more genuine than that of its government. Any broad improvement in this difference would be of great national benefit. Turning around an economy the size of ours is no easy matter, and we will need all our skill, intelligence and judgement.

It is an all too common form of public deception to suggest that we gradually work ourselves out of our present mess, as we are long past that point. It is too big, and getting bigger. We have built into our system mechanisms, both political and economic, which cannot be dislodged without great effort. Such an effort, to be successful, will impose its own pain and reality.

This will be the next great challenge to our people, our political and financial systems, our society and our way of life. We will engage in a new kind of arithmetic. We will have to add here and subtract there and maintain our balance throughout the constant change.

The old voices are hoarse and tired from repeating the slogans and mantras of the past. The old models will not work and new ones are yet to be tested, or trusted. We are at the edge, and the wind is rising.

Epilogue

And now we revisit our first visualization — the one trillion dollar, 67.9 miles high stack of thousand dollar bills. If the CBO estimate of $9.3 trillion of budget deficits over the next decade is correct, it would require a column of bills 630 miles high. That's outer space, beyond the earth's atmosphere, at a level used for space exploration and orbiting satellites.

End Notes

[1] <u>Crash Course</u> by Chris Martenson via Kathleen Parker, <u>Making nice with the beast,</u> Palm Beach Post, 3/9/09

[2] The original basis for the figures in this paragraph was the office of Management & Budget via the McClatchy-Tribune Information Service and Palm Beach Post 2/27/09. Their combination and averaging was done by the author

[3] Congressional Budget Office via the Associated Press and Palm Beach Post 2/24/09

[4] The Concord Coalition – Letter to members 2/09

[5] <u>Wall Street Under Oath</u>, by Judge Pecora, NYC, 1939, a book now long out of print, provided a detailed account with direct quotations from the official records.

[6] Palm Beach Post – 10/15/08 – "Plugging into... " Cynthia Tucker

[7] <u>Obama Unlikely to Change...</u> by Chilton Williamson Jr via Middle American News 3/09

[8] Associated Press via Palm Berach Post p 14A 3/20/09

[9] Middle American News 3/09

[10] Middle American News, 2/09

[11] "How We can Save Our Roads" by Earl Swift, Parade, 3/9/09

[12] Ibid

[13] Ibid

[14] Associated Press via Palm Beach Post, 3/21/09

[15] Ibid

[16] <u>Waste Watch,</u> Citizens Against Government Waste, 2008

[17] Reading Tea Party Leaves, Palm Beach Post, 4/16/09

[18] States in Crisis by Nill Novelli, AARP Bulletin, 3/09

ECD 4/25/09

Chapter Six —— July 2009

Here we trace the origins of the presence of Marxist socialism in America and the way in which it was adapted to our political process. We include discussion of both multiculturalism and political correctness.

Can Our Political Culture Survive Our Cultural Politics?

In the question above that poses two different circumstances the meaning of politics/political is clear and shared. Not so, however, for culture/cultural which carry differentiating nuances and shades of meaning. Culture is a word that can be put to multiple uses and can easily shift from one to another without warning. In thinking about culture it is helpful to keep this in mind and to check our focus from time to time before we find that we have taken the wrong path.

For our purpose culture is the combination of our individual and institutional identities that are reflected from our society. Included in these identities are elements such as government, history, religion, ethnicity, genetics, values, traditions, education, ethics, the law, language, art, geography and others. All are not necessarily present at the same time, but, even when absent, are ready and able to take their place when called.

In 21st century America, with money and power having vacated the political center and moved to the more extreme ends (and means), our historical culture finds itself under constant attack by elements which are incompatible with and seek to destroy or replace our national persona.

This is a tragedy of multiple parts. Cultures are not like weeds that quickly reappear if you cut them down. They are fragile and need to be nurtured. If attacked and suppressed, they often lack the internal strength or direction necessary for their revival. The great museums of the world provide records of once powerful and vibrant cultures which have come and gone and will not come again.

In addition to these many variables, cultures require human procreation to develop and evolve, there being no such thing as a one-generation culture. And cultures are also subject to intervention by other human impacts such as war, disease, absorption and folly.

There are many ways that the individual members of populations can choose to use their minds and live their lives. These individual choices gather and combine around common interests and form specific subgroups that can exist within the primary culture.

A political culture is a very specific classification, and our country has a political culture more specific than most others. This is because we started with a new continent and a clean slate that enabled us the freedom to form and pursue a new form of government of our own design. It was this absolutely unique circumstance that, challenged, empowered and colored the formation and early growth of our republic.

We, of course, had cultural ties of descent to England from whom we achieved a complete political separation, but we were never subjected to occupations by other cultures such as the political and territorial intrusions that marked European and Middle Eastern history for two thousand years.

Our new continent harbored both French and Spanish settlements that remained from their seventeenth century explorations, but our western migration served as an effective eviction notice, and by a combination of treaty and military force they were removed in the early 1800s.

What is absolutely key to our understanding of our present political/cultural quandary is that the establishment of our historical political culture and the founding of our republic were acts of extremely conscious and determined intent.

In our Declaration of Independence we served notice of our political philosophy, and thirteen years later with our Constitution we established the legal structure that would support the D of I and combine with it to form our government. We borrowed many aspects of our new government from the centuries of English law and thought that had evolved since the memorable moment of Magna Carta when King John was informed of the limits of royal power.

Most matters cultural are not the product of intent, but politics (and especially ours) are different. From our earliest eighteenth century origins to the present, through war and peace, prosperity and depression and exceptional growth, we have repeatedly, even when tested by secession and civil war, reaffirmed our political culture by our legislative and electoral processes. And, although these are far from perfect and subject to the usual political weaknesses, they have been able, over time, to maintain respect for our political identity and culture.

Time is the essential nutrient for culture and the phrase "over time" is important, as time provided us with the continuity that was hard to come by under the European monarchical system wherein the movement of its competing parts was determined by both marital and martial considerations. It is an interesting political cultural note that these monarchies which had ruled Europe for a thousand years marched willingly into the orchestrated chaos of WWI which did away with both their power and way of life.

Our country, even given our intent to maintain our political culture, has been very fortunate in its success. Most often the threats that we have faced have been external, and we have been protected by our physical isolation from other powerful nations. The two land borders we share with Mexico and Canada have not been sources of serious military danger.

Being contained in our transcontinental landmass and engaged in the common effort of settling it has provided us with a form of unity that has left a special mark upon our political culture. This has been helpful in maintaining our national values, vision and identity. And it is when these are attacked, as, for example, in the present argument over our use of torture, that we are most vulnerable.

Think back, how often in voice or verse we have invoked our founders; Washington, Franklin, Jefferson, Adams, and later Jackson, Lincoln, Wilson and the two Roosevelts. We have invested much of ourselves in our political culture and the role it has played in forming and framing our nation. Right or wrong, regardless of issues, consciously or unconsciously, it has exerted a unifying force.

Our present experience of cultural politics has a completely opposite effect, as it is based on identifying and dividing the country into an ever increasing number of distinct groups, or interests, which are assigned various "rights".

Sometimes these "rights" are seen as deriving from our Constitution or our legislative or judicial record. In other circumstances they are deemed to be "human rights" and to claim authority far beyond or above national experience.

One can fairly make the argument that by practice or by treaty (i.e., the UN Charter) we have expanded our view of what is fair, reasonable or desirable in our government's relation to its, or other, people. Such an argument is a delicate and difficult one, and not usually settled quickly because of its high probability of confrontation with our political culture.

But even more thorny than the argument over "rights" itself is the determination of by whom and how these newly conceived "rights" will be assigned. Our ultimate authority is the Constitution, and we have amended it sparingly over our history to modify the contract between government and its citizens. And at the next level we have used the legislative power of the Congress to pass laws or enter into treaties which can be done or undone far more quickly and easily than amending the Constitution.

Today, America finds itself host to a wide array of organizations, sometimes even funded by our own or other governments, dedicated to declaring, establishing and promoting special "rights" for special interests, even though such "rights" may run counter to our custom and law.

This is neither a pretty picture nor a proud moment in our history, cultural or otherwise, but big money is involved, and, when big money stands up, our Congress generally stands down.

Far from the unifying effect of our political culture, our cultural politics often appeal to the divisive elements within our society, as creating special interests on behalf of "rights" (or wrongs) favors one group at the expense of others. It chops the country up into smaller pieces each with its own goals, values and priorities. Carried to its extreme, we would become a mass of three hundred million squabbling "interests" and cease to be a nation. We would offer living proof of the sum of the parts being greater than the whole.

The Road From Frankfurt

How did we arrive at this impasse in our society where one element attacks and denies another? History can offer some clues and a reasonable perspective.

The collapse of the Czarist regime in Russia in 1917 and the assumption of power by the Bolsheviks imposed another complication upon a Europe totally engaged in war. Socialism, which had been confined mostly to labor and lecture halls and the turn of the century fringe press, overthrew the throne and assumed control of the world's largest and most troubled monarchy. With peace in 1918, the Bolsheviks began to carry their argument for international Communism into a weakened Europe, believing that the triumphant socialism of the Russian workers' revolution would easily convert the physically and economically exhausted European states.

In 1922 Lenin, who was at the peak of his power, and perhaps also in Stalin's cross-hairs, became frustrated by Europe's failure to immediately embrace socialism, and he called a meeting of the Comintern[1] in Moscow. Its purpose was to define and propose the new Marxist cultural revolution which would silently and secretly project Marxist thought and power to areas not suited to military conquest.

Two years later Lenin died and Stalin, in one of his many attempts to consolidate power in his own hands, dismissed the leaders of this group as a rogue element given to straying from the purity of the Communist dogma that had launched the glorious revolution seven years before. Some of this group were removed from further involvement by the NKVD[2]. Others removed themselves to other countries to practice socialism minus Stalin. One of these was a wealthy Hungarian, George Lukacs, who settled in Frankfurt, Germany.

There, he and others formed a group at the University of Frankfurt, known as The Frankfurt School, whose studies and teachings leaned heavily on Marxist theory. When Hitler took control of Germany's government in 1933, he shut down the Frankfurt group and expelled its members most of whom found new homes and employment at US universities.

From the safety and authority of their academic positions they launched a "quiet", cultural revolution which was able to gather academic support in the economically disastrous times of the 1930s when faculty compensation was notoriously low and union representation weak, if present at all.

As Marxist socialism sought to disguise and conceal itself in academia, it attempted to create a new, softer image and sell the idea that it was not all that different from our democracy. Playing against the background of mass purges in Russia, which the American socialists routinely denied, this was not an easy sale. Nevertheless, too many American individuals and institutions, seeking relief from the Great Depression (GD) and its root causes, were at first misled, and then mistaken.

For their purpose of spreading Marxist thought, words became the weapon of choice. They were more available and economical than military forces; they were more subtle in their method of attack and were even expressly permitted by our constitution; and they attacked the mind, leaving the body intact to perform other functions.

In its earliest days the Marxist experience in America was confined to the fringe with only an occasional bomb explosion to capture wide public notice. Those who planted the bombs or made fiery speeches in the streets or hired halls were referred to as Reds, Communists, anarchists, Bolsheviks, etc.

With the passage of time, however, and aided by the pain of the GD, the Marxist message was able to more quietly and quickly spread through our educational and other institutions and provide an effective counterpoint to violent oratory and street protests. Norman Thomas, a dignified and intelligent political writer, became that rarity, a political constant, by running for president on the Socialist Party ticket over a time span from the '30s thru the '60s.

Following the tremendous concentration of wealth in America in the late nineteenth and early twentieth centuries, the political and economic dislocations and loss of life as the result of WWI, the stock market crash and the GD, it is not surprising that Marxism found fertile ground in our academic institutions. This growth was substantially aided after WWII by the GI Bill which greatly expanded the faculties and student bodies of our college level educational system.

Over two generations have now passed since the arrival of the Frankfurt Group's members in this country. Since then, our academic world has undergone tremendous change. The pre-war "ivory tower" image has given way to a high degree of political activism. This is expressed in faculty writings, employment, curricula, student development and even fund raising. Some find these changes favorable, others see them as unacceptable, but, like them or not, they are today's reality.

Many of these changes over the past almost eighty years might have taken place without the contributions of the Frankfurt Group and its Marxist message, but the presence of the latter cannot be denied and it has, at the least, to be viewed as an accelerant. In the process it has moved from fringe to front row center.

Today the Marxist orientation of the liberal far left is as much a barrier to good government as is the conservative extreme right. Without making any judgement of their ideologies, the ways in which they position themselves reduce the chances of finding common, less ideological ground and, whether justified or not, offend a broad segment of the American public. This constant grinding wears down our political process and greatly reduces our chances of recognizing, let alone taking advantage of, those rare moments that offer us the possibility of fairly serving the national interest.

What is this Marxist presence that has grown amongst us over the past three quarters of a century? This is not an easy question and it evokes a wide variety of answers and emotions. There are, however, three aspects of it with which most people might agree:

1) It is extensive. It pervades all regions of our country and levels of our society, although in both cases some more than others. These differences are most keenly felt and difficult to overcome at the individual level.

2) Marxist thought, whether pure or diluted, challenges, if not directly contradicts, much of our Constitution. This unique document is the result of both our independence and heritage from our English origins. As those experiences are ones that Marxism will never know, its role in challenging our Constitution has been to refute or stretch it whenever possible. Both our Constitution and the Marxist forces carry with them a sense of destiny and their struggle has disturbed many of our most sensitive political areas.

3) It has its own agenda with which not all socialists agree, but from which its leaders do not deviate, and that is the winding down of white, western European culture wherever it exists. In the US and elsewhere that is socialism's leading, and cutting edge.

Socialism can appear in different forms with different faces. For instance, in England it took the identity of Fabian socialism which found support among both the upper and lower classes. It was moderate and intellectual and shunned the violence of Lenin's model which was suitable for the Russian, German and Balkan populations, but not for England. George Bernard Shaw, the great Irish dramatist who lived and wrote in England for most of his long life, was a Fabian, an elegant voice on behalf of socialism for many years, and provided an effective counterpoint to Lenin's extremism.

From the latter's earliest activities, however, the Marxist message was one of overthrow and revolution. These were needed to "liberate" the proletariat from its capitalistic bondage. And government was the means by which the physical, economic and political energy of the masses would be appropriated, directed and put to serve the purpose and privilege of the very few who wielded political power at the highest levels.

Under such a structure it was inevitable that violence and bloodshed would play an equally important part in establishing internal discipline as it would in external expansion.

Marxist socialism's arch enemy was fascism as it appeared in Spain, Germany, Italy and elsewhere between the two World Wars. With fascism's departure after WWII the lines of confrontation were redrawn so that world communism, which had absorbed most socialist political parties, faced the western democracies in the new Cold War struggle for dominance.

This war was fought globally, often using proxy countries and their troops to achieve local success. Like other wars, it contested markets, political regimes and sometimes territory, but at its core was the matter of identity. Whose would survive?

The considerable success of socialist thought establishing itself in our institutions of learning provides a platform from which the socialist left can attack our political culture as expressed in our Constitution, electoral process and legislation, as well as the many differing aspects of our social culture which are easily exploited by non-democratic interests.

Again, the socialist force in America today, as in other countries and times, is one of differing parts, and sometimes purposes, but it is by no means free of its origins, and there is a substantial, and probably dominant, element within it that seeks to eradicate our borders, our processes, our currency's value and our historical values — in short, <u>our identity.</u>

We have earned this status because we have become the strongest and most visible representation of western civilization and, therefore, we, like it, must go. It is a measure of Marxist weakness that co-existence is not an option. In this conclusion socialism refuses to part from its early origins of overthrow and revolution. Its present identity remains hostage to its past. This may turn out to be self-defeating or end in mutual destruction. Whatever the eventual outcome, we must be aware in our time and place that our identity, and that of our western culture, are under attack.

What we have offered here is a brief review of a situation that now faces our country and how it came about. We have tried to avoid staking out political party or ideological preferences, as they are matters to be decided by the reader. Our interest lies in improving our country's government and, therefore, how the history described here will impact that process and our national interest.

Getting Here From There

The early American Marxism of the Frankfurt School was centered around the activities of leaders such as Marcuse, Gramsci, Adorno, Foucault and Fromm. German-born social and political writer Herbert Marcuse enjoyed considerable longevity as Marxism's favored voice from the '30s into the '70s.

And if we look back to the early arguments of the 1930s we find that many of them have withstood eight decades of change and are surprisingly contemporary. For instance, consider these: viewing women as victims and males as their suppressors; creating racism as a <u>special</u> offense with separate legal status; the encouragement of uncontrollable legal and illegal immigration; the dumbing down and destruction of our traditionally independent investigative media; extension of government regulation and benefits into more numerous and extensive areas of our lives; the assault upon many areas of traditional authority but especially those of our schools, churches and the family[3]. The list goes on.

Having withstood almost a century of mixed economic depression, wars and prosperity, today's continued and active presence of Marxist social and political pressure strongly suggests that we are either unwilling or unable, or both, to make a stand in defense of our historical political culture against the encroachments of our current cultural politics.

How did this come to be? We must go back to the most significant non-event of the socialist movement — the failure of the industrial proletariat in Europe after WWI to launch the revolt by which Lenin hoped to transfer power from capitalist managers to workers and to bring down their elected governments.

Lenin's error was that he expected too much. Europe, after 1918 and into the 30s, was desolated by war, influenza, hyper-inflation, poverty and political failure. It had suffered the loss of its centuries old social order, as well as some 60 million deaths, casualties or other war related losses to its social/economic structure [4].

Had Stalin not been perceptive enough to change course, Marxist socialism might have not been able to survive, but the worsening economic circumstances of the GD years played to socialism's strength and bought time for its remaking.

Lenin had based his movement on political revolution, on using the laboring classes, mostly industrial workers, as its primary assault weapon. This Bolshevik battering ram was energized by agents that operated within the unions and work forces of European industry. Its success was often unpredictable; it was unwieldy and physically demanding and it called forth determined resistance and retribution.

The decimation of jobs and workers, as the GD took hold and as plants shut down, shrunk one of socialism's key targets, and Stalin made a quick substitution of cultural revolution for its political predecessor. From now on the key weapon of socialism's choice was to be the word and it was to spread through colleges and universities, print/broadcast media and private and public cultural institutions.

These outlets, which had historically acted as protectors of our cultural heritage were unable to withstand the invasion of the "new" language of socialism. They became the battlefield where the forces of the left began to deconstruct, alter and destroy our cultural cohesion. Quite simply, the war was widening, albeit unknownst to most Americans on and off campus.

With an agenda of such duration, and perhaps danger, were there no warning signs? Yes, there were and there continue to be. But do we not heed them? Apparently not, at least so far.

In the 1930s the Communist Party in the US undertook to launch a revolution here that was to be spearheaded by black Americans one of whom was a member of the Young Communist League named Albert Gaillard. This overthrow attempt failed for lack of black support. Looking back some years later from a different perspective, Gaillard appeared before the House Un-American Activities Committee in 1960 and voluntarily provided factual testimony as to the details of this plot and the deceptions employed to gain blacks' participation. He stated unequivocally that minorities were viewed by the Communists as the leading edge of their revolutionary efforts and as their preferred means of creating division and unrest[5].

Further warning might have been available from our participation in the Bretton Woods Conference in 1944 called to bring about reforms of the international financial system for the postwar period. Its most influential spokesman was England's John Maynard Keynes, a Fabian socialist and renowned commentator on economic theory. America's representative was Treasury Under-Secretary Harry Dexter White who, a few years later, was found to have acted as a Communist spy. With the war not yet concluded, it is easy to see how these two men dominated the Bretton Woods proceedings and decisions.

Currency degradation has played a critical role in many national declines, and yet for almost a century our government has pursued a policy of debt financing marked by seemingly unrestrainable spending. In peace or war, prosperity or recession, we have legislated our way from the world's largest creditor to its largest debtor, and, sadly, there is no sign of a will to change.

So much for warnings from the past; are there any now for our future? Fortunately, the answer is "yes", but it is doubtful whether we will be able to take the action necessary to change our present direction.

We refer to the creation of the North American Union (NAU) which contemplates the joining together of Mexico, Canada and the USA along many of the lines employed by the European Union (EU).

This project has been strongly pushed by the Bush and Obama administrations and is being gradually constructed and implemented, mostly out of the public's view, by executive order and by recently established and/or extended authorities within our active governmental departments, and also more remote and less visible sectors of our vast bureaucracy.

With this one move we would accomplish the eradication of our national borders, our language, our Constitution and our currency. Under already agreed to conditions our dollar would cease to exist and would be replaced by the Amero in such a way as to adjust upward the values of the Mexican peso and Canadian dollar. Unburdened by bureaucratic language, this would amount to a very sizeable transfer of wealth from the American public to its neighbors.

The government may write the rules, but it is the people who will pay. Without exception the NAU constitutes a unique threat, both imminent and continuing, to our republic, and asks in a very specific way whether our political culture can survive our cultural politics.

As the American socialist movement expanded under the guidance of its academic founders, it became evident that its tactics, weapons and targets were carefully considered parts of a precise plan from which very little deviation was permitted.

The privileges that democracies grant to their citizens often create opportunities for those who attack them. We have these soft, unarmored places unprotected by anything other than our ideals and intentions. In the world of global power conflicts it seems we have been issued a short lance, a dull sword and a sign that reads "kick me" to wear on our backs. And yet, quite surprisingly and fortunately, we have been able to endure equally the attacks of others and our own errors.

We saw in the testimony of Albert Gaillard how the US Communist Party used African-Americans as a leading edge assault wave to try to bring about revolution. Certainly, race relations is one of our most sensitive areas of democracy, and yet, although this tactic failed, it has been repeatedly used since then.

Today there are different circumstances. The most numerous

157

minority group is now Latino, and our immigration profile favors illegals over legals. Our Latino population is served by large and prosperous Latino "rights" organizations that are themselves inviting targets for the Marxist message.

In short, the Marxist tactic of using our abundant supply of minority groups to press its message of social and economic divisiveness is one that has stood the test of time and is expected to continue to be useful.

Language, especially in our media driven age, can undergo great change in time frames as small as a couple of decades or a half century. Often this change occurs because of new technology development. The computer and the internet for instance, have added so many nouns, verbs and adjectives to our language that it is undergoing a major transformation of both structure and style.

Words are weapons, and the two most frequently used in the Marxist arsenal are "politically correct" (PC) and "multiculturalism" (MC). These are very much weapons of choice and can be wielded with great efficiency, especially in a welcoming democracy.

PC had its origins in the early twentieth century Marxist-Leninist struggles. Its earliest appearance in print was in a Lenin speech in Russia in 1921. It traveled extensively, moving first to Communist China and then to western universities where it was softened and modified by the New Left. It first appeared in the US in the liberal writings of the 1960s and then expanded into public use around 1990.

It meant to be consistent with, not deviating from, the party line on any issue. It bolstered political purity, defined party theory and actions very narrowly and, by extension, projected party values from small to much larger numbers.

PC's strictness and its descent from Lenin to Stalin to Mao formed the lines of control by which their populations' feelings and thoughts were regulated. To stray beyond these boundaries was cause for imprisonment or death, and those who did, the politically incorrect, were charged with revisionism, factionalism and being the enemy of the people.

Leon Trotsky, an early Russian revolutionary writer, party leader, and Secretary of War (1918-25) was apt to stray towards independent thought and was labeled "revisionist" by Stalin. Trotsky fled Russia and created a new life and identity in a remote part of Mexico. Not so remote, however, that he could escape the NKVD, which after fifteen years tracked him down and executed him.

Indeed, these seemingly minor (from our democratic perspective) charges of political incorrectness provided the basis for the trials and convictions of Stalin's "Great Terror" and Mao's "Red Terror" which reduced the numbers of peasants, the military, the intelligentsia and party members by about 65 million people[6].

Lenin's socialism focused on power. If a small, revolutionary party was to take power, it must maintain its purpose, purity and discipline. He had no use for coffee klatch politics. Today PC is a determined, but somewhat diluted, form of its original model that has surprisingly survived almost a century of violent change and leadership within world socialism. We're not talking bean-bag here!

Marxism's other primary weapon today is multiculturalism (MC). Unlike PC's emphasis on the political individual, MC aims to declare and maintain an area of common, supposedly non-political thought where members of all cultures can congregate. This distinction cannot obscure the fact that PC has served as the base for MC.

The word multiculturalism, itself, is somewhat of a deception. The unsuspecting reader might well assume that it refers to a state or circumstance in which many cultures are present and by general consensus assigned equal value, and that this mass acceptance extends equally from each one to each other in the commercial, legal, cultural, political and ethical matters of their existence.

In today's America some people still feel that way, but their number is declining as our cultural wars heat up, and far fewer of us would consider the above definition appropriate to our time and place. Those who accept this benign characterization of MC perceive more comfort than reality, for the truth is that beneath MC's soft public pitch lies the hard, sharp edge of politicization. It is a weapon used to create resentment of our historical Western, Judaeo-Christian culture, and eventually to discredit it and replace it with a state-centered model controlled by the political leadership and state machinery.

The emotions underlying this politicization of MC and its use to attack our culture are searing envy and anger originally derived from Europe's 19th century economic disparities, but now seemingly more due to a combination of our wealth/power and the frustrating failures of global socialism to bring about the kind of mass revolt and overthrow that has been central to its thinking.

All cultures are unique to some extent and offer aspects of value. Politicized MC does not recognize those in the west, although it effusively celebrates and promotes others, and it views any claim on behalf of Western values as racism that demeans other cultures. They may celebrate; the west may not.

Today, militant Marxism continues to attempt to expand its culture throughout the world while trying to avoid being tagged for some of the bloody excesses of the Stalin and Mao eras. Its most persistent charge against the West has been the often cruel and unjust practices of 19th and 20th century colonialism for which there is neither doubt nor any excuse except that it was common practice.

It is true that the loss of life, property, liberty and identity under colonialism is a dark chapter in human conduct. But the same abuse has taken place in the Nazi concentration camps, the Russian gulags, the African diamond mines and our American cotton fields. For those who have been deprived in those places, the similarities would far outweigh the differences, and the political label of the oppressor would count for little.

All forms of government have relief valves by which internal pressures are dispersed. Elected governments are able to shed these pressures with more fairness and less violence than authoritarian state regimes, but each type has its own flash points.

There are some aspects of socialism's message that could be separated out and blended with our democratic system, but this is not permitted and they are absorbed and recast as weapons of war by the force of militant Marxism.

This is at the heart of the divisiveness of MC and PC. In the process of claiming to unify, the differences between disparate groups are actually emphasized. Consider the present battle over gender/sexual discrimination in which the original MC call was for an attitude of public equality between the sexes. That has been further divided into legal, judicial and political "rights" for homosexual and other orientations. And, of course, the more specific constituencies that can be created for an issue, the more opportunities are available to stir their volatile emotions.

For the culture under attack it means being besieged on multiple fronts and having to defend itself in voting booths, in the media when possible and at every level (state, appellate and supreme) of our judicial system. The objective is death by a thousand cuts.

Again, in MC and PC there are gradations of opinion as to ends and means, but these are largely overwhelmed by the ability of the central force to collect the variables and put them at the use of the mass movement. Such is the divisive nature of MC and PC.

Many of the voices that emanate from our government emphasize our "free market" system and our absolute commitment to its principles. This is not true, of course, but it spares our Congress and executive branch the need to think and act consistently. The truth is that we embrace the "free market" philosophy only up to the point when doing so becomes politically difficult or impossible. At no time has this been more evident than last fall when government intervened with massive amounts of public money to avoid complete collapses in our financial and automotive industries.

Our capitalist system has weaknesses like any other, but this is something that we find impossible to admit, let alone criticize. It is as if we admit error in one such important area, we will also find it elsewhere. Having to be right is a terrible burden for any system, and especially a free market one with wide individual choice. Ours is what it is, right and wrong, and we should not always expect the world's applause. But there's too much baggage to be carried. Capitalism is only as successful as those who control its policies and performance. And in these areas our financial services industry and our Congress, which has oversight responsibility, have put together a record of consistent failure.

The socialist, statist model is no better, but our errors provide it with grounds for criticism. The modern competitive tension between state controlled and free markets extends back for more than a century. Were it not for the power factor it might have been eliminated by mutual agreement. In our present age of economic globalism, which can seem like a new description of the old colonialism, that is not likely to occur.

We must remember that PC, which is strongly promoted and present in our culture today, was lifted from Lenin's playbook. It remains with us today because it proved to be useful to the Marxist argument. Similarly, Herbert Marcuse in his <u>Essay on Repressive Tolerance</u>[7] wrote *"all speech that advocated change in society (i.e., Western) should be encouraged and all speech that defended existing social structures should be repressed."* It takes no great leap of imagination to see that this, too, has endured into our own time and plays a key part in socialism's continuing push for recognition. And it puts the lie to MC's claims to being an exchange between equals of shared cultural value.

The mantras of today's social and political left (MC, PC and Diversity) are words that have been pushed past their customary meaning by their use as weapons.

For instance, we prefer "multiculturalism" to denote the harmonious coexistence of cultures that we suggested earlier, but that is no longer possible. The word's meaning has been extended and is now so loaded with antagonism and militancy as to overshadow any other interpretation. The same holds, to a somewhat lesser degree, for "diversity".

What they all have come to share is that they attack and seek to weaken our identity. Not all identities are created equal, but in a world of nations they serve as both ambassadors and boundaries. And in our politically polarized world it's quite possible that only they can provide the assurance that the Ideological Imperative demands.

The Ideological Imperative is a fixation shared by both parties and individuals whereby ordinary political preferences or choices are transformed into a rigid value system. This added identity factor, combined with its emotional charge, demands that its source be always right. And it robs our system of much of the intelligence and flexibility that are required in order for legislative bodies to produce good government.

It should be apparent that this need to be right derives from an underlying insecurity and discloses another area where our identity is challenged and uncertain. To complete the cycle, most of our confusion as to our national identity is traceable to our numerous and increasingly frequent failures of integrity, especially over the past half-century. The tension between ideology, identity and integrity is in constant play. And yet sometimes our many market and political forces can only combine to create a fatal inertia. We appear to be in one of those times.

In a way, we are fortunate to be able to observe this struggle within our society, although it is not by any means pretty. It lays charge to matters of our religion, race, ethnicity and identity and is fought out in our prisons, schools, media, language, work places, voting booths, playing fields, in our immigration and justice systems, our local police/fire services and at the highest levels of our government. It does not operate at full speed all the time, nor does it disappear. It has become part of us.

In these contests, justice and injustice are equally called upon for proof or support, and often 'whatever hurts, whatever works" seems to apply. Consistency is a quaint casualty of our time, much like assimilation, and on some of our college campuses in heavily immigrant states those students who march and call for multiculturalism see no contradiction in their requesting separate social and educational facilities for ethnic minorities.

In the MC wars the front is wide and skirmishes many, and yet there are places where reasonable minds have a chance to try to compromise or create common ground. But there are two areas in which any accommodation of one side by the other has proved impossible. These involve access to economic and political power. In our democratic system we define the rights to both private property ownership and elected government with distinct functions for each branch.

These are the dominant differences between Marxism and the western civilization that has opposed and thwarted its attempts to expand socialism throughout the world. As democracy and the institutions needed to support it have not achieved global acceptance either, these two very different political philosophies seem destined to continue their relationship of confrontation and opposition.

The central issue is one of statism — how much power and control should the state exercise over its people and, of course, also the reverse. This matter of authority is most fiercely contested at the highest political levels, but it extends downward into many other mundane areas of our lives as we have indicated above.

There, this constant friction can build up heat and pressure which is released by local agitation and the cycle can recommence, for the battle at the top must be able to claim support from the people below. The hard line, revolution-in-waiting socialism of Marx and Lenin was able to outlive the monarchies and fascist regimes that it encountered in early twentieth century Europe, but it has not been able to dislodge or do away with traditional democracy.

It has been "the quiet revolution", that expression of socialist thought and intention that was diverted to academia and the media, that has made possible the growth of the new, liberal left over the past half century.

Every political movement contains within itself a continuing argument between power and principle. Marxism is no exception and has increasingly favored the former. In the US, especially, its message and methods have been mismanaged, mostly notably in *its failure to understand the abiding connection between our economic and political freedom.*

Because of the emergence of the European Union (EU) from regional economic community to a form of political union and bureaucracy, the liberal political presence in Europe has gained far more power than could have been foreseen at the end of WWII. Europe remains an unfinished story. Will the EU's member countries be able to control it by the electoral process? Or will the enormous bureaucracy in Brussels prove strong and dense enough to overrule its members and establish a de facto managerial authority of its own?

Timing is a matter of real importance in all things cultural. For instance, we have had a recent and very emotional argument about our use of torture in Iraq, Guantanamo Bay and in CIA interrogation centers that we have established in other countries. As a nation, we have opposed the use of torture by others and ourselves by speech and treaty. It has seemed so incompatible with our standards and values that it came to be seen as part of our culture.

Then it became the basis of a painful contradiction. In 2006, in response to the release of information about the maltreatment of prisoners in our Abu Ghraib detention facilities, President Bush unequivocally denied that we used torture:

> "The U.S. does not torture. It is against our laws,
> and it is against our values. I have not authorized
> it — and I will not authorize it." [8]

This is interesting for two reasons. The first is that it was not true, as Bush had authorized the use of "enhanced interrogation", including water boarding, in '02, '03 and '04.

Far more interesting, however, is that he rejects the use of torture as being "against our laws and... our values". This sets it apart as being outside our culture and contrary to our identity. And identity is one of the three aspects of nationality, along with culture and currency, that are essential to orderly life and, therefore, prime targets for subversion.

Our identity has played an important role in our political culture from its earliest days when the colonists established values for their new society based on economic and political independence.

National identities can change significantly in some ways over time, but core values are usually retained by successful societies. We started as a primarily agricultural/rural society, then transform-ed ourselves into an industrial/urban economy and are now changing again into an information technology/media and entertainment economy.

These massive shifts are not achieved without considerable social dislocation and discomfort much of which is due to the difficulty of recognizing and accepting the involuntary change in our identity that they impose. Today we are living in just such a turbulent period which is made even more difficult because we have purposely dismantled our production capability in ways that mostly benefit a very small sector of our society, not the general public.

All nations or empires change over time, and we have been "in play" for only a brief time. In the course of this change process, there is usually a period of success or equilibrium followed by a more rapid decline. The latter can be the result of human failure such as greed, corruption, power fixation, militarism, etc. of which there always seems to be ready supply.

Sometimes just one of these faults is required to bring about a failed state rather quickly, but more commonly they combine to create a gradual decline over a longer period. In such a decline decadence often plays an important part, and decadence invariably involves a failure of the national identity mechanism.

We show many of the classic signs of decadence in our culture today that brought down great empires of the past — enormous wealth, superior weapons technology and power, extensive corruption in all branches of government and its lack of any effective ethical regulation, the erosion of our middle class leaving a wide gap between the rich and the poor, an expanding bureaucracy, a failing educational system, environmental degradation, an immigration system without controls and others. The list goes on, and everyone can make their own.

But now there is a critical difference. We are the USA in the twenty-first century. As the result of our computer age technology, we have ways to analyze, to predict, to review the past, to make comparisons — in other words, to command the knowledge of the forces that are acting upon us in a way that prior societies lacked.

We have cited before Jared Diamond's fascinating book, Collapse[2], in which he analyzes the economic, social and political circumstances that caused the collapse of some well known societies in the past. They, of course, did not know then what we know now about the reasons for their demise. But the same capability that allows us to determine the forces that led to their disappearance is available to us to apply the truth of our time to choices for our present and future.

This latter is crucial. Earlier societies had little technology which they could use to plan or imagine their future. For the most part, they were creatures of their present. Not so today, when we reach into outer space and can look ahead or behind millions of years.

Given this ability to see ourselves as we act out our destiny, the question that must be asked of our government is — will we take the necessary action and care to remain true to our original identity? More specifically, will we be able to reaffirm our early American idealism over present day ideology in the election and the functioning of our government? These are big, and not easy questions, and they must be answered.

There is another area of our identity that bears examination. It is our status as sole superpower. While there is growing evidence that this position is changing as China's and Russia's economics expand, we still seem to relish the role and title we have held since the implosion of the USSR.

It is a dangerous and expensive role, and perhaps someone has to fill it in spite of the billions of dollars that have been spent on the UN. It is the failure of the latter to function fairly and authoritatively as a leader that makes room for other power figures. In fairness to the UN, however, we and other countries are hesitant to give it the authority necessary to assume and command leadership. This is a chicken/egg problem with an omelet solution.

We have not lived with any sole superpower other than ourselves, and we would have a very different opinion of this responsibility if it were in other hands. To some degree, we seem to enjoy our international celebrity and reading our own press releases. But bathing in and reflecting the warm glow of constant publicity is not the best basis for successful foreign policy even when, as in Iraq, we are able to cow others into approving our Neocon adventure on the basis of flimsy evidence.

In our country, crowds frequently obsess with sports language and behavior even at non-sports events. In doing so, they often break into chants of "USA" or "We're #1" at a cue that only they recognize. Their need to be heard has spread and become a part of our culture, but not a necessary one. However, as with our superpower status, once established, it will require a conscious effort to remove.

Part of being a sole superpower is the sense that we are indispensable to solving the world's problems. This is a heady fragrance to those at the center of power and often carries them off in the wrong direction where solutions are not achievable.

Consider the nuclear triggers now in place in India and Pakistan. Their conflict was originally a religious one of Hindu vs Muslim enmity which was upgraded to national and political with the British partition in 1947. Today, both of these historical foes possess nuclear weapons to which we have given our approval, money and technology in spite of our professed opposition to the spread of nuclear arms.

We find ourselves in a quandary of our own making, but not, perhaps, design. Regional conflicts have a way of producing larger ones, and religious sparks can be an effective source of ignition. In the Asian subcontinent we can only hope that our investments and relations there, usually described as "to protect American interests", will not result in hostilities, nuclear or otherwise.

Again, identity is an important factor in how we govern ourselves — and others! We would benefit from not having to serve as the world's sole superpower if such a change could be made peacefully, as we could examine our policies and intentions unburdened by the world's largest defense department and armaments industry.

But the world is not that way and, in spite of our and others' efforts to prevent nuclear proliferation, there are now eight nations with nuclear capability and North Korea, Iran and perhaps South Africa attempting to join them. Libya has fortunately abandoned its pursuit. Others there may be who secretly bought information from the head of Pakistan's nuclear program and may now be trying to assemble weapons and delivery systems.

A small "dirty bomb" assembled and detonated here? A biological bomb on a ship offshore or in a harbor set off by remote control to take advantage of on-shore prevailing winds. Who knows? The only thing we can be sure of is that nuclear proliferation will continue and that in the process, as technology spreads, it will fall into less, not more, responsible hands.

And yet many of our chemical plants, ports, railway hubs and urban transportation systems, nuclear storage sites, etc. have not reached their scheduled security levels. The causes for this failure seem to be shared by Congress, the corporate sector, regulatory bodies and the executive branch. We can do better.

Its Midnight And Time To Remove Our Mask

America, our wonderful home-grown experiment in democratic representative government, now faces serious and urgent problems which have the potential to destroy what we have created if they are not acted upon forcefully.

Discussion and compromise, which have been at the center of our system since its founding, have recently come to be used to delay or avoid difficult action with the result that our government has become weaker and less effective. This deferment of political leadership defiles our Constitution and its promise to the people.

Perhaps the most tragic aspect of our present situation is that it goes unrecognized by those who control most of our government institutions, branches and departments. Here, for them, is a primer of what must be considered in any view or plan for our long or short term future.

The threats we face can be broken down into two basic groups of issues, the first of which revolves around our sense of integrity. Not surprisingly, this includes the warning of political, social and ethical failures that our nation waiting to be born made to its offspring in our Declaration of Independence and Constitution.

171

It includes our deep crisis of identity that gives rise to troubled arguments over torture, selective law enforcement, unilateral militarism, religion, race, homosexuality, executive privilege and others. A wide variety, to say the least, and many of which were non-issues when our country was formed.

But, as time and circumstance have changed, they have appeared — at first with little notice and then, in the glare of our modern media, acquiring first increasing political attention and then "rights". In our post war, egalitarian world the assertion of "right", whether legal, human, electoral or other, became the first step to laying claim to a new, more powerful and advantaged status.

However, from a governmental viewpoint the process of dividing our population into an ever expanding number of groups with different, or even similar, rights results in a widely fractured society which is ideally suited to exploitation by those who prefer to use, rather than to share, our values and intentions.

We have managed to return to MC, PC and our title question — Can Our Political Culture Survive Our Cultural Politics? MC, PC and other identity related interactions are mostly used to further the interests of groups within our society. As such, they are subsets of our national integrity. Of the latter we have a declining supply of "capital" which our recent policies and administrations have not been able to regenerate.

A close look at our society is not encouraging. We see wide-scale economic malfeasance from individuals such as Madoff and Stanford to the most prominent Wall Street firms. In between, there is no shortage of just plain, good old corporate fraud at Enron, Comcast, Health South, etc.

We have spawned from our pre-TV radio, newspaper and magazine media an entertainment industry dedicated to 24-

hour promotion of sex, pregnancy and body parts in all of its programming from smut humor to talk shows.

Another focus of our entertainment sector is the editorial celebration of drugs and violence, especially the latter which plays out all too predictably in the lives of our youth — both those who are trapped in our cities and those who have managed to escape to the highly compensated, continuing violence of professional sports.

From our social and political failures, what do we project as leadership to our own people? Or to the rest of the world? Do we imagine that we occupy some high ground which others cannot reach? Sadly, the answer seems to be "yes", and more often than not is provided by our Congress which has found it increasingly difficult to keep faith with our heritage. Presently, it no longer tries.

The members of Congress are both the product and protectors of our two-party system which has suffered a steady loss of ethics and efficiency since the century of its greatest success from 1860 to 1960. Still, for anyone contemplating a political career it sits just below the presidency on our political pyramid and beckons with the lure of federal pensions, highly paid post-Congressional employment, health care and the constant flow of money from Washington's resident lobbyists.

Our aspiring politicians must usually gain some lower level experience which can be had from serving on appointive boards or from local electoral office. At these levels, like those above, money is delivered and results are obtained. This is a basic instruction which applies equally to political ethics and efficiency. It goes unchallenged as the political novice rises to the state legislative level and then to higher office in Congress or, perhaps, as state governor.

There is another lesson that is taught at our entry level political offices, for in addition to revealing the entwined strands of money and power which form our political DNA, politics at the local level begins the process of forming the neophyte in a way that is flattering and ego-building, but that separates him from his fellow citizens. This is a character and value process made up of many small and silent parts in the media, the political parties, and local, regional or state interests that combine to give the young politician the sense that he is special, different from others, important and deserving of notice — i.e., a large fish in a small pond. In those instances where the political machinery is able to smoothly mesh with the public media this transformation is complete and a successful career usually follows.

Now we are at that critical divide that has marked the failure of American politics over the past half century. The congressional "newbie", riding a wave of local political publicity and power arrives in Washington. The dinners, photo-ops, press conferences and releases all continue, albeit with a new cast that now includes lobbyists representing every conceivable special interest.

But there is one enormous difference. He/she is no longer a big fish in a small pond, but just the opposite — one of 535 members of Congress most of whom are well entrenched by seniority and incumbency and who came to Washington by pretty much the same route and carrying the same baggage as our novice.

Our key question, as inheritors of our political culture, is how do we transform our elected members of government to see themselves as small fish in the big pond that is our national interest? How do we bring them across this deep and dangerous divide?

The course that we are on is a fatal one. Congress routinely invokes "the American people" at every public moment and yet in the privacy of drafting legislation it divides and packages its votes to meet the demands of special interest lobbyists. In recent years the "ear mark" has become the preferred means of applying anonymous influence to legislation in the making and thereby protecting oneself from public scrutiny.

Many first office politicians see the corruption of our process at the local level and decide they will "go along to get along" for a while and then try to change the system from within. One look at Congress indicates that this has not been an effective strategy.

In making these broad criticisms of Congress we recognize that there is a difference in motivation among its members. Some are outright manipulators of the system who make no pretense that anything other than their self-interest determines their action. The others are simply trapped by the political culture of which they are part and cannot even imagine a system in which the national interest would define the standard for service.

Whether this inability to recognize the national interest and be guided by it is intentional or not seems to make little difference. The end result is, unfortunately, the same. Recently, we have come to face serious economic and environmental threats to our nation and our planet that will demand more in the way of vision and understanding from our government. This prospect is not encouraging.

One of the most pernicious aspects of our two-party system in which access to the ballot is dominated by the two major parties is that it creates an atmosphere of continuing political warfare. It's "win or lose", "we versus them" and other extreme positions.

The difference between being a member of the winning or losing party is the difference between having a job, a paycheck, a pension, a funded campaign account, even a future, or not. These differences drive politicians, haunt their dreams and saturate their and their families existence. They are real.

As political office in the last half century has become richer and more powerful, the intensity of effort necessary to gain or retain it has also increased. This has given us the extremely polarized politics at all levels where much of our political time and energy by both parties is devoted to mostly minor, senseless, self-serving internecine attacks by one upon the other.

In the end, we are left with the Ideological Imperative, that circumstance when ideology for ideology's sake becomes the key mover of our political parties and policies. Our whole Congress operating under this culture of mutually assured destruction precludes any realizable national interest.

If we view this realistically, we must recognize that tomorrow's destiny can be no better than today's methods. For the America that comes from where we did and has been what we were, that is a painful admission. It is also a political prophecy and notice of decline that we cannot ignore. It will require us all — politicians, citizens and institutions — to play a different role if we are to survive.

This can be done, but it will demand great change by brave and objective people. Resistance will be strong, but can be overcome. Think back, think back to Philadelphia, 1776 and the way that vision and values produced government and then continued as its guide. Today, nothing less than a revolution is required — a revolution in how we have come to view and value our government. There could be no greater proof of our democracy than such a peaceful revolution.

The second area of failed thought and understanding on the part of our government's leadership is that of timing. We do not refer to internal qualities of character, but rather to the ability to comprehend and act upon the external natural forces that are inseparable from life on earth.

These are determined by the laws of physics and chemistry, not by legislation created by a representative from a man-made electoral district. The evident self-importance of members of Congress in how they treat these global issues is stunning.

The prime danger to our country is that they continue an argument to support their course of action or, more often, inaction and then convey it to their constituents as a correct and respectable government position. Spreading the lie instead of truth establishes a constituency of the uninformed and weakens our country. It is very much part of our national "dumbing down" process.

What are these issues whose agendas are set by national or numerical forces? There is population, global warming/climate change and the "end of oil". Subsets of these are species loss, aquifer degradation, immigration and others. This is a list that threatens every aspect of our lives with negative consequences, but fails to engage any proportional response in Congress.

The fact that we can look at the mathematics of these issues and not be stirred to serious engagement makes it clear that government hears and responds only to what it finds comfortable.

This introduces another enormous deception which has been foisted upon the American public for far too long, and that is the pursuit of eternal growth which translates into the politics and economics of "more", regardless of consequences. Every political campaign from local to presidential and every corporate budget, business plan or economic forecast is based upon the desirability and availability of continuing growth and expansion. The private sector is especially committed to these projections. Our population is presently increasing at the rate of about three million a year, or roughly 1%. If not adjusted, this will add another 100 million people to our population before the half century.

As our population grows, so do the markets, market shares, revenues and profits of corporate America. This type of market expansion comes with no cost to our private sector. Some of it is a gift from our bedrooms to our boardrooms to which lobbyists, their clients and the Congress are firmly addicted.

We have invoked before the Law of Limits, which states that there is a limit to any material that can be added to a confined space. We cannot pour two cups of water into one cup. No matter how many times or ways we attempt this, we will end up with one cup of water and a wet counter top.

There are politicians today, here and abroad, that give the impression that our global economic systems are close to a breakthrough moment when vast change will take place, when the errors and conflicts of the past will be gone and when we will all live in a world of peace and plenty made possible by new technology and trade.

Such utopian views ignore the fact that we already face severe economic problems in SE Asia, Africa and Latin America that are the result of too many people and too few jobs, water, food, schools, doctors, etc. Some of these populations are already attempting to migrate to the wealthier, developed countries that they see on television. Upon arrival, when they present their claims to employment, retirement benefits, housing, education, health care, electoral participation and religious inclusion, the newly selected host country is faced with difficult social problems.

We have arrived at a new time regarding these movements of people from one country or continent to another. Assimilation involves culture and identity which in the past have tended to change only slowly with the passage of time. Such time is no longer available, as the press of numbers and our instant communications technology act as political and emotional accelerants.

We are in a trap we have set for ourselves. Behind us, at every level and part of our society, are the demands and expectations of those who depend on "more". Ahead of us, just beyond our vision, is the realization that there is no "more", that we have engaged in a national delusion. That we have persuaded ourselves to be part of such a chimera is another clue to our identity problems, and we will not be able to restore our integrity until we again know who and what we are.

There is wide ground in this chapter — from Marxism and MC/PC to the Ideological Imperative and national integrity. Many of these topics are subject to different personal interpretations and conclusions. That is as it should be. We should be able to agree with some Keynesian economic or Shavian social goals without subscribing to Lenin's calls for revolution or Stalin's mass extinctions of Russian life.

Our American democracy was once the political pearl of the world, but has become contaminated by excessive corruption, ideology, congressional tenure and deference to special interests. These habits need to be changed, but such reform can only be accomplished by the voting public.

This is a problem because America's voters have become increasingly passive and mostly follow the hoopla and the directions of the two major parties. They are not passive when aroused, but they no longer seem to initiate change. They need a grain, a center around which they can coalesce.

In our colonial times the idea of freedom from British rule and forming an independent nation provided such a center and, following our successful revolution, it enabled our founders to make the necessary compromises and write the laws that transformed their vision into reality, and <u>government.</u>

Today we face the same kind of problem. The reality of our government bears little resemblance to what we think we are or what we want to be. Were the energy of American voters to coalesce around these historical visions, they could lead us out of the political swamp we now inhabit. The choice is ours.

These matters are joined in that they reflect a failure and loss of our national integrity. A restored sense of integrity will greatly facilitate our defining the national interest and electing to national office those who share that vision. This will not be quick nor easy, and everyone has a role.

We must start now. Do we have the will? Will we make the time?

End Notes

[1] The Communist International was the Russian administrative organization charged with spreading communism throughout the world.

[2] The Wanderer, 12/11/08 The Quiet Revolution Rolls Forward by Timothy Matthews

[3] Ibid

[4] The Rise and Fall of the Great Powers, by Paul Kennedy. Random House, Inc., NYC, NY 1987 Ch. 6, pg 278

[5] The Change Agents by Robert H. Goldsborough, Middle American News, June 2009

[6] Marxism, Multiculturalism and Free Speech by Frank Ellis. Published by the Council for Social and Economic Studies. This volume has been helpful in providing a background for parts of this chapter.

[7] Ibid. Intro. By David D. Murphy

[8] Palm Beach Post 10/22/08 "Another lie, another nail" by Leonard Pitts Jr

[9] Viking Penguin, NYC, NY 2005

ECD 7/25/09

Chapter Seven —— October 2009

We examine the widespread institutional failure
that has marked our country's passage through the
two generations of its postwar, Cold War and sole
superpower periods.

Institutional Failure: Our
Nation's Greatest Threat?

The process of institutional failure (IF) is alive and well in
contemporary America. As time passes and the quality of our
government continues its deterioration, IF can be seen as one of its
primary causes. It has spread its reach and accelerated its pace to
the degree that, if we are to honestly evaluate our present national
circumstance, it must now be recognized as a major force, rather
than a few unrelated instances.

Today, IF has occurred in every part of our government, in
both its elected offices and the administrative bureaucracies and
departments we have created to implement our policies.

But it is not our government alone that has built IF to its
present level of peril. Far from it, as government's role, perhaps in
a "me too" response, has been extended to a surprising number of
other institutions — media, economic, and even military.

IF in our society is ubiquitous. It touches all of us, like an invisible, odorless lethal gas, but where are the canaries' warnings? We seem anaesthetized by its frequency and steady repetition. Perhaps our national psyche blocks it out and considers that we are immune to its presence or consequences.

If so, we do ourselves a great disservice. There was such extensive IF during the two Bush II administrations that it would be natural to expect that we would do better under Obama, but early indications suggest that treating IF will not enjoy priority in his political agenda.

In fairness, as he has been faced with the need to come up with more damage control than most presidents and the big issues that lie ahead are extremely divisive ones, it is unlikely that he could find the political will and capital required to energize a national recognition of IF.

No inquiry into IF could be considered meaningful without laying most of the fault in the laps and halls of our Congress. Quite simply, our elected legislative branch has been the major source for our country's growing IF. Nothing can come close to what it has wrought, by omission or commission. Like Everest, it is unique and stands above all others.

The Congress is charged with helping to shape the president's budget and then translating it into legislation and, finally, actual funding. This is one of its primary national duties, like the exercise of its taxation or national security responsibilities.

In the last half century a variety of congresses has overseen the transformation of the US from the world's largest creditor to its foremost debtor. There is an unreal, or perhaps surreal, feeling to such a massive role reversal. And yet it happened and we are witnesses. There are several explanations, but they offer little solace when we recognize what we have allowed.

There is, as always now, the Ideological Imperative (II) to be considered. Each political party will blame the other and both will cloak their actions in ideology that is claimed to derive from our political founding and subsequent history.

The next most frequent and fervid explanation is that of representing the particular needs of local, state or regional constituencies. But this is as hollow and even more self-serving than the II. Today's truth of congressional representation is that it is mostly attached to reelection, funding for local projects, and the inclusion and service of "special interests" in federal programs.

A better, and more realistic, explanation is that our many congresses and their members underwent a separation from fiscal reality as the sums under their control grew from millions to billions to trillions. They seem to have operated under the illusion that America's wealth was endless and theirs to disburse in any and all ways they might wish. This, of course, was greatly facilitated by the use of "ear-marks" by which funding in amounts ranging from small to obscene was inserted in legislation without any indication of its source.

Congress' role as steward of our national wealth was checked in the cloak-room and not allowed "on the floor" except for the fleeting and rare moments of a trophy appearance.

When we discard the surreal atmosphere in which fifty years of congressional mismanagement has occurred, we face the shock of our having spent our way from mostly balanced budgets, surpluses and a debt-free economy to continually increasing budgetary and trade deficits, to a recognized national debt of close to $12 trillion that is expected to reach $20 trillion in the next decade and to total debt and/or unfunded obligations in the range of $50 to $100 trillion.

As shocking as these amounts are, in the tale of our descent into managerial madness they are minor in relation to the sense of national betrayal that emanates from Congress' abandonment of its stewardship responsibility.

Looking at our financial position today, the US is probably facing insolvency. The voices in Congress and at the Obama White House and Treasury tell us things will get better and that in ten years the deficits will have slowed and stopped, but such predictions are based on extremely serene circumstances.

Reality is different. It may include unplanned wars, pandemics, natural or nuclear disasters or public health crises. These are not events that can be forecast, but they are possible, as are others, and could render useless our financial projections.

Without any cushion, or reserves, and with our credibility in doubt at home and abroad, the outlines of our future may be left to chance, or to our friends or enemies.

In our twenty-first century, with its political, environmental, religious and social equilibrium all diminishing, our position is not one to be preferred. There are those who think it is improved by our superpower status. The truth is quite the opposite.

Another area of Congressional failure has been its treatment of the immigration problem, most notably its unwillingness to enforce existing legislation which has been repeatedly supported by polls that show about 65% of those questioned are in favor of reducing immigration. This selective law enforcement is the result of large and steady contributions to members of Congress by immigrants' rights groups.

Attempts were made during the Bush administration to rewrite present immigration law in favor of immigrant interests, but a strong expression of public opposition killed that effort. As a result, the law remains, but is not observed. And in the past, even when legislative action has been possible as with border enforcement, Congress has refused to fund the law it has enacted.

This is a poisonous situation which has existed for twenty-five years. In his electoral campaign Obama frequently expressed his intention to pass a new immigration bill in 2010, but post-election reality has downgraded this priority.

As immigration has grown and become a more divisive issue in our society, local sanctuary laws have been passed that often conflict with federal law. In Los Angeles local regulations prohibit police officers from contacting federal immigration officers regarding a suspect's status and often from making a direct inquiry to the suspect.

Such political accommodation can be readily found in communities with high immigrant population densities. While it can be useful "on the street", it is contrary to our Constitution. What Congress fails to understand in the matter of local law conflict is that it is a direct result of Congress' failure to honor its own laws. And even with as specific a matter as immigration, this failure spreads through our society and resurfaces in other forms of corruption such as labor, tax, documentation and credit fraud.

Not much further than a stone's throw, or a whistle's blow, from where our Congress sits are the offices of the Securities Exchange Commission (SEC). There, well paid lawyers practice what has become a highly specific area of our legal code relative to the issuance and trading of the nation's corporate securities.

The SEC was established to combat the laxity and abuses in our financial markets that had flowered in the late nineteenth century and which contributed in a major way to the severity of the 1929 stock market collapse.

The function of the SEC was regulatory protection for those who owned or traded securities. Charged with leveling a field that had a pronounced tilt, it early and frequently found itself in conflict with Wall Street interests which, however, over time came to accept its presence.

Repeat: The sole purpose of the SEC's regulatory function is to protect the investing public. Enter Bernie Madoff who aimed to attract real money from real investors by offering phony results and rates of return. The possibility of protective action by the SEC certainly seems clear and called for, especially as it had been contacted in writing and in detail by an informant who alerted it to Madoff's means and methods. Armed with this information and the substantial reach, staff and authority of our government, the SEC struck out! It visited Madoff's offices on a few occasions, but asked no tough questions nor requested the proper documentation.   Madoff continued his scam until his "take" reached about $75 billion when an investor's demand for a return of funds caused a complete collapse. So inept was the SEC procedure that Madoff was able to cite its inquiry as proof of his operation's soundness and legitimacy. In the IF hall of fame the SEC/Madoff affair occupies a very prominent place.

But our Congress is not alone in its failure to protect. Consider the Federal Reserve System which was established in 1913 to rid the country's economic system of the sudden and severe "panics" that struck often and without warning during the nineteenth century. These were liquidity crises that wreaked havoc with a system composed mostly of independent banks in the small towns and cities of our emerging nation and that had at their disposal only rudimentary forms of communication and control.

Looking back across the century behind them, the founders of the Fed put together a proposed system that would hopefully even out the painful swings (and bank failures) caused by panics and would protect both the economy and the public. *Who were these founders? They were the heads of the largest Wall Street banks.*

There was much congressional argument and huffing and puffing, but after extensive hearings and press coverage legislation was passed that met all of Wall Street's primary demands.

The Fed was established as an independent entity that operated in an area between the private banking sector and government's Treasury Department. A reading of its mission and methods as stated in its charter reveals an organization graced with extraordinary powers with little restraint upon their use, and any attempt to impose such restraint could be deemed an attack upon its independence. [1]

But it is the Fed's function to protect the public that we are most concerned with. G. Edmund Griffin in <u>The Creature from Jekyll Island</u> cites this record:

> "Since its inception, it has presided over the crashes of 1921 and 1929; the Great Depression of '29 to '39; recessions in '53, '57, '69, '75 and '81; a stock market "Black Monday" in '87 ..."[2]

We can add the brief downturn at the beginning of G. W. Bush's presidency and the wide financial calamity at its end.

These results cannot be considered separately from the policies that produced them and it is in the policy area that the Fed has most clearly failed to provide protection by persistently pursuing an inflationary policy that has eroded the value of the dollar by more than 90% since the pre-WWII period.[3]

The damage that is done to people in our economic system whose livelihood depends solely on earned wages is almost total. Lacking other assets that increase in value in inflationary periods, they are firmly but gently pushed down the financial ladder of competition and growth by which our economy and, in no small measure, our society have come to be defined.

The Fed, of course, was not alone in creating and maintaining inflationary policy, for, while suspended between them in its state of "independence", it enjoyed the whole-hearted cooperation of government (Treasury/Congress) and Wall Street's rapidly growing banking/financial services industry that served as guides in our transformation from the world's largest creditor to debtor status.

This low interest rates, easy credit, expansionist money policy fitted as neatly as pieces in a jig-saw puzzle with the myth of eternal growth that has dominated and dictated public, corporate and political thought during the course of our history.

Psychological precedent can be found in the settling of our large and rich landmass, but that time ended a century ago and we must employ a much greater adherence to reality in guiding our society through the next century.

It is true that our national wealth has increased greatly, but it is counted in dollars and, if we bear in mind their past loss of value and the probability that it will continue well into the future, a more realistic form of measurement could prove helpful.

Freddie And Fannie

A bit further from Capitol Hill, in their expensively landscaped corporate campuses, are the offices of Freddy Mac and Fannie Mae. These publicly owned and traded organizations, known as Government-Sponsored Enterprises (GSEs), were established to provide liquidity to our residential mortgage market. While not directly secured by the "full faith and credit" of the government, the latter's backing is assumed and they are plainly seen as "too big to fail".

Their rather special status has enabled them to operate with minimal regulation and oversight in spite of their debt and/or guarantee positions (est. at over $5 trillion)[4] and their debt-to-equity ratios that are far higher than the largest or most conservative commercial banks.

Our recent bailout legislation included up to $100 billion for them, but that will not suffice and what they need most is a new operating mind-set.

Managements at both have been the source of extensive corruption and self-dealing, most notably manipulating their public earnings statements in order to qualify for undeserved executive compensation bonuses. Many millions of unwarranted dollars were paid in this way and even more in separation pay when the participating executives were discovered and forced to leave.

It was a honey pot way of life. Stick your fist in the jar and whatever you were able to withdraw was yours. After all, they were tax payer dollars and Uncle Sugar was known to cast a lax eye.

When we mention corruption, oversight and regulation regarding F & F, we are entering an area of contradiction and denial that tests our credibility. The trail of malfeasance extends back to the Clinton administration two of whose appointees made $100M and $75M in fraudulent bonuses.[5]

And it's not as if Congress didn't know. In the last decade F&F have spent more than $180 million to lobby Congress, and Fannie Mae on its own made campaign contributions to the campaigns of 354 representatives and senators from both parties.[6]

Those members of Congress who received the most money from Fannie Mae were Senators Dodd, Obama and Schumer and Representative Barney Frank all of whom served on key committees that dealt with financial legislation.[7] Then Rep. Rahm Emmanuel received a lesser amount but also was paid $250,000 in 2000 and 2001 from Freddie Mac as a member of its overly acquiescent board of directors.[8]

This pattern of corporate corruption, and Congressional

closeness to it, has caused many comments and calls for investigation, but Congress protects its own and has succeeded in avoiding any significant inquiry.

One of the more puzzling aspects of our Congress is its handling, or more accurately non-handling, of ethical problems of which it certainly has more than its share. Both the Senate and House have Committees on Ethics, but on the rare occasions when matters are referred to them it is hard to discern any evidence of action.

There have certainly been no open hearings on members' ethically questionable conduct, no discussion on the floor and little in the way of cooperation with media requests. The Committees on Ethics act like astronomy's black holes. No matter what goes in, nothing comes out.

We are so accustomed to the absence of any functional ethical mechanism that we tend to accept it. This is a terrible mistake, as it only makes us less likely to seek and demand the good government that was promised in our Constitution.

Unfortunately, Congress does not see that its abdication of ethical leadership at the top of our government creates a numbing effect which spreads to other departments, agencies, etc.

Within its own halls and walls, it seems that Congress attempts to cover itself with a patina of decorum and respectability by referring to each other as "my honorable friend", "my esteemed colleague" or some similarly friendly title, but that's a tough sell. It's been argued that Congress operates on a "Don't tell" schoolboy sense of honor, but even that falls flat in face of the record. Most likely, unethical behavior has been condoned for so long and is so widespread because any accusation would engender a counter-attack. Better not to rock the boat; there are election campaigns, pensions, outside compensation, seniority, committee assignments all to be considered. Strike not; lest ye be struck!

You may recall the silence after Rep. Wm. Jefferson (D-LA) was caught on camera in an FBI sting taking a $100,000 bribe ($90,000 was found in his food freezer) after which the FBI obtained a warrant to search his office and files. This set off a panic alarm in Congress and the charge by both parties that the FBI's action violated the government's separation of powers!

No voice speaks with as much authority in the argument of public protection as that of pension holders. They are a recent (mostly post-WWII) addition to the contracts between people and their government or corporate employers, and their growing demand and acceptance can be seen as a direct response to the pain caused by the Great Depression of the 1930s.

Regular, repeated payments by many employers/employees can quickly build large accumulations of capital which then have to be managed to provide long term future benefits. With the ready participation of labor unions, industry and local/state/federal governments a major new element was added to our economy. But with major money more often than not comes major abuse or error, and pensions were no exception.

There is always the question, beyond human control, of whether the pensioner will be around to enjoy his benefits at the time they come due, and then its opposite, which is very much subject to human control, of whether the promised money will be there. The process of accumulating money over a prolonged period under someone else's care requires trust. And trust can be broken, especially when large sums are involved. People die. Greed lives.

The generation of the '50s thru the '70s were glory days for American industry. We made and shipped products to all parts of our globe. In this period, as pensions became more widespread, they also became one of the key elements in labor contract negotiations, as they allowed union leadership to claim that it had secured its members futures far beyond the 65 year retirement age. This was an enormously important benefit for both the practice and psychology of American trade unionism.

But the growth of pensions in labor contracts became an increasing cost factor to management. Pension expenses were calculated according to long-term actuarial forecasts with remote results, and they reduced present profits. Profits fed the flames on Wall Street and defined the value of salaries, bonuses, corporate retirement and incentive plans, etc.

Accordingly, many employers engaged in only partial funding of retirement benefits, thereby permitting both larger present profits and later pension payments. This practice, as time passed, led to more and more companies reporting increasing amounts of unfunded pension cost liabilities.

In 1974 Congress passed legislation creating the Pension Benefit Guaranty Corp (PBGC) to assure payments to workers enrolled in defined benefit pension plans in the event of insolvency or some other catastrophe occurring to the employer.

Notable bankruptcies such as Bethlehem Steel in 2002[9] and this year's General Motors' filing transferred billions of dollars of unfunded pensions to PBGC which now carries hundreds of billions of dollars of corporate pension fund obligations.

Bankruptcy courts regularly move these pension liabilities from their petitioners to the government via PBGC in order to complete the bankruptcy procedure and thereby provide some hope of an orderly dissolution or rebirth. In fairness, the PBGC was a well intended effort to provide protection to a large number of employees and their dollars. Today it appears that it may soon qualify for another massive taxpayer bailout.

The reason for this discrepancy, as in many other instances, is that the legislation's intention was not able to withstand the pressures applied by the private sector to critical elements such as penalties, vesting, fiduciary requirements and others. Because so many of the PBGC's obligations are long-term, it can continue to exist with occasional infusions of added funds, but even under these circumstances it is a time bomb — slowly ticking, perhaps, but still very much a bomb!

We must recognize, however, that pension problems can cut both ways, as many communities, anxious to maintain both municipal services and labor peace, sign off on absurdly rich contracts that encourage excessive overtime accumulation, early retirement at or around age 50 and retirement benefits at full or nearly full compensation.

Many of the board or commission members who approve unworkably rich contracts serve short terms and will not be in office when the results are felt. Then, it is not uncommon for police, fire and other public service personnel to commence retirement with payments in the $100,000 to $400,000 range. The impact of these policies grows markedly as community population and service personnel expand and impose larger payments.

Medical retirement benefits constitute another serious drain on community finances, as police and firemen can be guaranteed health benefits for the rest of their lives after five years of employment.

It is easy to see how these contract obligations can quickly increase with the passage of time, and Credit Suisse has estimated "that state and local governments have a cumulative $1.5 trillion shortfall in commitments for retiree health care".[10]

Media Madness

This betrayal visited upon our country is like no other. It spares no one today and reaches down to generations to come. It is a profit motivated participation in a broad dumbing down of our population, especially youth, sponsored by our educational and commercial sectors and other "special" interests.

Rather than serving as an elevator, it imposes actual and psychological limitations that inhibit upward mobility by those at the lower levels of our society. And its view of our national capabilities even creates a drag on our leadership.

Time was when our public media consisted only of print publications — newspapers in every city and town and a few magazines with mostly local readers. Mass marketing techniques and mailing methods expanded our print media to national reach which formed the foundation of our postwar consumer economy. With the addition first of radio, and then TV, we engaged in a marketing and distribution explosion of enormous variety that continues today and accounts for about two-thirds of our GDP.

Why do we include it here? Unlike in many other democratic countries our broadcast media are privately owned and operated, and yet our media sector is very much a national institution in close and constant contact with our sensibilities. It is private and yet it depends upon use of our public air waves to deliver its message.

The dividing line, or the line where public and private meet, is the Federal Communications Commission (FCC) that is charged very specifically with some functions such as determining transmission frequencies, granting and renewing licenses and collecting the revenues therefrom.

It is also charged far more broadly with responsibility for the broadcast media's product content so that it meets standards of decency and the public interest. The key question, of course, is whose standards?

With the exception, perhaps, of the Federal Drug Administration (FDA), whose relationship with the pharmaceutical industry is notoriously close, it would be hard to find a government agency that has shown more supine deference to the industry it regulates than the FCC. Until recently, fines were infrequent and for only token amounts that lacked any deterrent effect.

The entertainment industry is awash in money and can spend millions in legal challenges to FCC rulings. Not surprisingly considering the amounts of money involved, the latter are frequently overturned on appeal.

The content of most TV entertainment is now built around sex and violence of any and all kinds. There is a decided majority of public and professional opinion that holds that repeated exposure to highly graphic and detailed images of sexuality and brutality have had a very unhealthy cumulative effect on our culture, and especially our children. Hollywood and its counterparts blow away such criticism and continue to try to stretch public acceptance to embrace ever higher levels of shock value.

There is one question, however, behind which both sides gather their weapons and mount their attacks or defenses.

Read the accounts of youth gang trials, or young homicide/ rape/assault cases. Denial is always present, but visibly diminishes as prosecutors make their cases. At the end, the contest between truth and pretense can often appear to have been decided.

The origins of our public media lie in the free press that is guaranteed by our Constitution. This is their first tie to government. The second is that of the power of enforcement lodged in the FCC. And the third is that Congress has the power to create the legislation that could strengthen both enforcement and industry standards for its products.

Congress, however, lacks the ability to withstand the constant pressure applied by the lobbyists who represent the media/ entertainment complex. Money talks and Congress listens. and that is why one of our great national institutions fails to protect the public and why our government is complicit in this failure.

Watch the mayhem, rape, incest, sodomy, decapitation and torture that appear on TV 24/7 and then ask whether, for the benefit of our society, we have the right to insist that government, through its control of the broadcast spectrum, take corrective action.

Part private and part public, our public media sector is one of the most powerful institutions in our country — not only because of its wealth, but also because of its reach. It has access to most of our nation's households, and presents an image of our culture to ourselves and to others around the world. But by presenting our culture it also creates it, and it is this result that ensures our media a prominent place among our institutional failures.

The North American Union

Perhaps no failure of protection is as broad as that of the North American Union which was initiated by Pres. Bush II and has been continued by his successor.

This plan establishes a union of Canada, Mexico and the US which would eliminate the physical borders on our north and south that now separate these three countries.

Physical separation, however, is not all that is scheduled for elimination. Our currency would be replaced by a new common unit. And the effect upon our judiciary system would also do away with many traditional protections. For example, it is stated in present NAU regulations that any litigation or disagreement involving any aspect of NAU's operation would be assigned to special NAU courts whose judges or arbiters would be appointed, not elected, and from which there could be no appeal. Under such a structure the US would be perpetually faced with the possibility, if not the reality, of a 2 to 1 opposition.

The NAU is an across-the-board intended elimination of

many of our nation's constitutional guarantees. It strikes equally at our culture, our currency, our security, our judiciary and our representative political system, and, as if these were not enough, throughout its language there is the spectra that the US will find its range of choice greatly compromised.

Quite consistent with these future prospects is the way the NAU has been sponsored so far. It was announced by Presidents Bush II and Fox of Mexico and Canadian Prime Minister Harper in 2005 without any prior public exposure. Since then, each country has established and funded various committees and working groups to "harmonize" the necessary operating elements. These groups are also not afforded any contact with the public.

They exist in our bureaucratic shadows and are spread through various departments and agencies of our government. It is intended that they remain out of sight until they can "go public" in the form of a *fait accompli*. This strategy probably recognizes the amount of opposition from American voters/taxpayers that is almost certain to be aroused.

The political footwork will be tricky. The rhetoric will be sly and false. Congress has avoided any meaningful oversight and will probably fail in its duty when the time comes. So, the answer for us, as with other crises we face, is "Will there be time?" And also, "Will we have the means?"

If the American people want to engage in a three-way merger with our neighbors with a resultant change in our form of government, and if they express that wish through a public vote, or referendum, then the public would have to try to be guided by such a decision. The NAU project has been wrapped in secrecy and deception. On those rare occasions when it is mentioned publicly it is referred to as a "trade agreement".

It may well be that, but it is also much more with, behind its masks, the power to alter and do away with much of our democratic republic's structure and history. NAU is a cautionary tale in the making which very clearly reveals the willingness of our Congress and two recent presidents to abdicate their constitutional duties.

Mirror, Mirror On The Wall

Over the course of the last century and a half America has found itself fighting in many different foreign lands where economies and political structures were much less developed than ours and where, whatever the proximate reason for our presence, our efforts came to include nation building.

This has been spectacularly and expensively true in Iraq and the pattern seems to be about to repeat itself in Afghanistan and Pakistan. There, when things prove more difficult than we had anticipated, the lack of strong, functional governmental institutions is often cited as a complicating factor that works against our "success".

While we may sincerely denounce nation building as of no interest to us in our early comments about military ventures, it seems to have an uncanny knack for appearing later and joining the mission. It is a task that becomes very difficult to avoid because it can be used to define the difference between "success", or the lack of it.

Transplanting home-grown institutions to foreign soil is a tricky business and requires a deft touch. The British were masters at the game in the nineteenth century colonial era. Our turn comes in a different world, but, even so, we do not function at the same level of commitment or skill.

Americans talk knowingly, and sometimes glowingly, about nation building and the institutions it requires to favor success for a new local government. We spend $800 million on an embassy in Baghdad and a billion in Islamabad. We have tried to help the

Iraqis form a new government and to rebuild its structure along many of our own lines. All of these are matters of public comment and record.

There is, however, an enormous disconnect here. The nation building in which America should be more pressingly engaged is its own. Institutions that fail to protect fall short in our country on the same scale, if not more, than those in the lands where our troops are sent to fight.

But here is the critical difference. The president, vice-president or member of Congress. who frequently cites our duty or success in these matters abroad, says absolutely nothing about the failure of spirit and performance in our protective institutions! They fail, and continue to fail, our history and our people in ways that are mean, miserable, unfair, cruel, cheap and dishonest.

Sadly, over time they have developed acceptance for these ways among themselves and among the people. The result is that in our government pervasive corruption is joined to pervasive cynicism. This is an absolutely lethal combination which, if allowed to continue, will destroy whatever we have created and built, whether in the public or private sectors, and lead us to a dreadful end, whether at our own or other hands.

Our enemies are many. Republicans or Democrats, it makes no difference. The same for the over 90% reelection rate of incumbent members of Congress. The extreme right or left fringes? There's no help there. The money gang — Wall Street, the Federal Reserve, the globalist crowd? No, they're too busy making money! The Department of Justice? Afraid not; too many misconceptions there, although the FBI has done some really fine counter terrorism work.

No, if America is going to cure itself, its people will have to do it. And therein lies another problem. The vox populi in America has been muted by two generations of dumbing down of its public

199

educational system and media. It is not that the American people don't have great energy and good intentions. They do, but they no longer have the sense of political initiative that they once did. For the most part they are willing to let the two major parties set both the pace and the goals of public politics.

The two parties were quick to exploit this move away from individual to mass group consciousness. They now spend billions of dollars in presidential elections on many forms of promotion — meaningless debates, advertising and, of course, parades, crowd control and other forms of manipulative hoopla. What is missing is factual explanation, but today on the campaign trail, as in Congress and throughout our government, the volume is turned on "high" and the sound overwhelms the message.

In our world of IF, Congress, acting on behalf of the legislative branch, dominates the contamination and erosion of our representative government.

To achieve the widespread failure to protect that marks its action takes power. Congress has that power. It can legislate; it can excuse; it can conceal; it can pardon; it can specify rewards and penalties; and, perhaps most cynically, it can delay, deny, deflect and ignore any reasonable criticism or request for responsible oversight or inquiry.

In the early '30s Representative Arsene Pujo of LA with the sole assistance of an extraordinary attorney, Ferdinand J. Pecora (later a distinguished federal judge in NY), held hearings to determine the contributory causes of the 1929 stock market crash. The heads of all the major Wall Street banks appeared under subpoena to testify. The questions were pointed and not allowed to go unanswered. It was a unique exercise in the questioning of enormous power in a democratic government.

Today, one year after Wall Street's second meltdown in the past century, there is no contemplation, let alone mention, of any public congressional inquiry into the collapse that required hundreds of billions of dollars of taxpayer money to repair. There will be no questions and there will be no answers. The signs that mark the way from Wall Street to Washington and back are dollar signs.

Regarding Congress, which is at the center of our widening circle of institutional failures, there are two things we must understand. Congress has long been the law of the land. And, it is now a law unto itself!

Government, however, does not live by legislation alone. It depends upon an increasingly large web of departments and agencies to implement its policies. Washington offers these in abundance. Some are well known to the public; others operate in considerable secrecy.

Theoretically, they exist to serve the public, or some part or parts of it. This concept of service often includes protection of one kind or another, and in the matter of bureaucratic protective failure the record of the Dept. of Interior's Bureau of Indian Affairs (BIA) is notable by any standard.

This was examined in detail in a previous book[11]. Suffice it to say that for more than a century the BIA, which was formed to protect our Native Americans' interests, engaged in a massive, purposeful program of fraud, deception and theft claimed by the Indian tribes in court proceedings to exceed $130 billion. It is a grimly fascinating tale which, by the nature of its extent, interest and result, assigns to the BIA unchallenged leadership in institutional protective failure within our govern-ment's managerial bureaucracy.

Our bureaucratic failure to protect does not occur only in our large or important government entities. It is carried out on a daily basis in transactions large and small (by government standards) at all levels.

A decade ago Congress authorized the use of government credit cards to pay for federal employees' work-related travel. While the cards were intended to reduce waste and abuse, the result was quite the opposite, as charges have almost doubled from $4.4 billion in 1999 to $8.3 billion in 2008.[12]

Other charges which have worked their way through our system unimpeded include $1,100 for internet dating services by a US postmaster; $642,000 by a Dept. of Agriculture employee for personal expenses identified as car loans, gambling, etc.; and $3,700 for laser eye surgery.[13]

Even more incredible among a list of incredible items was $100 million of unclaimed refunds for airline tickets that had been purchased, but not used.[14] All in all, the General Accounting Office (GAO) audit that provided some of these figures revealed that 41 percent of all credit card transactions were questionable for a variety of reasons.[15]

Sadly, other audits or investigations confirm this pattern of gross neglect and abuse. The information is routinely made available to the Congress, but the practice continues.

Government contracts are also an area of faulty management and unnecessary expense. All government contracts over $100,000 are supposed to be evaluated for performance, but the GAO, in a survey of 23,000 such contracts, discovered that less than a third had been reviewed,[16] and found that multiple contracts here and in Iraq, including one for $280 million, had been awarded to contractors with records of prior defaults.[17] As government contracts amounted to over $500 billion last year, its failures in this area are of real consequence.

In its stewardship role, Congress often acts with government institutions. For example, it became evident as we developed increasing nuclear power generating capacity that we were creating a polluted waste problem that had to be dealt with. A joint study by our Atomic Energy Commission (AEC) and Congress' nuclear regulatory committee proposed about a dozen sites for waste storage. The nature of the problem invited a strong public response. After many hearings and conferences with the states involved, Yucca mountain in NV was chosen. More hearings and legal arguments followed, but eventually the process was completed and construction commenced on an enormous underground storage facility for the nation's radioactive waste. It is now completed at a cost of $13.5 billion, but has been declared unsafe and will not be used, at least for its intended purpose. There has been no public comment by the AEC or Congress as to whether an alternate use would be possible.

Another prime area of government's protective function is that of the security of our territory and borders. A report by the Department of Homeland Security has stated that over the past decade there have been over 215 instances of Mexican armed troops entering the US.[18] Their presence usually serves to protect smugglers of illegal drugs or aliens. It doesn't make much difference, as both are illegal, but what shocks the most is that these incursions are never reported and are allowed to continue without objection.

There is a movement afoot today in our country to grant voting rights to non-citizens. This has commenced at the local level and has been successful in several municipalities, notably Takoma Park, MD; and the Center for Immigration Studies reports that "legislation has been formally introduced in a number of cities, including NYC and Washington, DC, and in at least two states – New York and Minnesota – to allow non-citizens to vote in local elections". [19]

Our voting privilege is one of our earliest and most treasured institutions, and it is easy to see where these efforts to weaken it are coming from and what they hold for the future. For, once non-citizens are allowed on local voting rolls, pressure for state and national acceptance is sure to follow, most likely under the argument that their exclusion would constitute discrimination and a denial of "human rights".

A Man And His Dog

And, finally, one last poignant image which at the institutional level reveals an exercise of contemporary cruelty that we have come to accept in our society and which for the victim caused great personal pain and helplessness:

Tyler Hurd was a student last year at St. Cloud University (MN). Because a childhood injury has left him subject to frequent brain seizures, he is always accompanied by his black lab service dog, Emmit, who carries a pouch with instructions for anyone willing and able to help Tyler in the event of a seizure.

St. Cloud's student body also included some Muslim Somali immigrants who, following the Islamic line, considered dogs "unclean" and taunted and threatened to kill Emmit. Hurd was deemed unable to continue in his classes because of the Somalis' religious beliefs, and the school has reported it was trying to reach a compromise so that he could complete his studies without attending classes with the offended Somalis. *The dean of education referred to this circumstance as "part of the growth process when we become more diverse".* [20]

It would be understandable if Tyler Hurd and many other Americans had a take on this matter that centered more on our sense of history and fairness.

Our Institutions Now And Then

We did not come easily to the institutions that define and sometimes provide necessary support to our system of government. We tend to take them for granted today, but many of them were created simultaneously with our country, and have had to grow, survive attacks, gain experience and develop the character and credibility necessary to justify their existence. Our form of government has, for the most part, been helpful in this process.

Institutions as a form of protection, however, are a relatively recent emergence. Before their arrival, going back in history, man obtained protection from monarchs, tribal chieftains, and deities, whether Christian monotheism or the earlier multiple deities of the Greek, Roman, and Egyptian eras.

Prior to Christianity the innumerable wars that were waged throughout the known world were often claimed by their sponsors as means of protecting their people even when territorial ambitions were also in play.

But the Christian monotheism of the Old Testament and God's covenant with his people introduced a new element by which civil government came to be seen as having been delegated the authority to provide order, fairness, justice, mercy and other qualities of life by God in return for worship.

This pact that offered protection in return for faith through the medium of government marked the beginning of institutional development and its role in government.

Although hereditary monarchies would remain the dominant form of government until the early twentieth century, most monarchs took advantage of the concept of civil government with a divine flavor and made appropriate religious connections between their religions and their thrones.

As bloodlines proved to be considerably less than error-free in the selection of heads of state, institutions gradually assumed a more important role in transferring the civil benefits from one generation to the next, providing continuity and, then, tradition that could survive the excesses and inadequacies of monarchic procreation.

When our colonists came to create a government for our newly independent state, it had on hand the benefits of both centuries of Christian government tradition and the years of erratic rule by George III. This template proved useful in forming institutions and in nourishing their early growth.

But there is another element that successful institutions must develop and sustain, if they are to support government and stay true to their original purpose. This is a sense of shared mission between government, the institution and the public. Looking back over the institutions we have cited here, it is evident that what is shared is not mission, but rather its absence. Without this shared sense of mission, as we have seen, our institutions are bound to fail in their protective function and will not be able to pass their historic values on to their successors.

We are now at that stage where too little is demanded of them, where former goals may no longer serve and new ones may not be enunciated as the result of our political polarization. This is a dangerous time for our republic, if its institutions cannot provide the strength and support they have in the past.

IF plays no favorites; it cuts both ways, with double edges. Whether in the private sector (Wall Street and our media, for example) or in government (Congress, the BIA) its effect on the people and our government is equally damaging.

The problem comes partially from the duality of our institutions. To some degree they are monolithic with distinctly individual identities. On the other hand, they depend upon government to feed (i.e. fund) and staff them and to determine their relevance through enabling legislation that issues licenses or creates charters.

What our institutions receive from our government today is the same fuel that powers government — corruption, fraud, lack of ethics, conflicts of interest and control by special interests/lobbyists. Is it any wonder that so many of our institutions fail in their protective functions? Our government and institutions may be eating at different tables, but their meals come from the same kitchen.

We are faced again, as we have been before regarding immigration law and other aspects of our democracy, with America's dual personality, split screen and often schizophrenic tendency to speak one way and act another. We see our institutions as noble, independent, fair and strong public benefactors, and yet have turned them into compromised extensions of all that is wrong and regrettable in our government.

And in the private sector which is only indirectly financed by government, but makes use of the same lobbyists and congressional control, its leaders are able to find their way to avoid public responsibility without any assistance. Again; different tables, but the same kitchen.   Only the American people, the vox populi, can bring about the changes that are necessary.

Political GPS

America confronts a series of major issues any one of which could bring disaster on a grand scale. The failure of our protective institutions is only one of these. We are also exposed to dangers from population, immigration, climate change, religious jihad, excessive national debt and others.

In the best of times any one of these would be formidable. We are not in the best of times. Mr. Obama made many promises in his campaign speeches, but purposefully did not indicate how they would be kept. He has had a brief honeymoon in Congress which will not get easier. Some of his methods have disappointed, but his weakest effort has been the people with whom he has surrounded himself.

Regardless of how the health bill now turns out, he has lost support among independents and moderates of both parties. The congressional elections next year will bring some wide-open races and inflamed rhetoric.

Our present view is that the Democrats will be net losers of seats in both the Senate and the House which will tighten votes on key issues, will fail to keep their control on others and, as a result, will make government in the next two years more polarized and contentious.

Good government comes from policies fairly and carefully crafted in the public interest. Policies, when orderly enacted, produce consequences that are beneficial and, unless confused by external forces, controllable. America has not had such government for a long time.

The Ideological Imperative

Democracy does not strive to make every commoner a king, but is designed to spread evenly among the people the benefits and responsibilities of government. This, of course, is not possible in our presently polarized state ruled by the Ideological Imperative (II).

The latter is how we armor ourselves against change, humanity, reason and rationality. As our resistance to these values grows, so does the likelihood that we will damage our cultural and societal machinery beyond repair.

It used to be that science provided us with broad proof that we accepted, but now even science is challenged by ideology. Will our political insecurities now deny science, and us, that comfort?

The path to political power in our country is not marked by nuances. This is because our political process is dominated by our two party system whereby access to the ballot for all elections is controlled at the state and local levels. It is there where money, effort and organization have their greatest impact, where candidates are selected and where ballot content is determined.

The two parties are meeting places designed to attract votes, money and political emotion by forging one identity with the broadest possible appeal. Their messages require the continuous exposure that only broadcast media can provide to be effective.

This is a match made in marketing heaven. The political parties are able to reach almost every segment of our national audience with messages that can be specifically tailored to local constituencies. And the broadcasters are the beneficiaries of enormous revenues from the frequently repeated, 24/7 commercials.

Everything operates on a mass scale when our two party system shifts into its electoral mode. Each party has repeatedly proclaimed, and actually believes, that only it can provide solutions to our national problems. This is nonsense, of course. We go from Bill Clinton to Bush II and then to Pres. Obama without any real improvement in our government.

Leading up to last year's presidential election we were treated to a series of televised "debates" among the multiple candidates for nomination. There was much rhetoric about issues, some real and some not, and about claims as to what he/she would do, or not do. There was no statement by any candidate that embraced a commitment to improve the quality of our government.

This attitude readily transfers itself to the general public in the form of a widely held, cynical belief that we are captive to the ethics, patterns and structures that we have allowed to shape our government.

One of the main purposes of our multi-billion dollar campaign process is to keep the voters of each party in their own tents — no crossing over, no leakage. This attempts to diminish the importance of the independent voter, and has proved in recent years, as campaigns have become increasingly expensive, to lessen our democracy.

However, the recent Obama/McCain campaign was marked by several image factors which encourage independent and cross-over votes. These factors were the contrasts between young/old, black/white and conservative/liberal images.

Mr. Obama created and carried a larger than usual independent vote which found his promise of change appealing and moved the election to his favor.

It's quite possible that he has overestimated his mandate and allowed the political pendulum to move along its arc beyond the point of national acceptance. Such is the way of the II. It drives us in too many wrong directions and the only way we will shake it loose is for both parties to find ways to bring back centrist, moderate elements to our political ambitions.

One of the reasons that the II is so damaging to our government is that it encourages the erosion of our institutional protection. This failure is a terrible thing. It is a form of mutually assured destruction within our government which separates us from our history. It engenders fear and leaves us to the not so tender mercies of the worst among us.

Our world rotates smoothly in its majestic orbit of the sun, but our history moves in fits and starts — a war here, a plague there, a well-timed assassination someplace else. It is a moving mass of technology, personalities, wealth, fear, ambition, natural resources, politics and chance always ready to defy predictability.

Leaders come and go; nations appear and vanish; empires emerge and dominate, but they, too, wind down and recede into the past. *There has never been a permanent superpower.* The global greatness of the British Empire lasted a century. Hitler's Thousand Year Reich came and went in twelve years. Napoleon was the scourge of Europe, but only for a decade.

Twenty years ago America was the sole superpower; today we are now the leading superpower, as China and Russia push their challenges. We must recognize that being sole superpower is a term-limited status. The "We're #1" crowd cannot accept this fact of history, and their denial is combined with a potentially fatal sense of entitlement.

Many of the policies we adopt require choices that set short term goals against long ones, and vice-versa, and these considerations, whether economic, political or military, tend to favor term limits. Error is never more than a phrase or phone call away. The calculations required of a sole superpower in our nuclear armed, computerized, instant everything and globalized world are so complex as to be unimaginable as recently as a generation ago.

Looking ahead to America's place in history's flux, we will need our institutions' protections more than ever. They will have to be able, not only to protect the people, but also to support our government, to maintain their missions. In return government will have to clean its own stables, to do away with its extensive corruption and conflicts of interest.

Few people in America today know/understand our history/ Constitution. In politics this means that arguments are not grounded in a common identity and people both in and out of government are easily led to extremes — i.e. polarization, the II.

The cycle continues, for, as the quality of government is reduced by conflict, so is the mission it can convey to the public and our institutions.

This is a key moment for our country. It will require a concerted effort on the part of the public, the Congress, the executive branch, the private sector and our governmental institutions.

We have to ask a very important question of everyone mentioned above. Are we satisfied with the quality of our government? If we are, then we can sit back and continue to slide along as we now are. If not, we had better get the repair program started. We should not leave this to history; for, if we do, the outcome could be most unhappy.

Today. America finds itself having its government, its politics and its culture pushed, pulled and stretched into forms it has not known before. As this process has been mostly undertaken without exposure to the public (i.e., the NAU, for example), its legitimacy is questionable.

Further drift will only serve those interests who have taken us this far. We have created a massive kleptocracy by which our government has quietly taken from us many of our historical ideals and values. This process will continue and accelerate unless the American people can speak with one voice to reverse it.

End Notes

[1] Readers interested in an extensive analysis of the Fed's origins and history should refer to The Creature From Jekyll Island by G. Edmund Griffin, American Media, Westlake Village, CA 1994. This fascinating account has had 24 printings in 4 US and 3 foreign editions.

[2] Ibid

[3] The American Sentinel, Charlotte, NC – "...more than 90-percent of the dollar's value since 1933 has been eroded through inflation..." The McAlvany Intelligence Advisor – "In the US the dollar has lost 98% of its purchasing power via inflation from 1940 to 2005. In 1940 dollars, $1 is now worth a paltry 2 cents."

[4] Citizens Against Government Waste

[5] Judicial Watch, letter 4/10/09 from Chris Ferrell, Director of Research & Investigations

[6] Ibid

[7] Ibid

[8] Ibid

[9] Citizens Against Government Waste, letter 9/3/04

[10] Palm Beach Post, 9/12/08 In Extremis … by George Will

[11] Matters of Conscience, Aug., 2005 and Eminent Disdain. Author House, Bloomington, IN; 9/09, Chapter 8

[12] Parade, 7/5/09, p.6

[13] Middle American News 8/08, p. 6

[14] Cf. #12

[15] Cf. #13

[16] Parade, 7/19/09, p.6

[17] ibid

[18] American Border Patrol - Letter 10/2/09

[19] Backgrounder, 4/08

[20] Middle American News, 8/08

ECD 10/25/09

Chapter Eight —— January 2010

Changing circumstances require Islam and the U.S.
to more clearly define themselves.

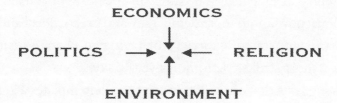

Approaching the Intersection

Ours is a world of extreme and imminent danger. It crackles with messages of political, economic and religious conflict and, when tensions build and words fail, as they often do, violence is visited by one group upon another. If that were not enough, our planet shudders from the spasms that changes in technology, population, wealth distribution and our natural environment are forcing upon its social structures.

As a former sole superpower, and now still a leading one, America's role in crossing these cultural quicksands is a risky one. It is made incalculably more so by the fact that we wear two masks, that we regard ourselves in two different mirrors, that we speak with two voices and that the language of one is not that of the other. This confusion of our identity poses difficult political policy questions here and abroad.

Consider this example of our conflict in Afghanistan. There, as elsewhere, we confront the jihadists that are descendents of those we armed and supported against the Russians. Our presence and policy have been enabling factors in both the Taliban's success and the subsequent growing popularity of Osama Bin Laden. Unfortunately, whether in Iraq, Afghanistan or Pakistan, our efforts have been marked by widening conflict and regional instability.

Secretary of Defense Bob Gates, in speaking of transforming our military power into more democracy and greater local authority in Afghanistan, stated "I'm leery of trying to change history in dramatic, short strokes. I think it's very risky." [1]

This suggests that our policy is one that contemplates a long and gradual process, but the truth is that we are neither militarily nor financially capable of long term occupations and nation building in remote areas where our efforts fuel local insurgencies.

The world watches and analyzes every move we make and we cannot expect to get the results right unless our policy is a clear expression of our identity.

America and, indeed, the rest of our world face the distinct possibility that the four forces shown above are possessed of elements so powerful and volatile that, should they collide, much of our planet could be consumed by events of either natural or human origin.

Our country's role in this impending confrontation of interests is made immensely more difficult because we have been the world's sole superpower for the last two decades — a role to which we brought little in the way of training or suitability other than military and financial superiority, these being the two elements of danger that Pres. Eisenhower specified when he advised us to "beware the military/industrial complex".

Today's variety and reach of our nuclear weaponry is far beyond anything Ike could have imagined and no longer is ours alone. This is one of the commanding facts of our present status — the "sole" in "sole superpower" no longer means what it used to. It has been diminished over recent time by the development of other nations and systems, and this process will probably continue until an approximate technological parity emerges, but even parity among nations offers no protection from the same technology in the hands of an extremist martyr-to-be.

This flux in world affairs, caused by differing roles of economic and military growth, is an historical fact of life which, as the advantage of our relative power contracts, we must be able to grasp both intellectually and politically.

Our first step should be to recognize that we are no longer the sole superpower and that our reduced status is the result of the combination of others' successes with our failures of policy and practice. "Sole" should be removed from both our superpower conception and our vocabulary.

The area in which readjustment will be made most visible, and for us necessary, is that of foreign policy where all major powers will have to move their thinking towards a more internationally oriented process.

In its original concept the UN was viewed as being capable of facilitating the shading and shaping of its members' positions in a generally acceptable way. Because the present political, religious and intellectual polarization of the UN makes such a broad process of accommodation highly unlikely, the necessary policy reviews and revisions will have to be undertaken by individual states or regional groupings to which they are committed.

Looking ahead, as more powers come to wear the "super"

label, the formulation and expression of foreign policy is bound to change. It will have to seek specified, achievable results that will enlist cooperation and benefit others as well as ourselves. And it will have to include stated and agreed to costs whenever possible.

England dominated the world and most foreign policy in the nineteenth century. That period ended abruptly in the mud and blood of WWI, and is no more. In its wake, WWII, our advances in communications and weaponry technology and the existence of the UN have imposed real changes in the ways that we, and others, will express and exercise our international initiatives.

Each one of the forces in our title illustration is supremely powerful in its own way and approaches their intersection with the gathering momentum of recent history. Fueled by technology, faith and, all too often, extremism, they indicate the likelihood of a highly dangerous collision.

Underlying and exacerbating all four of these global issues is the quiet and persistent pressure of population increase. However, as complex and intertwined as these challenges are, there are two questions that must be heard and answered in order to make any real progress possible.

Definitions

These are behavioral questions which are rarely addressed directly because of their political/ cultural delicacy, but now must be faced.

The first deals with the conflicting nature of Islam and its varied interpretations. There is the violent, jihadist Wahhabi view of Islam as the flaming sword conquering and destroying all differing forms of faith, government, ethics, art, commerce, etc.

And there is the moderate Islam whose followers see it as capable of co-existing with other belief systems.

Islam is a dominant religion in SE Asia, the Middle East and Africa and is an expanding presence in Germany, France, England, Holland and the Balkans. In the course of its mission, it has delivered a mixed message that has served different purposes in different times and places. As confrontation and violence increases, this tactic loses credibility.

The moderate Islamic identity is the only one capable of producing long term peace and political/economic improvement for its followers. To do so, it must declare itself opposed to the jihadist movement and bear the risk of internal division and perhaps conflict.

The question of which Islam is the real Islam, of which voice should be believed, is one that moderate Islam has been unwilling to publicly address. Again, this is a behavioral matter within the Islamic family to which no outside agency can bring credentials.

It's quite possible that the moderate elements within Islam fear that any condemnation by them of their jihadist brethren will put their own lives at risk. This may be so and the prospect of an internal Muslim war to determine "the true faith" is a bloody one.

Nevertheless, the case of Islam's true identity is one that should be resolved. It may not yield an instant answer, but continued silence on the part of moderate Muslims seems unsustainable in view of Islam's growing numbers and violent politicization.

The second behavioral question of global consequence involves our own country and identity. The latter we have dealt with in some detail in previous chapters, but in this case we refer to that specific aspect of our identity that seems to have grown out of our role as "sole superpower". This is our almost obsessive compulsion to recreate in other places our own values and society.

We have labeled this "nation building", but that does not indicate the extent of our insistence upon having our own homegrown extension of self in foreign lands. The situations in which we display this fear of separation usually commence, and are first presented, as security threats, but it is not long before we are called upon to engage in nation building and to provide the institutions, training, ethical guidelines, personnel and funding that is required to replicate our systems.

Faced by what we view as a security challenge, our response reveals a psychological insecurity that insists upon the familiar patterns and props of our free market, democratic, capitalistic, non-sectarian model.

We are, it seems, unable to view other countries' landscapes without wanting to attach to them the malls, condos, high rises, super highways, sports stadia, jet ports and ubiquitous media forms that we have built in excess at home. This questionably beneficial approach to other lands and people is only partially a matter of politics, as behind the political drapery those who represent our commercial sector can be heard as they persuade, advise and demand the action that best serves their interests.

Nation building is difficult at best and is made more so when deep cultural differences are present. In Muslim countries our attitudes clash head-on with local ones regarding such basics as the human body, sex, marriage, divorce, clothing, punishment, art, faith, etc. And the latter, we have found, cedes little to interpretation.

There is nothing new about the combination of foreign policy with commercial goals. What is different is the ability by which the increasing population and technology of a leading superpower such as ourselves can move mass marketing in a way that alters centuries-old lifestyles and cultures.

Our armed interventions are not risk free for us. At a time

when our economy is in an extremely precarious condition they constitute a viable economic threat. A recent report[2] indicates that we have spent $53 billion in Iraq since 2003 for reconstruction of infrastructure and relief. And yet many of the hospitals, H_2O treatment and electrical plants, schools, bridges, etc. are not operating as planned, or at all, because Iraqis are not able enough or available for their operation, and American contractors have been paid and returned home.

Stuart Bowen, inspector general of the Government Accounting Office (GAO) for Iraq, has reported that the GAO "regularly raised concerns about the potential waste of US taxpayer money resulting from reconstruction projects that were poorly planned, badly transferred, or insufficiently sustained by the Iraqi government"[3].

Bear in mind this $53 billion is only from one source of waste. There were additional billions lost by private contractors and the military. Still, today "more than 40% of Iraqis lack access to clean water" and " 90% of Iraq's 180 hospitals do not have basic medical and surgical supplies"[4].

Indeed, the use of private contractors has changed our way of war. There are about 600 contractors in Iraq, Afghanistan & Pakistan whose employees number about the same as our 260,000 military personnel.[5] In addition to normal civilian functions they provide security, special ops, snatch & grab abductions and targeted assassinations which can pose ethical or constitutional questions.

The line between private contractors and our military's tasks is becoming increasingly blurred with private services moving higher up the chain of command and often without Congress' knowledge or approval.

This is not good. These groups operate in the confusion of wartime, when legal/social restrictions are not in place, and are able to establish extralegal powers that become the basis for a military/

political complex. Consider Rome's Praetorian Guards, Hitler's SS and Saddam Hussein's and Iran's Revolutionary Guards. They all provided political security in return for special authority capable of being exercised at the highest political levels.

But Iraq is only the beginning. There is now Afghanistan with its own peculiar problems such as the extremely high desertion rate of 20% to 25% in its security forces[6] which require a continuing new supply of thousands just to avoid troop loss. And, numbers aside, such high turnover and its constant drain must cause a loss of efficiency.

Increasingly, our plans in Afghanistan are couched in nation building terms, and our participation in the spreading conflict in nuclear capable Pakistan may be seen in Washington as having to be increased. Poverty there is endemic and extensive and billions could be spent without any notable effect. We should not confuse results with purpose, but our press releases often make no distinction.

This pattern of destroying infrastructure so that we can rebuild it only makes sense to those who profit from it, whether there or here. The saddest part is that America needs rebuilding, that many of the same installations we pay for abroad are on our list of things that we must provide to our own society at local, state and federal levels.

Throughout our history our government has observed a general sense of fairness in its conduct towards most of the people. In the last half century this attitude has changed and the taxpayer has been increasingly burdened with unwelcome and unnecessary expenses.

There is considerable electoral anger in our country now, most prominently about the Wall Street bail-outs. Whether government can see it or not, the taxpayer, contemplating massive infrastructure costs in foreign countries where we have elected to wage war, may not regard this addition to his burden as justified or of primary importance. Sometimes government can make a persuasive case, but our Congressional attitudes towards the amount and type of expense the taxpayer should be forced to assume has built real and wide resentment, not so much because of the amount, but because of the fairness factor.

Americans are fair and pay their share when it is called for. Unfortunately, the Congress can no longer act credibly as an arbiter of fairness.

For those who may choose, or be forced, to answer these two defining questions there are considerable, although different, risks involved. Regarding Islam — whether in its wars of conquest or in the conduct of Sharia law at its most local level — all Muslims are aware of the physical violence and terror it harbors and justifies as divinely sanctioned. And they have no reason to believe that in the event of an internal struggle over the control of dogma or identity they would be spared.

Must it not be a sobering experience for the clergy or members of a mosque to consider the random destruction of <u>their</u> friends, families and selves that would result from a bomb's detonation at <u>their</u> mosque? And might it not cause them to seek the safety of avoidance, to turn away and to leave the extremists to their own interpretation of Islam?

But, without control from moderate elements, it is the way of violence, the way of the flaming sword that is extending Islam's grip on minds and territory.

This threat of fraternal violence is especially difficult because it is grounded in shared faith. It is a kind of spiritual blackmail from which the only relief, although moderates resist it, is its recognition and acknowledgement. Even then lives will be lost and brother will fight brother.

Our response is crucial to the world. Our many speeches of

respect, affection and tolerance for Islam have not had any success in containing its extreme element. At all our policy levels we should now call for an authoritative Muslim statement of identity. Muslim political leaders will resist, but this step is one that only they can take. We cannot take it for them. *It must be a matter of their choice, not our dollars and soldiers.*

This raises some delicate questions for everyone. Does moderate Islam's leadership know the real numbers of extremists? Do they care? Do we know? And do we care? Enough to ask? Finally, is there a moderate Islamic leadership?

Matters of faith have a right to privacy, while matters of behavior in our conflicted world are all too often public. The persuasion of public behavior has been the goal of all international and regional cooperative efforts — the League of Nations, the UN, NATO, EU, etc. At its inception the UN was structured to play such a role, but it has allowed the General Assembly to be hijacked and split along the same ideological and parochial fault lines that plague its individual members with the result that it is largely unable to bring about solutions acceptable to all or most of its various power blocs.

The U.S. situation is somewhat different, as both its nature and penalties are more political. The leader(s) who would attempt to break free of the political pack mentality would suffer loss of support from the military/industrial complex which, in spite of Pres. Eisenhower's fair warning, has become the dominant voice in our economic and foreign policy decisions. In his time no one could have imagined our recent embrace of globalism and its effect of sucking out our economic innards. We have become what we were warned against, and to regain our freedom will not be easy. Talk, of course, will be plentiful, but our political structure is now largely supported by special interests and, as the chance for any meaningful movement away from this control and towards political independence is remote, our government may find itself behind the curve in the major issues of our time and be forced to deal with them by reaction rather than foresight.

Entwinement

One cannot contemplate our situation for long without recognizing the impact of how thoroughly the four issues in our diagram are interconnected. Consider the almost inseparable religion/politics quandary of the Middle East, the mix of money, nature and geopolitics in the environmental issue and many others.

In most major issues of our time, national and global, there are two, three, or even all four of these elements present. And, again, underlying all is the unique and ubiquitous pressure of our planet's expanding population for which both its cause and solution are matters of personal procreational choice.

It is true that over time most of our planet's cultures have been conditioned to promote and accept unrestricted population increase, and this has established a global cultural momentum that will not be reversed easily, especially as excessive population's penalties still appear vague and remote in time to most individuals. But their resistance will hold the day only until nature's arithmetic decides otherwise at which time its impact will be anything but vague and remote. Although we are at the early beginning of this moment of civilization destiny, there are few sounds, and fewer actions, to indicate we are aware of it.

Americans must now take a realistic look at our world and how some of its key parts react to each other. To do this we must note some evident similarities and even more evident distinctions.

Global warming (CC/GW), for instance, if it progresses will

impact all parts of our planet, but will be felt far more severely by the atoll island nations in the Indian and Pacific oceans which face complete destruction. Similarly, agricultural output, food prices and institutional values will be altered in different ways in different areas as the result of widespread change in the natural processes that determine the quantity and quality of water, and the availability of light and moderate temperatures throughout our world. As CC/GW is not limited by our man-made boundaries, it can intensify human economic, political and religious conflicts wherever they exist.

The history of our world's human civilizations over the past 5,000 years is witness to a variety of cultural, economic and military movements most of which have taken place horizontally in an East/West or West/East direction.

In the temperate zones travel avoided the threats to navigation, health and food availability posed by the extreme weather conditions of our northern and southern polar zones. In centuries of early exploration trade was the motivating force, and for Europeans that meant moving east by land. Later in the Great Age of Exploration of the fifteenth and sixteenth centuries, as navigational science and instrumentation improved dramatically, the lure of oriental trade led to eastern sea routes around the Cape of Good Hope at Africa's tip and westward across the Atlantic.

The Northern Tier

Our cultural/historical reference to our world divides it into zones —— Europe, the Orient, the Middle East, Africa and the New World of the north, central and southern Americas which, because of Europe's exportation of government, religion and language to them, have become extensions of their parents.

The Near East has long been a unique part of the world that

was the only land bridge between Europe and the Orient. It was populated by a mixture of Africans, Europeans, Orientals, Mongolians and native or nomadic tribes all of whom served, in one way or another, the great trade route between Europe and Asia. Its conjoined interests of politics and economics are obvious and with the birth of Islam in the early seventh century a new, volatile and eventually defining element was added to the mix.

Lines can join and they can just as easily separate. Trade routes, phone lines, highways all join. Lines of geometry and genetics both join and separate. Fortifications, boundaries and ethnic lines mostly separate. Whether joining or separating, lines have the ability to make distinctions, and are so used with regard to places, people, politics, resources, religions and other elements. Our national policies, especially our foreign policy, are generally drawn to recognize such distinctions.

Look at a world map and imagine a line drawn from California's most southern and western point along our border with Mexico, then east through the Gulf of Mexico, around FL, north and east to Gibraltar, through the Mediterranean, through the Bosporus and Black Sea and eastward along the southern border of Russia to the Pacific Ocean north of Japan, across the Pacific to Alaska and then south along Canada's and our western coast to our starting point.

This is a line that cannot be found on any map. It is a line of distinction and separation that reveals startling differences between what lies above and below it. Not surprisingly, these differences are strongly present in the four forces of our intersection illustration.

By citing these differences we will see what an extraordinarily important line this is. The countries north of it lie mostly in the temperate zone. They include the U.S., Canada, Europe and the Russian Confederation, although their northern rims are not temperate, but polar by climate, flora and fauna.

227

This largely temperate territory is blessed with natural benefits for agriculture, livestock and human productivity, most importantly providing its human populations with abundant animal and vegetable proteins and reliable supplies of clean water from infancy on.

Below our line vastly different conditions prevail in the tropical zones whose debilitating heat imposes less productive life styles and far more precarious community health standards. In many arid areas the water supply is threatened and reduced by extensive dry seasons and has to be renewed by rainfall to provide for the next year. This is usually accomplished by monsoons which carry their own health risks and can remove much needed topsoil.

Another clear distinction drawn by this line is cultural. Above are the countries that have given the world what we call western civilization — mostly Christian and white which derived from Rome and Greece and then embraced Christianity and spread east thru Russia and west to the "New World".

This combination of classical and Christian backgrounds, as Europe moved out of the Dark Ages that followed the collapse of the Roman Empire, provided Europe with an important cultural identity and unity which flourished in its system of monarchical states and survived, although somewhat altered, the major upheavals of the Moorish invasion and the internal schism of the Protestant Reformation.

Equally as significant north of the line is its political character and its economic resources. Politically, most of the nations have elected representative governments of a democratic nature with the largest, Russia, being the least conforming, as it suffers from a lingering attachment to the centralized power and methods of its Communist past.

As Russia's size and climate are indistinguish-able from its politics, they place it in a category entirely by itself in terms of natural resources. It enjoys an abundance of oil, gas, timber, fisheries, rare metals, diamonds, water and agriculture with space for growing and grazing.

Like China, India and the U.S., its industrialization has caused pollution and waste, and it must set about repairing the environmental damage it has caused, but Russia is uniquely spared the view of future scarcity that faces many other nations, as in a world of widespread, out-of-control population increase Russia's population has remained stable or declined somewhat. This is a contradiction in our time that results from the political/economic harshness remaining from Communism and from Russia being mostly successful in controlling its borders, although there now exists a significant problem along its southeast boundary which we will discuss later.

Economically, again, the circumstances that prevail above our dividing line are unusually favorable. The nations in this zone have all the natural resources necessary for the operation of a developed economy and the capability to feed themselves — not the rest of the world, but themselves. This last is important because, if CC/GW continues, it will turn arid and hot many areas that are now temperate and will shift the temperate zone north. This will have the benefit of moderating temperatures and changing land usage in large areas of northern Canada, Greenland and Russia. It will also increase the pressure from populations to the south to migrate to these newly temperate regions, bringing with them their unresolved economic, ethnic and religious problems.

If these northern nations are not blocked by political inertia they will have to be technologically inventive enough to adapt their economies and production systems to the environmental realities of our time. It can be done, as this northern tier has in place the educational and medical infrastructure capable of meeting future demands.

There are, of course, anomalies. Australia lies far to the south of our dividing line, but is a staunch insular outpost of British culture and government. Its heritage is more defining than its geography. Japan, is a curious hybrid with two generations of westernization applied to it's traditional Asian history.

South Of The Border

The atmosphere and view south of our line is entirely different. There, forces which we accept with reluctance in our zone, control its politics and cultures.

This southern zone is enormous. It includes Central and South America, Africa, the Near East, India, China and Southeast Asia with some penetration of the Philippines. On the governmental scale it ranges from small, isolated tribes in the interiors of the South American and African jungles to the highly centralized authoritarianism of China. It is a moving mass of different faiths, accumulations of wealth and political systems through which a high level of corruption is constant. And in every aspect of its existence there is reflected the punishing equatorial heat of its tropical areas.

The population that lies to the south of our line is vastly larger than its northern counterpart including, as it does, both India and China, and all its large populations are increasing.

Within this area there is nothing as dominant as the combined classical/Christian inheritance of the north. Instead we are faced with a mix of tribal mythology, Egyptian, Hindu, Muslim, Christian and Communist ideologies and religions.

For perspective, we should note that worldwide the Roman Catholic Church counts about 1.1 billion numbers. Ranked next among Christians is the Eastern Orthodox and then the Anglican communion of about 80 million, half of which are located in sub-Saharan Africa[7].

Starting in Latin America, the main influences are the Catholic Church and in the interior jungles the local tribal beliefs with some Communism added where local activists have formed cells. Moving east to Africa, again there are tribal societies with their particular myths, legends and laws and the missionary efforts of the Roman Catholic, Anglican and other Christian churches.

But in Africa everything changes because of the widespread presence of Islamic faith and its companion, Sharia law. In the Middle East, Islamic split-off faiths exist along with Judaism and some Christian sects which more aptly belong north of our line. After the Middle East, India provides a refuge for Hinduism and then from Pakistan on through SE Asia, Islam dominates.

Because the Islamic faith calls for adherence to both its own spiritual and legal demands, Islam exerts a dual religious and political pressure in the area of its influence. That area constitutes a substantial share of our world's territory and populations. Islam is not static. It is very much in motion and flexing itself in ways that impact much of our world and our foreign policy.

The economies of the southern zone are as curious a mix as its faiths. There are the emerging industrial engines of China and India, the oil producing states mostly in the Middle East and SE Asia, but also in Africa and Latin America, and the more broadly developed and balanced systems such as Brazil, Argentina, Turkey and South Africa. Spread throughout this zone, in Latin America, Africa and Asia are the subsistence economies of native tribes whose ways rarely change and whose lives are marked by their arduous poverty, climate and terrain.

Corruption exists in all places, at all times and at every level from the baksheesh payment to a minor state bureau functionary to the millions paid by drug cartels to cabinet level government officials and, even, heads of state. In Muslim countries, for instance, where payment of interest is prohibited, baksheesh, "a little something extra", is an accepted economic element.

But the consequences of corruption and the degree to which it can penetrate and influence an economy are most clearly evident in our neighbor to the south, Mexico.

There is reasonable doubt that Mexico can bring its corruption and violence under control. The highest levels of the police and military security branches have been compromised so that the drug lords operate with impunity in an atmosphere of wide lawlessness. This extends across our border in the form of increased gang activities and drug commerce.

We have a growing trade in weapons to Mexico, many of which are obtained by the drug cartels and then used in the drug wars. Our response seems to not be willing to say or do anything that might offend Mexico. This may be long on courtesy, but not an effective tactic in a fifty year old "war on drugs".

Our map line is one that draws real religious, political, economic and environmental distinctions. For the observer, perspective is everything and, looking at our world divided horizontally as we have done, we see two very different zones marked by varying degrees of cohesion of which the upper one contains about a third of the earth's landmass. Perhaps without undue political or other pressure these two areas could sort themselves out and coexist as two benign entities peacefully pursuing their own futures.

But there are pressures — the increasingly urgent and difficult ones in our diagram that lie within the purview of our political, religious, financial and scientific leaders. To meet their ends, regional, global and national organizations engage in continuing, well-intentioned debate, but not all issues are solvable by discussion and priority is difficult to achieve

The underlying effect of population exemplifies this difficulty. It impacts all people and all issues and yet has gained very little governmental recognition or response. It offends and is ignored by important constituencies, and yet it will be heard. And it will have the last word. Not the last laugh, mind you, as it is no laughing matter, but the last word.

Inconvenient Truths

Why should we be concerned about what the world looks like? It has for centuries had different appearances — sometimes created by quick military rearrangements of populations and wealth and, at other times, more gradual accommodations of cultures, religions, languages, etc.

Indeed, the cultural/religious cohesion in the area north of our line presently exists in spite of centuries marked by frequent political and religious wars. Is the present peace only a temporary truce, a lull between wars, or is it a societal marker of future importance? Answers to defining questions such as this should be emphasized in determining our foreign policy, but with all our current potential crises they are often assigned lesser priority than more immediate issues.

On both sides of Russia's southeastern border that runs from the Caspian Sea to Mongolia live hundreds of millions of Muslims, probably the largest ethnic/religious border minority in the world. They have inhabited this area for centuries and have been given unusual autonomy by both Czarist and Communist regimes. Because of their strategic location the Muslim members of the present Russian Confederation have been assiduously courted by both Russia's and our governments.

But life along this border has changed greatly since Czarist days, and even since Stalin's era. A few days after last Thanksgiving, a bomb derailed a Moscow to St. Petersburg train killing 26 and wounding many more. Responsibility was claimed by a Muslim group. Conflicts in Armenia, Georgia, and Azerbaijan reoccur frequently and the Chechen rebel movement poses a continuing threat to Russian control. In all these areas the Muslim religious element is a key factor.

And Al-Qaeda has not limited its destabilizing efforts to attacks upon the US. From Afghanistan it is also attempting to spread its message of jihad north into Russia and Central Asia — a message that Moscow now views with new and legitimate concern.

In that part of the world, as in others, where religion, economics, populations and politics are joined, their resulting volatility poses a constant threat to well intentioned efforts towards compromise or consensus.

Islam's "flaming sword" is at work in bombings in Iraq, Afghanistan, Pakistan, Indonesia, the Philippines and parts of Africa, and yet there seems to be little expressed recognition of this at our policy levels. The southern borders of Europe have, like those in Russia, become areas of entry and occupation by any means possible, legal or illegal. This has now produced a second generation of native born Muslim Europeans armed with citizenship and determination to forge an Islamic identity in Europe by both procreation and politics.

Were religion the only change applied by Islam, it might be accommodated, but with faith often comes the law (Islamic Sharia) which is totally antithetical to our western values. Western democracies pride themselves on being able to host differing faiths and cultures and to tolerate the changes in dress, language, worship and custom they bring. If they believe they can also provide a home for a second legal system derived from a foreign faith, they are deluding themselves.

In a surprising statement last year the Archbishop of Canterbury proposed allowing some aspects of Sharia law to be recognized in England. In all probability, this would be deeply resented by most British citizens and would create strong arguments over what might constitute proper sentencing, punishment and imprisonment procedures, but some local politicians' acute sense of hearing has picked up his message in those numerous urban areas where mosques, language and trade have tilted to Muslim advantage.

In our country our "leaders" issue calls for multicultural acceptance of Islam and its followers. But which Islam? What is not heard is any demand for clarification of Islamic identity. Is the Islam that multiculturalism requires us to honor the moderate Islam of gracious welcome and peaceful coexistence? Or is it Islam of "the flaming sword"? We cannot make this decision. It is one of elemental dogma where sharply contrasting interpretations defy our understanding.

Islam's division was clearly evident in the actions that followed the Christmas bombing attempt on Northwest Airlines #253 to Detroit. A 2006 internet posting by Abdulmutallab stated "I imagine…how the Muslims … will rule the whole world and establish the greatest empire once again"[8]. Meanwhile, outside the courthouse where he was arraigned some Islamic protesters carried messages such as "we are Americans" and "not in the name of Islam".[9] Other major faiths have shown deep divisions over the years. The early Christian church split into Roman Catholic and Eastern Orthodox branches and then again when the Protestant Reformation separated from the Roman papacy. Likewise, Judaism has grown into two distinct forms — Orthodox and Reform.

Most of these groups have a structure of authority that recognizes an individual leader and spokesman — i.e., the Pope, the Archbishop of Canterbury, the Patriarch of Constantinople — and this practice extends to other groups. However, it appears that there is no one person who can speak for all of Islam, or even each of its two very opposite images. This hampers our, and others', ability to develop realistic and effective policy in Islamic areas. Any movement towards clarifying the nature of Islam would benefit international policy formulation, but is unlikely to gain wide traction for two reasons. First, the location of oil and gas resources; and, secondly, the fear of violence that targets anyone who opposes jihadist Islam.

The latter cannot be underestimated as moderates witness the random killing and maiming of Muslim vs. Muslim when suicide bombers detonate themselves in markets, in mosques at time of prayer or other public places.

The divided personality of Islam is no less than that of our own conflicted identity. Consider our military, for example. In our revolutionary days we were the light, quick force that by stealth, flexibility and hit-and-run tactics outmaneuvered the British in their dress parade costumes and battle formations.

Look at Iraq/Afghanistan where the roles have been reversed. Every US soldier carries fifty pounds or more of equipment and is accompanied by tanks, trucks, artillery, aircraft, etc. of which the combined firepower is truly awesome. Our foes have no uniforms, no mechanized mobile fire power and their weapons of choice consist of AK-47 automatic rifles, along with small scale explosives such as rockets and bombs that can be moved by their light trucks and quickly planted or fired and dismantled by two or three fighters.

The insurgents that we now face move as quietly and unnoticed through their towns and cities as we did in our forests. At that time, although England was embarking upon a century of being the world's superpower, we were able to deliver a military defeat and win our freedom.

There is another role reversal of which we should be aware that cries out for notice, but to which we do not respond. About twenty years ago the Soviet Union collapsed because its centralized economic system was unable to meet the increasingly expensive demands of its Cold War competition with the US. Technology played two important parts in this failure, as Cold War weapons became progressively more complex and expensive to produce, maintain and operate.

Its second contribution to the Russian implosion was that the emerging computer/internet/communications web was based on information sharing. Such openness was a direct challenge to the decades of secrecy and control that lay at the heart of the Communist system, and those in charge of the Communist Party, media and intelligence/security functions were unable to part with their past ways and embrace the cyber future.

The computer/internet path has changed our society in ways we could not imagine and, to a much lesser degree, Russia's also, but the parallel that we should be aware of is the economic one. As Russia was in the 1980s, *we find ourselves engaged in expensive overseas wars of our initiation that must be paid for by an exhausted economy.*

Then, in Afghanistan we backed the locals against the foreign invader. Now, we are the foreign force. Then, we engaged in an alliance of common interest. Now, we must persuade the Afghan people that the war in their homeland is in their interest. This is not an easy argument to make and the Afghan people have been able to forcibly reject it in the past.

The price of empire eventually becomes too high. Our sole superpower role has confused our policies and principles and led us to try to establish cookie cutter copies of our democracy in areas and cultures where our values and methods are alien and unwanted.

This thought process that "If it's good for us, it must be good for others" is a political conceit that serves the purposes of our military/industrial complex. It provides new space in which generals can fight, contractors can build, the private sector can market and those who make up our volunteer armed services can die.

But look at the map. The world is vast. Who can say where our next pursuit of security or our "national interests" will take us? Some wars, some involvements are more necessary than others. Will we reach or pass the point when <u>we</u> can distinguish between the real and the bogus? This is a question to which the answer will change as our ability to finance war also changes, bearing in mind our weakened financial condition and our reliance upon growing debt to fund our expenses.

It is a sobering thought, in looking at our world map, to see how many lives and dollars we have invested in just two countries in which the final results and costs of our involvement may not be known for many years.

As our reduced financial circumstances limit our choices, we should be formulating a specific policy for response to real security issues. This should be shared with our allies and must have their commitment as well as ours. If we spare the political rhetoric and make it understandable to all, we may be able to reach a consensus — first, perhaps, in NATO, then in the EU and the UN.

In Afghanistan, policy pursued is no assurance of policy achieved. There are too many elements to whom the distant conference rooms in Brussels, London, and Washington mean nothing. These are the war lords, drug dealers and corrupt office holders who control the flow of political power and money there. They make up the hard, sharp edge of cultural resistance that lurks beneath the more frequently and publicly pronounced values and customs.

It was recently announced that we and the Afghan government have secured the loyalty and support of a powerful warlord with a payment of a million dollars in return for which he will keep the Taliban out of his area. And after we leave? Shifting alliances lie at the heart of Mideastern politics and suggest that diplomacy of this sort is an exercise in naiveté. Bob Gates expressed doubt about changing history in short strokes. He knows the Muslim memory is long.

We think we know what we will find if we only press on, "finish the job", etc., but we may not. Afghanistan's history, it's political DNA and its preferring things the way they are to becoming an exercise in western nation building may prevail. It's possible that, say, in three, five or eight years we could see a clear enough imprint upon the country to "declare victory" and leave. But it's equally possible that such a vision would be flawed; that beneath our imprint the outlines of old Afghanistan would remain firm and inviting; that, whether gradually or quickly, their invitation would be accepted, the country would revert to its roots, and the voices of earlier generations would be heard again at night in the high, dark mountain passes.

Muslim extremism and activism is a problem in China, Russia, Europe and Africa, but, like us, no one there has asked the Muslim community to declare its identity. Again, like us, they may be afraid they will offend, but extreme Islam is active and expanding its numbers and territory. It is unlikely that a collective silence will act as a deterrent.

Islam is a difficult political mixture of oil and religion. Were we to suddenly rid ourselves of our reliance on petroleum, we would have more freedom in dealing with the Islamic Middle East, but without our petro-dollars living standards in this area would be depressed, and any such economic dislocation could well have the adverse effect of fanning flames of resentment and increasing activist fervor.

Take another look at the world map and Islam's present borders. It may well be that we are poised at a moment of massive expansion which will overrun our western civilization. Or we may be at its zenith from which it will retreat, for one reason or another, into insignificance. Or it may remain, as it is, an opposing and violent force, in a state of continuing conflict with other faiths and cultures. These are questions only history can answer.

In 732 AD at the battle of Tours Charles Martel decisively defeated the Saracen forces at their furthest point of Muslim penetration into Europe, but the latter only became evident much later. The most we can know is where we are now, and try to make the best of things without making them worse.

More of the earth is home to Islam today than it was at the time of its reach into Europe in the eighth century. It will not go away, but must be dealt with on a continuing basis. Armed intervention may be necessary or appropriate at some times and places, but not at others. What is in our real national interest is to offer a policy to which others can subscribe that recognizes the overall reality and can also make distinctions as to the type of response the international community should make, bearing in mind that Islam in our present political world is an "active ingredient".

Corruption is ever present in third world countries in which power is controlled and expressed by tribal entities rather than open, public elections. This is especially true in Islamic governments in which political office is held or traded as the result of personal power bases.

The issue of corruption in Afghanistan has been one of frequent comment since our earliest presence there, and burst into full bloom in the recent reelection of Hamid Karzai as president that UN inspectors deemed fraudulent.

Afghanistan's institutions, political and commercial, are far from seamless. At the places where people, power or money are joined they often have to be stitched together to bridge a gap. These places provide excellent opportunities for money to change hands, for it to leave the system, for it to be transformed from public funds to personal wealth.

A report issued by the UN Office on Drugs and Crime on January 19 provides a measure of scale. It stated that in the past year half of all Afghans paid at least one kickback to a public official, and that the total amount of bribes paid reached $2.5 billion. This figure is almost equal to the $2.8 billion estimate of the Afghanistan's opium trade, and amounts to about 25% of the country's annual gross domestic product.[10]

On many occasions we have made public statements committing ourselves to the eradication of corruption in Afghanistan's government as part of our nation building process. This is a worthwhile goal, but it won't be easy. We will have to face the reality of different language, methods, standards, values, structures and practices. Perhaps the best we can anticipate is a few token arrests and/or trial convictions with light sentences as punishment. More likely, the Afghan system will find ways to modify its corrupt practices, to include them in our nation building activities and retain them for the future after our departure.

There is another side to the corruption coin and it has USA stamped on it. This is the growing amount of theft, waste and corruption that we have allowed in the conduct of civilian contractors employed to feed, reconstruct, fund, secure and manage an increasing number of projects and people where we have undertaken military intervention.

The civilian contractor has become part of our military action plan. In an operating atmosphere where regulation is loose and often of the moment, where oversight is not possible and opportunity ever present, civilian contractors have been very successful in finding ways to divert money/goods to their own use. When exposed, media coverage is intense for a brief period, but then passes and often, even after conviction, these companies or individuals are returned to bidding lists for future projects.

Civilian contractors are big business, with their contracts running into billions of dollars, and have changed the way our military operates. As they operate in an area somewhere between the Pentagon and the Dept. of State, scrutiny tends to be lax.

Their increased presence has had a significant impact upon our use of military forces. First, much, if not all, of their funding has been "off budget". The work that has been done by these contractors in conjunction with our volunteer army has reduced the number of actual military personnel required and helped to make our military efforts possible without having to use a national draft.

Another impact has been conflict between the military and the civilian contractors over, authority, discipline, areas of operation, etc. The last, and perhaps most important, impact has been civilian contractors' emergence as a newly accepted element in the funding, bidding and managing of war. In past years our funding and bidding procedures have proved to be inefficient and highly costly with the result that the nation's security and financial interests have suffered, and our military procurement process has come in for much justified criticism. Will the addition of another profit seeking participant be an improvement? Not likely, in our opinion, but the military/industrial complex now has a new member with a large appetite and a loud voice.

Crescent, Cross And Candelabra

The Middle East has been the battle ground of choice and history for the wars of survival and aggression between the three major desert religions — Islam, Christianity and Judaism. Over two thousand years the cast of characters has changed from time to time, but the events and texts that inspire religious faith have endured to the point where they now seem to be protected by genetic code and transfer. They cross and recross history's stage, sometimes as prayerful monks and at others as conquering warriors.

In the nuclear game the cards in the Islamic deck have no images such as King, Queen, Jack, etc. —only Arabic lettering which we cannot read — and the martyr-to-be is the wild card. The card game, the arms game and the diplomatic game all go on simultaneously. There is no time or reason for friendly jokes, pats on the back, compliments, time-outs, applause, or demonstrations. What is shared is only silence, a corrosive lack of trust, the need to continue and the knowledge that any misstep could be fatal for all.

In some quarters, and at some times, there is hope that it can end, that all the players will throw their cards face down in the middle of the table and walk away with their backs to each other. But such hopes must be kept at a distance lest they interfere with the moment's continuing play, lest they become distractions and create weakness.

Here, for the present, is the paradox of superpower. Islam's power to create martyrdom, to destroy millions of lives, both Muslim and others, is one that only its followers can grant or withhold. If unleashed, how do superpowers respond? Bomb Afghanistan? Not much there. Or do we retaliate against other Islamic nations?

And going beyond actual retaliation, on a level with religious roots, do we face the possibility of WWIII scale destruction because the three desert religions cannot peacefully coexist? Just this month in Northern Nigeria, Muslim youths set fire to a Catholic church filled with worshippers. This set off widespread destruction of mosques and homes over a period of several days during which over three hundred people were killed, many more wounded and thousands lost their homes.[11] This is religious warfare at the parish level.

History In The Making

The original nuclear club consisted of the five permanent members of the UN Security Council. Non-proliferation was theoretically embraced by all but not enforced, and others — South Africa, Israel, Iran (in process), North Korea, Pakistan, India — have entered without knocking and taken seats at the table.

The UN was unable to control this issue due to sovereignty concerns of its members and to philosophic/political tensions between its General Assembly and Security Council. Also in the UN, the ghost of the old colonialism has been joined by a somewhat different contemporary form in which the five permanent members of the Security Council account for about a third of the world's population and far more of its wealth and land.

This imbalance is not lost upon the growing numbers of the world's poor. The diminishing resources and shares of world wealth available to them may also be further exacerbated by economic and natural disturbances such as the present record drought in much of Africa and the tsunamis and earthquakes in SE Asia and Haiti.

In attempting to deal with the broad changes in nature's patterns that are becoming more frequent and more evident, we must pay close attention to two factors — time and flexibility.

Even in only the first decade of our present century things

are moving much faster than they did in the previous one. Our old timetables for national, regional or global action are no longer workable. Our thoughts, actions, methods and managements must be correspondingly accelerated. This is no easy task, but nor can it be avoided. We are what we are where we are — a threatened species of the twenty-first century faced with the need to take prompt, cooperative action.

Many defining moments in history are not readily recognizable as such when they occur. They must be put in the kind of perspective that only time and history can provide.

Our present moment seems to be clearly different. Nuclear and/or environmental catastrophes fueled by nature's laws have the ability to extinguish urban life, to poison the air, the ground and the water of vast areas and to reduce societies to insignificance.

There is a horrible irony in that mankind's great progress in peaceful pursuits can be trumped by weaponry and warfare. In the past we have been able to work our way around this, but we now face the anonymous, random destruction of the jihadist mind.

Randomness is present in an unusual degree in both our nuclear and natural threats. The suicide bomber, the hijacked airliner, the anthrax release, the exploded train or truck all come without warning to their victims. The same is true of nature's increasingly destructive patterns. A tornado here, a tsunami there, an earthquake or a flood — all are the products of natural law, but strike at random.

Random is. Random rules! In nature we can precisely map the genetic code and develop formulas to express the laws of physics that govern electricity, but we cannot know in what form or when a mutation may occur, nor where lightening will strike.

Similarly in politics, tensions can build, diplomacy intensify and demands increase, but we do not know where or when the first spark of war or revolution will ignite.

The forces shown in our diagram are actively present throughout our world and, no matter how we think or what we do, they will require our attention. None of them will simply go away. While our illustration shows an inevitable head-on collision, perhaps by a change in our thinking we could change this intersection to a roundabout. The potential for collision would still exist, but its damage could be lessened.

Islam's acceptance of violence in expanding its faith and imposing Sharia law could qualify for debate in the UN as a matter of human rights, but the reality is that the UN is not ready to participate in such a discussion. There are too many Muslim nations in the General Assembly who would take offense and label even such a tentative exercise in global government as an intrusion upon their religious freedom.

This is the UN's main weakness. Although created to engage in matters of broad global governance, it cannot muster the necessary objectivity to do so. In this case, the Muslim nations would act as executioner, but other political, economic and environmental issues also have strong constituencies opposed to the degree of change that global progress may require.

Our role as a leading, but no longer sole, superpower finds us now at war in several Muslim countries — Iraq, Afghanistan, Pakistan and perhaps Yemen — with no readily achievable goals in sight. One of the main problems of these wars is that our stated purpose has been nation building — to establish a new democratic political reality in the countries in which we intervene. We have offered and pursued this goal without making it clear to ourselves and to others what an enormous make-over we have in mind.

In Iraq we found that in spite of our unlimited firepower, which enabled us to win battles and skirmishes and reduce to rubble anything we chose, our nation building goal remained frustratingly distant.

This is a different kind of war. We talk of exiting Iraq in a year or two when it should be able to maintain its own security with the help of "a few military advisors" presumably working out of our new $800 million embassy. But what if it can't? If, as time passes, either quickly or slowly, old divisions and enmities reappear? What if the old tribal lines are redrawn and even reinforced by the pain we have imposed and the money we have spent in the course of a decade of military occupation?

When we have answered these questions, if we can, we will have to ask them again of Afghanistan.

The amount of money we are spending, and the waste and corruption that accompanies it, is staggering. Our politicians of both parties pretend that we have this money, that whether our wars are ones of choice or necessity, they have a claim of priority against our human and physical resources.

None of this is true. The costs of these interventions are wreaking havoc upon our economic system which will continue to be felt by our debt, our currency and our standard of living for many years after our departure.

What is the true nature of our involvement in wars such as Afghanistan and Iraq? This is not an easy question because wars can combine multiple purposes. They can be fought to provide access to natural resources (i.e. – Iraq's oil), for the control of seaways or for the establishment of military bases in strategic locations. It's clear that in these different circumstances, and most others also, the political and commercial considerations are joined and would prove difficult, if not impossible, to separate.

This puts to the US a question of identity, not unlike that facing Islam, as to who we are and how we wish to be seen (and judged) by others. Our military/industrial complex is a major player in our foreign policies and wars. It would be useless to try to deny this in view of the record of Halliburton's and Blackwater's activities. There are many others.

There are admittedly practical problems in any attempt to clarify public statements about ourselves or our strategies. Security concerns limit any comments to the broadest generalities expressed in time-worn clichés lest we give notice of our intentions that could give advantage to those who oppose, or who are likely to oppose, us. Similarly, given our debtor status, we are forced to portray our financial circumstances and intentions as stronger than they are to our creditors to avoid as much as possible rumors or comments capable of roiling the global money markets.

We have emphasized, in calling attention to the identity problems of Islam and the US, the close connection between religion and politics. More recently they have been joined by environmental concerns that cross all borders. Planetary in its scope and impact, our current environmental threat cannot be met by a piecemeal response.

There is some truth in the claims that the activities of the developed economies since the beginning of the industrial revolution have been most responsible for the present cumulative level of carbon dioxide (CO_2) and other pollutants. There is just as much truth that in today's overheating world the damage done by a molecule of developing economy CO_2 is the same as that of a developed country. And that deforestation in undeveloped areas annually prevents the absorption by trees of more CO_2 than is produced by the world's automobiles.

Our intersection symbol conveys the truth of the world as it is. This is not the world we would like. It is the one, however, that we have fashioned.

In our country with its many forms of polarization it is difficult to bring ourselves to believe that we might create an open, moderate conversation between government and the people about any of the four forces in our illustration. And yet, it is desperately needed.

Even the two that are closest to the center of our government, economics and politics, prove too inflammatory for a cooperative effort. This would be especially true of economics, with our emotional and differing views of capitalism's faults and benefits.

And, as if these four pressures were not enough for us (America and the world) to contend with, they are all subject to the constant pressure of out-of- control population and its negative effects.

Author and teacher Frosty Wooldridge, in <u>America on the Brink: The Next Added 100 million Americans</u>[12], states we are projected to increase our population by a third, or 100 million, well before the half century. This is a projection that requires real thought and the answers to serious questions.

Where will they live and work? And how can we provide housing and jobs for them? How will they be educated? Our schools are already overcrowded and many physically deteriorated. The new numbers would require thousands of new schools, parking lots, teachers, etc., as well as highways, bridges, sewers and other infrastructure elements.

But population will cause even more problems elsewhere. By 2050, according to the UN, world population is expected to grow from 6.7 to 9.2 billion, most of which will occur in less developed areas which will increase from 5.4 to 7.9 billion. This projected growth of 2.5 billion in less than half a century is equal to the world's total population in 1950.[13] Most importantly, how will the US, facing enormous deficits for the next decade, be able to pay for the added costs of these 100 million? There will be no tax income from jobs in steel plants, textile mills or shoe factories. Our manufacturing capability has been sold and dismantled.

Where will we find the necessary additional water? And how

will we prevent the price of food for all of us from rising as land for growing and grazing is diminished while demand increases?

Our attitudes, if they exist, regarding these problems range from uninformed to unrealistic ("It can't happen here") to outright denial. These are not issues for which we can find solutions by throwing around a lot of money which we do not have. They require sensitive and determined deliberation among ourselves and with others.

In all of these we must recognize the consequences of our and others' actions. For too long we have all danced to the music in our own heads and now are approaching a midnight of our own making when the music will stop and all masques must be removed.

End Notes

[1] Palm Beach Post, 12/17/09 Maureen Dowd. Via NY Times
[2] Palm Beach Post 11/21/09 Timothy Williams via NY Times
[3] Ibid
[4] Ibid
[5] Fresh Air, National Public Radio, 12/16/09
[6] Palm Beach Post – 11/6/09
[7] Palm Beach Post 12/25/09 George F. Will via Washington Post
[8] Palm Beach Post 1/8/10 Thomas Friedman via NY Times
[9] Palm Beach Post 1/9/10 via Associated Press
[10] Palm Beach Post 1/20/10 via Los Angeles Times
[11] Palm Beach Post 1/19/10 via Post Wire Services
[12] Published 2009 by AuthorHouse, Bloomington, IN Tel 1-800-839-8640 www.authorhouse.com
[13] UN Population Report 2006 Via NY Times 11/18/09 Thomas Friedman

ECD 1/25/10

Chapter Nine —— April 2010

At the deeper levels of our society we harbor conflicts between population and wealth including capitalism and government.

Ends at Odds

A careful look at our recent government attitudes and operations will reveal that they are more often than not at variance with our stated traditional values and goals. In capsule form, our ends are at odds with the results that we seek. This would provide a fitting sound byte for a presidential campaign debate, a State of the Union speech, a major congressional policy discussion or a presidential whistle-stop tour to present the party line to the public. It is a sound byte, however, that, despite its tragic truth, you will never hear.

What's more indicative of the intensity of our commitment to this pattern of conflicted thought and behavior is that we steadfastly maintain it in denial of what is often seen by us and others as accepted scientific, economic, political or religious truth of our time. If these are the foundations of our, or any, society, the damage done by our denial is now extensive and may become irreparable.

Any attempt to change course will be marked by twin truths.

It will cause public discomfort and it cannot succeed without a concerted effort of multiple segments of our society each of which will be called upon to recognize that *the whole cannot be saved without pain to its parts.*

Population

In our last issue we identified overpopulation as a major threat that will impact economics, religion, politics and the environment throughout our planet. Now, we continue our examination of it from a different perspective.

Overpopulation imperils all aspects of human life and society wherever they exist in our world. It has the capacity to alter and ultimately to destroy the economic, religious, political and environmental structures that have emerged in the course of our development from animals to sentient human beings.

The irony here is obvious. This evolution from animal to primitive and then to modern man could not have taken place without our various forms of existence being able to extend themselves from one generation to the next and to do so by increasing their numbers.

But that was then and this is now. The numbers are not the same; nor are their effects which are now greatly magnified. Without interference man's ability to multiply is infinite; our planet's resources are limited. Whether on a global or national scale, the process that created benefits in a largely undeveloped world now carries with it multiple forms of natural and human dislocation.

In the beginning of our twenty-first century overpopulation is potentially the most extensive and efficient form of destruction that faces mankind.

Overpopulation equates to a mathematical problem. It is

possessed of that same beautiful, and sometimes deadly, precision that we find in $E=MC^2$ or $a^2+b^2=c^2$. It is constant and gradual. There will be no blinding flash or mushroom cloud, but, like all processes that lack a natural or imposed balance, it will have its tipping point which we will only be able to identity after the fact, as we struggle with its consequences. Presently, it is still subject to our control, but the passage of time without understanding and action will move it beyond our reach and authority.

There is no major issue today that is not exacerbated by the effects of our geometrically increasing population within the confines of our limited physical space. Our rapidly growing world and national population is the "mother of all" issues, and is reflected in its derivatives such as public health, species loss, environmental degradation, aquifer depletion, climate stabilization, economics, diminishing natural resources, population migrations, religious conflicts, political wars, expansion of contagious diseases and many other aspects of our global and local society.

The population of Bangladesh last July, according to google, was about 157 million — approximately half that of the USA. This statement will probably elicit only mild surprise from most readers, but here's the kicker that elevates it to shock level. Bangladesh is about the same size as Iowa, and it has boundaries. It is a confined space.

Similarly, the UK's population is now about 62 million and is projected to increase by 11 million. High growth rates are particularly damaging in the UK because there is little open land and most of what appears "open" is under private ownership of wealthy titled families, the crown or conservation interests. The UK's anticipated 73 million will have to exist, compete and survive in a space the size of Oregon.

Unrelenting pressure as in these examples will raise the costs for all public services and facilities. Arable land will shrink and bring about higher food prices, and there will be far less water per capita coming from finite supplies.

We are not familiar with long-term scarcity of our basic needs in America. We know that elsewhere such shortages can produce civic protest and unrest, but our "leaders" view these as local or regional events. They cannot see them or feel them as interrelated by their primary cause — all life on our planet being dependent upon the same sources of water and air and the animal/vegetable food chain which is the common menu from which all forms derive their sustenance.

Population is a subject that does not come easily to most Americans because they have been encouraged, and even conditioned, by some of our most important and powerful constituencies to view it as remote and not part of our national experience. This, combined with our more than healthy degree of egocentrism in our national character, have led us to "look the other way" in matters of population.

And yet, as a continuing presence it has drawn some very clear and strong lines across the map of history. One of those lines traces its economic impact, most importantly proposed by economist and clergyman Rev. Thomas R. Malthus who lived the first thirty-four years of his life in the eighteenth century and the second in the nineteenth.

Malthus stated that over time population's geometric increase would favor demand over the arithmetic growth of the supply needed to support it, and he called attention to wars of territorial expansion caused by this imbalance.

Another broad brush consequence of our disregard of population growth is found throughout our environment as we consume global natural resources faster and in greater quantities than they can be replaced.

In politics, if we trace the surges of populations in motion

254

across the years and our globe, they invariably result in political upheaval and change.

Religion, too, has been greatly influenced by population factors. The world's two largest religious groups — Muslims and Roman Catholics — push for large families and high birth rates. Population growth is divinely ordained in their scriptures and has served as a highly efficient propellant for their missions and memberships.

Still, in spite of population's evident ability to disturb key elements within our global society, America and Americans remain largely unaware and uninformed of what is taking place around them.

Why?

From the moment of our birth America has been able to create itself in a way far different from those of its European forebears. Most prominently we enjoyed the opportunities of a blank political slate and a vast continent which could be ours for very little taking.

This abundance of free, open space, time and resources was key to our developing our throw-it-away, tear-it-down and start-all-over character and economy which would have been impossible in Europe.

Over years, we developed from an individual on horseback to a group mobility which progressed from our covered wagons to railroads and then was enshrined in Henry Ford's automobile.

All these factors combined to produce an expansionist social, political and economic philosophy. It honored growth for growth's sake and was greatly abetted by the new capitalism of the industrial revolution. It is never easy to align social, political and economic interests, but emerging America was a unique case in which all three forces were often joined in the common effort required to extend our territorial frontier, complete our political structure and settle the nation. There were few critics and those who spoke out had little impact on the powerful forces that opposed them.

Today, the most powerful and wealthy sectors of our society still hold to a belief in continual growth, sometimes described as sustainable, which will produce prolonged prosperity. But such growth, which must operate within the confined space of our planet and draw upon its finite resources, is an illusion.

In twenty-first century America the voices that call for population awareness are ignored and resisted by politicians, religious leaders, the media and both the business and labor interests of our commercial sector. All of these are heavily dependent upon the politics of "more". They want more numbers, more sales, more souls, more consumers, more voters, more viewers/listeners, etc. They have become accustomed to the steady enlargement of their market bases by millions of added population every year at no cost to them. It is part of the system — a very important and profitable part.

China is the only large country to successfully adopt and enforce population control measures. It did so when it was clearly the world's most populous country and was faced with serious consequences if it made no effort to limit its population growth.

The West was mostly highly critical of this communist country's one child per family rule when it was initiated, but it has stabilized China's population. India, which used to rank second to China, attempted a national vasectomy program and then abandoned it. Today it is quite close in size to China and is scheduled to become the world's most populous country within a few years.

But India may also become the world's population poster boy as a result. It has large numbers of the extremely poor and uneducated in its society which, even in an expanding economy, will remain a burden and will suffer most as basic prices rise.

Another problem facing India is the reduction of its water supply from drought and from the current melting of the Himalayan glaciers. Given the nature of these circumstances and the vast divide between the wealthy and the poor, India must be alert to the possibility of public unrest.

Around the world those who favor the status quo are mostly in control of its power centers. Big population numbers for labor, for industry, for agriculture, for armed services and for politics have translated into big money and big power.

America has shared in this equation and it has also developed a cultural conscience which views ourselves as #1 by having tamed, settled and inhabited a continent in a century, and, finally, by being inheritors of unlimited capability and opportunity. In short, we have come to regard ourselves as an unstoppable force.

There are those in our government and other areas of our public and private life who completely disregard the population factor, who actually recommend as much growth as possible and believe that the track we are now on, which will add another 100 million to our present population well before mid-century, will benefit the country.

Theirs is a dated model for an increasingly challenged future which can be disproved in many places on our planet. The point they regularly fail to grasp is that the global forces of increasing numbers and media-driven consumerism cannot be sustained indefinitely by the finite resources of our world. These two forces lie at the root of the population problem and each reinforces the other. Adding people in geometric increase applies one pressure against our natural resources. Mass consumerism promoted 24/7 by media/marketing interests then launches the second wave by stimulating and increasing the appetites and needs of the whole population.

The most basic of our resources — land, water, food, clean air — have to be shared by all of our life forms. This is a system that can only function successfully in a state of balance between self-interest and mutual responsibility without which it will fail.

Our country, more than others, desperately needs a public discussion of overpopulation, bearing in mind that we are only part of our world. The arguments pro and con should be made rationally and as factually as possible although we know that big money is at stake and the Ideological Imperative will be called upon. At some point this question will be asked: *Can Bangladesh, or the UK, with their enlarging population problems, grow their ways out of them?*

Like other important issues, this one elicits rancor and hyperbole, and the population growth proponents apply labels such as alarmist, racist, elitist, social Darwinist, conspiracist, etc. to those who favor policies of balance.

But population is not about labels. It's about numbers. Both its truth and its warning are in its numbers, as those who care will see. It can occur anywhere and spread from one region to another. For Americans and Europeans it occurs mostly out of the reach of our eyes and ears in places so widely spread around our world that only the concerted action of many can be effective in combating it.

Population's numbers play a unique statistical role and are central to our understanding (and often misunderstanding) of their broad consequences. Government and other statistics are frequently isssued in per capita figures, in order to facilitate our understanding of them and to emphasize what has been accomplished.

But this focus on the admittedly more easy to grasp human scale often conflicts with total results. For example, during the peak period of its gasoline and electric power crises, CA emphasized long term per capita usage decreases whereas total consumption increased substantially due to added population.

It is within both the interests and intentions of most nations to produce policies that are clearly stated, readily enforceable and capable of delivering effective results, and population is no exception, but in managing some of our other most important issues such as health care, fiscal responsibility and immigration we have not been able to do this. These are classic examples of how we have chosen and pursued ends that are at odds with our historical national values and interests.

Capitalism
In 21st Century America

No discussion of American capitalism can be meaningful unless we declare in advance what it is and, perhaps more importantly, what it is not. Otherwise, the emotional components of greed and power will dominate or preclude objective considerations

Capitalism is an economic philosophy for the creation of wealth and, through the use of public and private resources, for the development, production and exchange of goods and services in ways that maximize efficiency and profit via private ownership and unregulated markets. To work most efficiently it requires mass markets and consumption -— institutions, systems and large mobile populations committed to the satisfaction of spending.

It established its presence with the arrival of the industrial revolution at the beginning of the nineteenth century and has put to its use and purpose four critical masses – mass population, mass communications, mass consumption and mass distribution. The combination of these factors provided a kind of "perfect storm" which transformed our commercial world. Capitalism was never free of fault or excess or error, but was built upon a lack of regulation that appealed to the entrepreneurial Zeitgeist and produced enormous profits that were able to control political machinery wherever and whenever necessary.

Again, capitalism is an economic system designed to profitably convert natural resources into wealth and to facilitate broad commerce (enter the middleman) in goods and services. It has forebears to which it is indebted in varying degrees. These are barter, feudalism, mercantilism and the isolated economic landscapes of the Russian Czars, Indian Maharajas and the Muslim caliphates.

All of capitalism's predecessor systems have dropped away into obscurity. They are, after all, only systems to which we were attached by time and technology. There is no need to mourn them; they "were", but no longer "are". The same fate probably awaits capitalism, as it may self-destruct or evolve or become irrelevant. It will become the past, and we will need all our energies for the present that will then face us and command our efforts.

Looking back over the rapid technological advances of the twentieth century, we must assume that, as technology builds upon technology, progress and change in the next century will be even greater. Can we imagine our contemporary capitalism transported to and functioning in an extraterrestrial economic space? Can we imagine a judicial system of the kind that capitalism relies on for its protection operating on some other planet? Can we imagine an orderly resident work force, a sensible form of compensation or, considering the cost of building and supplying off-planet production facilities, the cost per unit of production that would result?

These things may come into being eventually, but they will not come from a world or an era that thinks as we do.

Empire eventually becomes too expensive. For centuries we have seen this play out. The more territory and people that are absorbed, the more expensive their political, physical and economic maintenance becomes.

Our capitalists, and their politicians in hand, already tout outer space exploration and colonization as means of solving some of our present earthly social/economic problems. This is part of their commitment and visceral attachment to the process of continual growth. It is delusional. There are too many weak links that question such theory — human nature, units of population, money, social inertia, religious confusion, etc.

All of capitalism's forbears were efficient for their time and place. Barter? One-on-one; as no money was involved, there was no price and value was set by the quality of the goods and the need of those involved. Feudalism? With land the primary resource and means of wealth, what could be more useful than having it controlled by few people who could transfer it intact to their inheritors? Bear in mind that those who worked the land lived on it and raised their families to do the same. Feudalism had a certain efficiency to it, but was unable to survive the movement towards central government and improved transportation and weaponry technology.

The list goes on. *Capitalism is a system and, like any other, it will have to adapt to survive. It is here now but it is not a fixture of our time or technology and, as the latter change, most probably so will we and our systems.*

Still, the calculation of the capitalist equation in America has been neither complete nor accurate and leaves us with the age-old question of what might have been.

It has been a natural progression from the early days of the Industrial Revolution's machine age, high volume production to today's global markets and mass consumption by large, mobile populations committed to 24/7 spending on necessities, luxuries and media-marketed products portrayed as both. In the process, capitalism has been able to reward those who pursue/control money/power and those who wish to be viewed as close to them.

Our present capitalism is far different than it was at its nineteenth century peak. Then, with little supervision, it indulged in excesses which entailed social and political costs in the form of government controls and public resistance. It also enjoyed steadily available sources of raw materials and orderly means of distribution which cannot be assured given the rapidly, changing economic/political circumstances of our world.

Looking ahead a century, the conditions that have been favorable to capitalism in the past may no longer exist, and anyone who thinks that it can continue unchanged is almost certain to be wrong. It is likely that nothing will be the same.

For instance, anticipated changes in populations and our environment could totally alter what have come to be recognized values of such basics as land, water, air, food, shelter, etc. While such changes are not assured, but reasonably anticipated, they could do away with much of capitalism's necessary social and structural support. At a time of public disaster and peril when basic goods/services are no longer available, as in New Orleans, Haiti, etc., we allow government to provide the necessary goods and services because it is the only force large enough to activate the required money, personnel and equipment. In spite of capitalism's many benefits, conditions of public catastrophe are not those that would be best suited to its pursuit of profits. And roving groups of migrant poor separated from their accustomed social or political space do not meet capitalism's requirement of a "mobile population".

Like any other system, capitalism contains its own contradictions. In its early stage it depends upon aggressive and competitive pricing to obtain and expand markets. Once this has taken place and competition has been diminished or eliminated, prices increase and service can be consolidated and/or reduced. The definitive example of the operation of this cycle is provided by the growth of John D. Rockefeller's Standard Oil Co. The multiple execution of this technique was flawless and well served Rockefeller's goal of efficiency.

One contradiction that doggedly trails capital-ism is that its stated goals of private ownership, lack of regulation and open markets lead it eventually towards lesser competition, monopoly and the concentration of greater wealth in fewer hands. This shrinkage of the purchasing pool will then produce a decline in goods sold. A constantly increasing population, of course, can sustain demand.

There can be no higher testament to the achievements of capitalism than the development in less than a century of our petroleum, electric utility and railroad systems, especially the latter, but they were of another age. In the interim, what seems to resuggest itself is that the closely wound circle of capitalism has trouble making contact with the human or practical forces that surround it. Certainly the changes brought about by the UN, the Cold War and our pursuit of economic globalism have rewritten many economic rules. The Cold War, then a major struggle between Russia and the U.S. to prove economic and political supremacy for their different systems, is now an historical footnote in spite of the fact that trillions of dollars and millions of lives were lost in its pursuit.

The chemistry of coming change will alter our values, practices and measurements of everything from success to survival, and capitalism will not be spared.

There are lessons to be learned — for capitalists, socialists and terrorists; for all governments; for liberals and conservatives; for private sectors and public citizens; for religions of all kinds and for those who deny religion; for those who live in the past and those who will have to live in the future. They all share the same classroom and population is the teacher.

The skeletons of prior systems lie at our feet. Their eyes are long gone, and yet their sightless sockets stare questioningly up at us, but we must remember that in their time they were sources of answers, not questions.

If we do not make an effort to view the future of capitalism, of our country and of our world thru the lenses of greatly increased population and environmental pressures, it is likely that our responses will be too little and too late. Unfortunately, our government shows no ability to either understand or react to emerging paradigms. We have managed to "play catch-up" before and have pulled it off, but such success becomes increasingly more improbable as our and others' roles change.

In <u>Dr. Jekyll and Mr. Hyde</u> Robert Louis Stevenson explored the co-existence of evil and good in one man. Islam is a translation of this metaphor into a religious text. Capitalism, as well as other systems, performs the same function for economics.

These two important areas of human existence, religion and money, are at the roots of many of the problems we have encountered in Iraq and Afghanistan. There, widespread extremes of religious faith and economic deprivation mark their societies in a way that is generally unknown in ours.

Members of our State Dept. and Congress regularly make the case for democracy by rambling on about the benefits of capitalism's free markets and private ownership, as if telling Iraqis and Afghans how rich and successful we are will provide the stimulus necessary to change their lives. There is a very real disconnect here because our real message of freedom is not only burdened by economic ideology but is delivered by our military forces.

Capitalism has been an incredibly successful economic system since the advent of the industrial revolution. It has served nations and created great personal wealth throughout our western world, but most notably here, where we could pretty much start from scratch and write our own rules as we grew.

That time is now over, and capitalism must abide by rules of our state, local and federal government imposed by our judicial, executive and legislative branches. For the determined capitalist, even though the old ideology calls and commands, this is the new reality. Globalism is designed to buy time, to create wiggle room. But how much and for how long?

In fairness, it may be said that we have done more damage to capitalism than it has done to us. We exalted it and worshipped at its altar to validate ourselves, to make us appear better, stronger, larger than life. As freedom's message is burdened by capitalism, so capitalism's message has been burdened by our need to inflate it (and us) to an all conquering ideology. Economics are tough enough without having to carry ideological baggage — personal, corporate or political.

In the deserts, mountains, jungles, islands and floodplains of the third world and in the corridors and conference rooms of the UN it is not surprising that the scent of the old colonialism is being raised again.

In its time it brought some good, took a lot and didn't leave much. The new colonialism goes under the name of globalism and employs different methods of funding, of management and of ownership.

The old system at its peak lasted for about a century from the mid nineteenth century to its post WWII break-up when the world's cumulative political changes could no longer be resisted. That pace may seem leisurely as we look ahead to the next century, for, as the world speeds up in every way, we will probably have no choice but to face more sudden and severe change — in politics, in economics, in commerce, the environment and, of course, population.

Unfortunately, time and pressure leave messy marks on our political leaders and, unless we are able to notably improve their quality and redefine our national interests, our range of response will be limited and inadequate to the tasks ahead. To avoid such a failure we must regularly ask ourselves whether the ends we choose to implement our policies are in keeping or conflict with our historical values.

Men And Money; Money And Men

These are not isolated issues. Quite to the contrary, many of the major issues facing our government have resulted in legislation or other actions that challenge our traditional roles or beliefs. At any point in their transit through Congress they could have been challenged and identified as bearing the risk of questionable results.

But in today's Washington, calling attention to the public's interest other than by overblown rhetoric is a non-starter. There are too many lobbyists working the congressional corridors. The rot is deep and if you penetrate the surface, you'll find it underlies all of our elected, and a good part of our appointed, offices.

AARP recently disclosed that five industry groups with important stakes in the passage of Pres. Obama's health care bill have spent just over $600 million in their lobbying efforts.[1] With 535 members of Congress that averages out to over $1.1 million for every senator and representative. We know, however, these funds were not distributed equally to each member, as some members who hold key committee positions relative to a particular bill are more generously funded than others.

This $600 million was directed to just one bill. If we consider the number of local and national interests which target every member of Congress, we can begin to imagine the scale of special interest money at work in our government. Although it cannot help but disturb our political conscience, it does offer an explanation of why our government entertains policies or legislative efforts that significantly vary from, or run counter to, our stated goals and/or character.

The two examples of "ends at odds" that we have covered so far, population and our capitalistic economic foundation, are of prime importance. But they do not stand alone or exist only in their own political isolation. The error they share and display so clearly encompasses a wide range of the ways in which we experience our national government.

Two other major issues of our time that threaten our political will and ability to function are immigration and our out-of-control national debt. With the former we are treated to a view of representative government at its worst. This is because our policy has become disconnected from our legislation and the Congress refuses to enforce its own laws. In government, this is a double whammy that over time can bring about complete collapse.

Immigration, as an issue, is somewhat similar to what slavery was in the nineteenth century, as it invokes constitutional, social, moral, economic, security, religious, fairness and electoral considerations. If we wish to see ends that conflict with our own professed interests, we need to go no further.

Our immigration policy underwent enormous change with the passage of the 1965 reform act — far more than was intended by many in Congress who voted for its passage. This is because its proponents sold it on the basis of false and misleading information which turned years of immigration law upside down.

Congress did not revisit the subject until twenty-one years

later during Reagan's second term when a "one time" amnesty was passed for illegals then living/working in the US. Again the "one time" claim turned out to be false, as the 1986 act was followed by several more. Whether correct in their purpose or fair in their function, these further amnesties extended the reach and results of the 1986 act.

The horrendous hypocrisy we face today, and which was accepted by Presidents Bush I, Clinton, Bush II and Obama during their twenty years in office, is that of the Congress refusing to take the actions necessary to fund and enforce its own legislation.

This is tellingly symptomatic of current government in America. What it says to all who can vote, or write checks, is "We can have it both ways. We'll pass a law to appeal to some voters and then work the other side and not enforce it to please others". This may be a win/win situation for Congress and its money sources, but it's lose/lose for electoral democracy.

After the health care squeaker in the House, immigration may be the next big and bitter piece of legislation Pres. Obama chooses to pursue. It is highly charged with money and emotion, and it's quite possible that in numbers and intensity its public demonstrations will surpass those of the health care argument. It is more than likely that any attempt to move immigration reform through Congress will produce even greater acrimony and partisan ideology than health care. And at its end, there will still be the problem of effective enforcement.

This forces our attention to another failed aspect of our government. We have been strongly critical of the Congress, and rightly so, but they are not alone. The immigration mess has been largely permitted and continued by each of the presidents we named. The executive branch is involved — not only by the direct presidential role, but also by the many actions taken in the field and at headquarters by enforcement agencies such as the Departments of Justice and Homeland Security, the Border Patrol, the Drug Enforcement Agency, Customs, Coast Guard, Treasury Dept., etc. Today all of these agencies operate in a kind of nether land in which actions taken in the field in compliance with our laws can be ignored, subverted or overturned at any point up the chain of command including cabinet level secretaries and the White House. This is a "suckerpunch" on law enforcement and on the public. It is what it is.

Nor is our judicial branch free of criticism in matters of our immigration intention. It is customary for most illegal entrants, unless they pose security risks, to be released until some future trial date by which time they have disappeared or obtained new identification papers, or both. Our local immigration courts operate under the combined weight of voluminous paper work and the broken system above them. In spirit and performance they reflect the failed bureaucracy of which they are a part.

The damage done to our society by our present immigration policy of not affirming or enforcing our law is substantial and spread throughout our structure and process. If we do not deal with it decisively, effectively and permanently, the rot will spread to other parts of our government. *This is political gangrene in the making.*

It is doubtful whether anyone from even the fringes of the Right or Left over the past generation would have wanted our country to be in its present state of financial insolvency. And yet that is the shore upon which our ship of state has deposited us, and it is now and here that we must set about finding our way home.

In a half century or less we were transformed from the world's richest lender to its largest debtor, much like Dr. Jekyll and Mr. Hyde. From those in both parties who orchestrated this needless transition we have little in the way of explanation or responsibility.

Their ends were not our ends; nor their purposes; nor their values.

On a daily basis, they regularly, quietly and purposefully constructed a habit and level of debt that has put our country at great risk and will keep it there, if we survive in our present form, for many years and, unless we can contrive a means of escape, perhaps forever.

Congress recently approved an increase in our national debt limit to about $14 trillion dollars so that it can continue to operate in the red until we are past the mid-term congressional elections in November. If past is prologue, the limit will have to be raised again before year-end.

At $14 trillion our annual interest payment at last year's rate of 3.3% will be about $448 billion[2]. This is more than the combined total of what we spend on our Departments of Transportation, Education, Veterans Affairs, Homeland Security, State, Housing/Urban Development and a few others.

But this is only our "official" national debt. In addition, we have trillions of dollars of unfunded obligations which could increase our exposure to over $50 trillion.

As startling as the amount of our debt is the fact that it has grown to its current size in the span of only one generation, from the beginning of the Reagan presidency to now. In this briefest of historical moments, four presidents, two political parties and fifteen sitting Congresses undertook to reverse many of our traditional economic concepts about security, risk, thrift, debt, currency, government's role and how they combine to form our national character.

Day by day, in an apparently endless sequence, votes were taken; funding was approved; projects were initiated, authorized and assigned to government agencies; loans were generated or structured for direct payment; budget increases were proposed, revised and always approved; grants were made; social programs were created; earmarks were inserted; hiring expanded; operating expenses grew; etc.

An occasional voice was raised as elections drew close, but the people we had elected to run and be our government were mentally elsewhere. Our government no longer had its traditional sense of stewardship.

We used to talk about America being embarked upon a wonderful and unique political experiment. True; but what we have embarked upon now is a financial debacle similar to those that have befallen many other nations and forms of government in the course of history.

This may sound like the desperate cry of the lonely pessimist in a time of plenty. It is not. It is based on numbers which provide the structure and architecture for all our policies — social, political and foreign. As with population, it's not about labels. It's about numbers.

We must face the truth that from 1980 to the present, with the exception of a brief period of surplus at the beginning of the Clinton presidency, we have persisted in a program of widening deficit spending. Although occupants of the White House and the Congress often signaled that they were temporary and would soon be succeeded by balanced budgets and even "surpluses as far as the eye can see", these growing deficits reached their highest levels during the eight years of Bush II and then escalated sharply again under Pres. Obama's stimulus program designed to slow the recession and avoid a major depression.

There are always mechanisms at hand to increase deficits. The act of spending is a finely developed skill in Washington with no need for restraint if reelection is assured. But turning deficits into surpluses is something else. Like a speeding car, you first have to decelerate, then apply brakes and, finally, actually shift into reverse.

And the "crowd" mentality is an important element, as one congressman looking around and seeing most of his counterparts committed to popular spending programs, especially ones that may impact his/her home district, is unlikely to assume the role of the lone voice of reason.

The key to our present financial circumstance and the possibility of change and hope for the future lies in our three stage automobile analogy. First, we must decelerate, slow the flow of dollars. Then we must hit the brakes with new and reduced budgets and cutting or eliminating the scope of most programs. Finally, we must shift hard into reverse by changing both the number and method of funding procedures in Congress and establishing efficient ways to assure that our intended economies are targeted and carried out in the multiple departments and agencies of our burgeoning bureaucracy.

None of this will come easily. It is too abrasive, and grinds against the grain of our government. The first hurdle to overcome involves the immensity of the scale of our multi-trillion dollar debt which defies our human and political comprehension.

In early March the Congressional Budget Office (CBO) increased its estimate of budget deficits in the next decade to $9.8 trillion, or $1.2 trillion more than the White House's February prediction.[3] This is one scale.

Here's another: Freddie Mac and Fannie Mae, which serve as national mortgage market makers and had to be taken over by the government in 2008, have received $111 billion of taxpayer funds in order to survive, but are not yet stabilized and are anticipated to receive $77 billion more in the next year and a half and to eventually reach $400 billion.[4] The securities marketed by these two very powerful companies used to be regarded as informally guaranteed by the government. Today they pose to the American taxpayer a formal and unlimited risk exposure.

While the Freddie and Fannie figures are only billions, even they test our ability to comprehend their relative sizes. Here's a basis of comparison:

One billion seconds equals almost 32 years.
One trillion seconds equals almost 32,000 years.
And if you had spent one million dollars every day since the birth of Christ, you still would not have spent one trillion dollars.[5]

It is only when we attempt to convert government spending into a human scale and experience that we can begin to realize the senseless recklessness of our political class. This is what we have permitted and what we must now face if we are to repair our country, and we should not count on help from either party.

The language of politicians tends not to be precise. This makes it difficult for the public to fully understand the issue behind the words. For example, let's take the present conversation about deficits which implies that by eliminating deficits we will solve our financial problems.

This is only partially true. We will improve our position in one way but will not accomplish a cure-all. Let's suppose we start with a trillion dollar deficit and reduce it by $200 billion each year for five years. At the end of the first year we will have lowered our annual deficit to $800 billion which is then added to our national debt. At the end of five years our annual deficit theoretically would have disappeared while our national debt would have grown by $2 trillion. *In other words, reducing the deficit may be a helpful change of course, but only surpluses will reduce our debt. Where are these trillions of dollars of surpluses to come from?*

273

Politicians avoid this trap by rarely embracing specific time periods in economic matters or, if they do, extending them so far that projections are meaningless. We have seen this in the Health Care bill debate's claim by the administration that we will experience ten years of rising deficits followed by balanced budgets.

Financial projections are so complex and subject to so many variables that they offer little chance of accuracy beyond three years. To suggest that the CBO, or any other government bureau, can provide accurate forecasts of events and results a decade or two ahead is simply not credible.

There is another aspect to such projections that is not mentioned but should be questioned. Given that the numbers might work out as projected, what would be the basis of their success? What would be the actual physical force, the engine, that would drive and enable such a broad recovery from our present circumstance?

What will be the mechanism that will permit us to improve the performance of the Congress? Term limits? Eliminating gerrymandering and removing the redistricting function from the control of the two parties, as CA has done? In Washington, all are possible, but none is popular, or probable.

The time-tested way of digging out of a mess is to pull ourselves up by our own bootstraps (i.e., taxes), but with taxes we may be reaching a tipping point. We have heard the cry of "wolf, wolf" too many times.

We have spent $800 million on a new embassy in Baghdad cited by our State Dept as being necessary for our security and the protection of American interests, and this cost must be paid by the US taxpayer. Suppose we were to take to the streets and randomly ask 16 million people to pay fifty dollars each for the security provided by the new embassy. No naming rights; just cash, please. Sixteen million people – about 5% of our population

– would constitute a valid sample, but the results would probably be disappointing.

There is another area of failed government which must be recognized and changed. It is the process by which our bureaucracies achieve a kind of perpetual growth by increasing their budgets and employees. It's a chicken/egg process without an intended balance. Budgets are proposed, employees hired and results claimed that support increased funding followed by more hiring, etc.

In the ways of bureaucratic government, mostly staffed by civil service employees, distinction does not come from results or individual effort, as it does in the private sector, but more from the size of the entity's budget and staff. This can result in excessive real estate, over employment with insufficient productivity, overspending on office equipment and disproportionately high labor costs.

The Congress would most likely be unsuited and unwilling to involve itself in any effort to cure Washington's managerial problems. And yet it makes the nation's laws and, more importantly, controls the funding for the many and varied elements of our national bureaucracy.

Managerial inefficiency is a nettle that neither the executive nor the legislative branch wants to grasp. And so it will continue, as it has in the past, to be largely ignored. But it is expensive, although not perhaps by congressional standards, and it gathers momentum which at some point will prove capable of deflecting our occasional efforts towards change or improvement.

Population and wealth at one level of language translate into people and money at another. Either way, constructing a valid equation between these two elements is one of the most difficult and demanding tasks faced by all societies, and many have been destroyed by their failure to do so.

We have devoted most of this chapter to them because our population and financial problems seem to be moving on parallel tracks and approaching tipping points before mid-century. And because our political structure (i.e., parties, "leaders", class, elected representatives, or whatever label you prefer) is both unaware of the seriousness of these threats and unable to take sensible action because of its ties to a variety of special interests.

This latter obligation has developed such wide acceptance within our government that it casts serious and equal doubt on both the performance and the value of our representative democracy. This is not doomsday pessimism; it is a plausible (whether prophetic or not remains to be proved) view of immensely important events over which, due to our lack of attention and interest, we may not be able to exercise the control required by an orderly society.

President Obama made extensive promises during his election campaign regarding aspects of health care and regulation of our financial markets/practices. In office, he has turned away from many of these positions and, in some cases (i.e., health care), reversed himself.

The health care bill that passed is a mixed bag — some pluses and some minuses. Overall, we see it as a negative because of its potential for unwanted financial results, most particularly the failure to make any significant reduction in the insurance industry's ability to generate revenues and profits from all parts of the health care system. This is a far cry from the Obama campaign oratory.

It is evident to us that in other areas, as well as health care, Pres. Obama has misread the voters' mandate and extended it to areas they did not anticipate. Yes, those who provided the "swing" votes for Obama voted for change, but change of the kind that moved away from the errors of two Bush II terms to a more moderate government that would operate in a range from center right to center left. At his inauguration, Pres. Obama had a historic opportunity to reaffirm centrist government and even to launch a counter attack against our long-running ideological wars and the choking grip of the Ideological Imperative on our democracy.

The health care bill just passed is not what half of our country wants, nor what candidate Obama offered. It may be amended and improved in time, but, looking ahead, the insurance companies look like the biggest winners.

Again, as a matter of scale, consider these numbers. In 2009, Washington's army of lobbyists received $200 million from the banking segment of our financial system. This does not include contributions from other entities such as insurance companies, hedge funds, venture capital groups, etc.[6] And further, in the last two years the members of the Senate and House Banking Committees as a group have received around $60 million[7]. These committees usually consist of about 20 members each.

In every aspect of our nation's life, as it has grown larger, scale becomes more and more important. As it changes and is enlarged beyond our prior experience, our ethical, social, historical, political and even scientific perspectives are altered.

For instance, the lobbying expenditures quoted above were received from only our financial services sector. There are other groups with extensive interests and funds that are applied to our legislative branch. These include agriculture, retail, mining, pharmaceutical, apparel, appliance, construction, transportation, tourism, utilities, communication and many more.

Now the true scale of Congress' receipt of lobbying funds is beginning to emerge. It surely runs into more than a billion dollars annually. But, in addition to what is officially reported, there are many forms of favor that are not official and exist in a world of their own. Finally, we must also include the billions of dollars that make their way into the system by campaign contributions.

In twenty-first century America this is the truth of money pushing politics. It is not pretty, but it is what it is. It works wonderfully well for those who participate, and it will not be dislodged easily.

Financial Regulatory Reform

The above comments regarding lobbying are prologue to the issue of financial regulatory reform and the intense level of voter emotion raised by the collapse of our financial system and the actions of its leaders. This is an issue that ebbs and flows in the public conscience but which, even when it lies dormant beneath the surface, can be recalled by the failures of fairness of our political and financial "leaders", including our Federal Reserve central bank.

In the run-up to the '08 elections all of the nine Democratic candidates engaged in their multi-city "debate" professed their undying love for open and transparent government including regulation, when excess called for it, of our financial markets. As markets, deteriorated and corporate and banking failures required bail-outs, regulation became a prime issue. It was promised to an angry electorate, but time passes and it has been delayed.

The party line is that health care is the administration's front line, and that other issues have had to wait until its passage in order to benefit from its political momentum. A wider truth is that the financial services industry is calling in its many markers (of which it seems to have an endless supply) in order to slow, weaken, neutralize and, hopefully, defeat any meaningful reform.

In any definitive record of quid pro quo financing the Clinton administration's repeal of the Glass-Steagall Act would probably rank somewhere between overnight rentals of the Lincoln Room to party donors and the transfer of our missile technology to China. Glass-Steagall separated commercial from investment banking and for over half a century provided discipline over some of the forces that brought about the 1929 crash.

Its repeal was met with delight on Wall Street where changes in market practices and products to reflect the new freedom soon appeared. Today, a year and a half after our recent meltdown, the public's mood is still one of strong anger and betrayal.

Has the time come for the Return of Glass-Steagall? We may be approaching a Frankenstein meets Wolfman moment -— the power of public anger aroused against the ever increasing flow of private purpose funds through Congress. President Obama has spoken frequently of financial regulatory reform, and it seems that he will have to make a political effort in this direction.

The systemic question that begs an answer here is "Can campaign oratory survive legislation?" This is important because if, in fact, it can't, then voter disillusion and distrust is bound to increase and our system will be diminished. And here again, our political ends seem to be at odds with our claimed values.

Odds And Ends

There is probably no area of congressional action in which the public interest suffers more than in our military procurement process. Its faults and traps are many, and are shared by Congress and the Dept. of Defense (DOD). Like Scylla and Charybdis[8], these two bodies often transform or destroy the projects that must pass their scrutiny in order to satisfy Congress' local political interests and the financial interests of retired officers employed by contract bidders. These military retirees act as consultants in matters as varied as design, engineering, pricing and especially purchasing, where they are likely to be dealing with comrades or associates from their service days.

The DOD is presently involved in a development program for a new aircraft named the Joint Strike Fighter for which both General Electric (GE) and Pratt & Whitney (PW) are designing an engine with a determination now scheduled for 2016.

The GE entry has suffered an unusually high rate of test failures which have caused multiple delays and increased the cost of the program. It is designated as "the alternate engine" and will require its own spare parts, maintenance procedures and production facilities[9] which will add tens of billions of dollars to the system's cost.

Defense programs have a way of developing lives of their own which can defy sensible judgement. In the case of "the alternate engine", opposition has been voiced by the White House and even some parts of the Pentagon, but Congress pushes ahead usually citing "national security" as its justification.

Even passing reference to our procurement process should include mention of Congress' recent attempts to transfer $23.5 billion from our defense budget to the Air Force for the lease of 100 Boeing 767 civilian airliners which would then be converted to military tankers at the expense of U.S. taxpayers.

Fortunately, this effort was blocked, with Senator John McCain leading its opposition. McCain is a man of many political parts and directions not all of which appear to be synchronized. His exceptional military service, which includes years of imprisonment and torture by the Viet Cong, gives him a unique authority within Congress on military matters. He has referred to the Air Force/ Boeing lease deal as "one of the greatest rip-offs of taxpayers and the nation's defenses in history" [10]

The aircraft that the converted Boeing 767 was intended to replace is our C-130. A $50 million propeller driven plane that can carry troops, supplies and light field weapons and transport vehicles, it has been a mainstay of our global military role.

In the last two decades of the last century the Air Force requested five of these planes but received 262 of them! "They are built in the home districts of some of Congress's most influential members"[11], and the consideration of local employment and economic interests took precedence over military needs. In such cases the failure of the Congress to articulate and pursue our national interest is all too evident.

Reading reports of government activities on a steady basis usually reveals the existence of a subtle form of deception which shades the truth and of which the public should be aware.

First is the use of emergency spending bills designed to cover the costs of unforeseeable internal catastrophes such as floods, earthquakes, fires, tornadoes etc. These costs are not included in the national budget or the annual deficit, but are added to the national debt. The bills that authorize this form of spending are often referred to as "supplementals". They provide a way for the government not to disclose the actual amount of money it spends, a prime example being Pres. Bush II's funding of the war in Iraq entirely by emergency spending bills.

Another trick takes place in the way the government defines inflation which acts as a key element in determining payments for Social Security (SS) and other programs. During the Clinton administration inflation measurements were changed to reduce indexed SS payments with the result that we now have two bases for reporting — the broad-based Consumer Price Index (CPI) and the more narrow Core Inflation which does not include food and energy.

As these last two items account for a significant part of the American family's budget, their exclusion lowers the rate of inflation, cost-of-living increases and interest rates. Supermarket shoppers and gas purchasers have experienced consistent price increases in recent years, and the CPI has shown annual increases double that of Core Inflation.

Finally, our government again uses two different systems to report on its budgets. There is the Audited Federal Budget which employs the accrual method of accounting for revenues and liabilities as they are incurred. The other method is the Official Budget calculated on a cash basis that treats only actual income received and expenses paid.

This last basis paints a far rosier picture of our financial condition than that presented by the Audited Federal Budget. In fact, dual reporting by the Treasury Dept. has revealed some startling differences such as in the nine year period 1997-2005 the Audited Federal Budget indicated deficits of $2.9 trillion as compared to the official Budget's $729 billion.[12] The differences are, indeed, dramatic, but even if they were far more modest, there should be no need for keeping two sets of books.

The lower figure is useful to Congress because it makes passage of a bill and funding of programs easier to obtain, but the abuse factor is high and getting higher. We have tracked the growth of the Capitol Visitor Center over the time from its first announcement to its completion. It was originally announced at a cost of $265 million, but attracted a lot of Congressional self-glorification and ego-exercising additions, and ended up costing over $600 million.[13]

Population Awareness

The first step in dealing with any problem is to recognize it. With population, its lack of exposure and discussion through the usual public channels of government, media, commerce, education, religion, etc. have worked to keep it out of both sight and mind.

There is information available that is startling not only because of its factual scientific content, but also because of its ability to relate the consequences of humanity's development over the past three thousand years to our planet's natural capacity for supporting and interacting with its native life forms.

Today, the global existence of "off-the-chart" population growth is not mere theory. It is a fact, and one that we must come to understand.

Its consequences have only recently begun to be recognized although they have been silently at work beneath our consciousness level for the past two centuries. The issue of unsustainable, geometric population increase cannot be kept out of public sight and awareness forever. The only question is whether we want to recognize it now and have the benefit of time on our side in responding to it, or whether we defer to chance, let nature set the schedule and find ourselves with neither the time nor the means for a valid response.

This is too important an issue to ignore. There must be at least a conversation about population's numbers and consequences in America, and it should start soon.

End Notes

[1] Aarp Bulletin, March 2010. Sources: U.S. Chamber Of Commerce, Insurance Industry, Trial Lawyers, Doctors/Hospitals And Food/Beverage.

[2] Waste Watch, Winter 2009, From Citizens Against Government Waste

[3] Palm Beach Post 3/6/10

[4] Associated Press Via Palm Beach Post 2/25/10

[5] Cf. Note 2 Above

[6] Bill Moyers Journal, PBS 3/26/10

[7] Ibid

[8] Scylla & Charybdis refer to a rock and whirlpool that threatened mythological mariners in The Strait of Messina. They are used in contemporary language to signify two equally perilous alternatives, neither of which can be passed without encountering and probably falling victim to the other. – Webster's New Universal Unabridged Dictionary, 1996

[9] Cf. Note 2 Above

[10] Citizens Against Government Waste. Letter 3/15/10 From Senator John McCain.

[11] Ibid

[12] Citizens Against Government Waste, Letter 5/28/08

[13] Waste Watch, Fall 2009, From Citizens Against Government Waste

ECD 4/25/10